EDUCATIONAL GUIDANCE AND COUNSELLING

EDUCATIONAL GUIDANCE AND COUNSELLING

Editor

V. C. Pandey

ISHA BOOKS

DELHI-110 033

Educational Guidance and Counselling

ISBN: **9788182051713**

Reprinted in 2011 in India by
Isha Books
B-63, Ist Floor
New Gupta Colony
Near DDA Market
Delhi-110009

Printed at: G. Print Process, Delhi

PREFACE

Students are challenged daily to make decisions in an environment fraught with tension and uncertainty. Faced with social, economic, and cultural issues to a degree not experienced by previous generations, students must have proactive choices to nurture the potential they each have to become successful learners. Guidance and counselling programmes, as educational programmes, creates options for students to develop and emphasise strategies which enhance this potential.

Guidance and counselling programmes are integral part of each school's total educational program. It is developmental by design and includes sequential activities organised and implemented by certified school counsellors with the support of teachers, administrators, students, and parents. Generally a guidance and counselling programme include guidance curriculum, individual planning, responsive services and system support. Through counselling individuals may be facilitated in working towards living a more satisfying and enjoyable life.

The present book provides a vivid and in-depth description of all fundamental aspects related with educational guidance and counselling. The nature, purpose, techniques, procedures and scope of educational guidance and counselling programmes are covered comprehensively. The skills needed by counsellors, significance of carrier development, techniques of counselling students with special needs etc., are also described in detail. This book will assist guidance counsellors, guidance supervisors, teachers and parents.

Editor

CONTENTS

1

Understanding Guidance and Counselling

The Counselling Service aims to provide a professional and supportive service to the clients who are in need of help. The main activity of the Service is in providing individual counselling sessions to students within a confidential and supportive setting. The counsellors working for the service endeavour to conduct these counselling relationships in ways that respect the individual's values, rights and personal resources for coping. Through counselling individuals may be facilitated in working towards living a more satisfying and enjoyable life. Counselling offers an opportunity to talk with someone in a confidential and supportive setting. The counsellor will not advise the you about what you should think and feel in relation to their situation, or even what action you should take. Instead, they will facilitate you in exploring the issues that are concerning you and that you wish to address in counselling.

The purpose of counselling is not to tell you what to do. This is partly because it would stop you developing your own resourcefulness, but mostly because the counsellor cannot possibly know what is best for you in your particular situation. The emphasis, therefore, will be on offering you non-judgmental support and trying to understand, with you, what you are going through. It is hoped that by doing this you will be able to develop your own answers and ways of overcoming your difficulties. People come for counselling for different reasons.

A particular event may have caused distress or a person may want to deal with something that has been going on for some time. In addition, the concerns that people bring to counselling vary enormously. These concerns can include: relationships (with friends, partners or family); self-harm; eating disorders; study problems; loneliness; depression; self-confidence; sexuality; bereavement; cultural issues; and self-esteem. There is also wide variation in the degree of distress that a person is experiencing when they come for counselling. Some people are aware that something is troubling them, although they're not experiencing too much difficulty, whereas others are already extremely distressed, perhaps feeling suicidal.

Therefore some people may be experiencing crisis, whereas others may feel their situation is not so urgent. But whatever the nature of your situation, you may find counselling to be of some help. The Counselling Service has a core staff team of professionally trained and qualified counsellors who are used to working with people experiencing a wide variety of difficulties.

HISTORY OF COUNSELLING AND PSYCHOTHERAPIES

Although psychological therapies trace their history back to the contributions of Freud, many modern approaches to counselling and psychotherapy are now much more firmly grounded in other bodies of thought. Modern psychological therapies trace their history back to the work of Sigmund Freud in Vienna in the 1880s. Trained as a neurologist, Freud entered private practice in 1886 and by 1896 had developed a method of working with hysterical patients which he called 'psychoanalysis'. Others such as Alfred Adler, Snador Ferenczi, Karl Abraham and Otto Rank were also analysed by Freud and had brief apprentice-type training from him before becoming psychoanalysts in their own right.

In the early 1900s, Ernest Jones and A.A. Brill, from the UK and US respectively, visited Freud in Vienna and returned to their own countries to promote Freud's methods; Freud himself began a lecture tour of North America in 1909. Gradually many such as Ferenczi, Adler, Rank, Stekel and Reich began to develop their own theories and approaches, which sometimes differed markedly from Freud's. Jung in particular, a close collaborator of Freud's from 1907-1913 who was in some sense 'groomed' as Freud's intellectual successor, eventually split from Freud and pursued the development of his own school of analytical psychology, drawing heavily on both Freud's and Adler's ideas. All these immediate descendants of Freud's approach are characterized by a focus on the dynamics of the relationships between different parts of the psyche and the external world; thus the term 'psychodynamics'.

A separate strand of psychological therapies developed later under the influence of psychology and learning theory and leading thinkers such as B.F. Skinner. Rejecting the notion of 'hidden' aspects of the psyche which cannot be examined empirically (such as Freud's rendition of the 'unconscious'), practitioners in the behavioural tradition began to focus on what could actually be observed in the outside world. Finally, under the influence of Adler and Rank, a 'third way' was pioneered by the US psychologist Carl Rogers.

Originally called 'client-centred' and later 'person-centred', Rogers's approach focuses on the experience of the person, neither adopting elaborate and empirically untestable theoretical constructs of the type common in psychodynamic traditions, nor neglecting the internal world of the client in the way of early behaviourists. Other approaches also developed under what came to be called the 'humanistic' branch of psychotherapy, including Gestalt therapy and the psychodrama of J.L. Moreno. The figure below illustrates some of the historical links between these three main strands which developed from Freud's original contributions.

Medical vs. Non-Medical Split

Freud strongly supported the idea of lay analysts without medical training, and he analysed several lay people who later went on to become leading psychoanalysts, including Oskar Pfister, Otto Rank and his own daughter Anna Freud. He published two staunch defenses of lay analysis in 1926 and 1927, arguing that medicine and the practice of analysis were two different things. When Ernest Jones brought psychoanalysis to the UK in 1913, he followed Freud's preferences in this area, and the tradition of lay involvement continues to this day in the UK, where most psychoanalysts, psychotherapists and counsellors have a lay background.

In the US, however, Freud's analysand A.A. Brill insisted that analysts should be medically qualified — even though there were already many lay analysts practising in the US who, like Brill, had trained with Freud in Vienna. Brill prevailed, however: in 1926 the state of New York made lay analysis illegal, and shortly thereafter the American Medical Association warned its members not to cooperate with lay analysts. To this day, almost all US psychoanalysts are medically qualified, and counsellors typically study psychology as undergraduates before becoming counsellors.

Counselling vs. Psychotherapy Divide

It was largely in response to the US prejudice against lay therapists that Carl Rogers adopted the word 'counseling', originally used by social activist Frank Parsons in 1908. As a psychologist, Rogers was not originally permitted by the psychiatry profession to call himself a 'psychotherapist'. Ironically, Rogers himself became renowned as one of the most influential empirical scientists in the fields of psychology and psychiatry, introducing rigorous scientific methods to psychology and psychotherapy that psychoanalysts themselves had long resisted (and, in the view of many, still largely resist today). He became a joint Professor in the Departments of Psychology and Psychiatry at the University of Wisconsin as well as Head of the Psychotherapy Research Section of the Wisconsin Psychiatric Institute.

In the field as it now stands, the argument as to whether counselling differs significantly from psychotherapy is largely academic. Those from psychodynamic traditions sometimes equate 'psychoanalysis' and 'psychotherapy' — suggesting that only psychoanalysts are really psychotherapists — but this view is not common anywhere else.

Others use 'psychotherapy' to refer to longer-term work (even though some psychotherapists offer brief therapy) and 'counselling' to refer to shorter term work (even though some counsellors may work with clients for years). The two terms are commonly used interchangeably in the US, with the obvious exception of 'guidance counseling', which is often provided in educational settings and focuses on career and social issues.

Modern counselling and psychotherapy have benefited tremendously from the empirical tradition which was given such impetus by Carl Rogers, even though the research agendas of psychology and counselling have diverged greatly over the last half century. Additional work in cognitive psychology, learning theory and behaviour has informed many therapeutic approaches. The richness of the bodies of both empirical and theoretical work which are now available, coupled with the raw complexity of human beings, has led to a profusion of different approaches to the field.

By some accounts, the different strands of counselling and psychotherapy now number in the hundreds. Mainstream approaches, however, are much fewer in number, and over time it is likely that many of the less well-grounded schools of thought will fade away, while more new ones will emerge to take their place. While the main approaches continue to develop, and others appear and then fade away, clients are left to choose for themselves what might be best for them.

TYPES OF PSYCHOTHERAPY

Psychotherapy is a method of talking with a psychotherapist, psychiatrist, psychologist or professional counselor. Many forms of psychotherapy can help people having difficulty in life, those who wish to make some kind of change in their personal or professional life, or people suffering from depression, anxiety or other serious mental health problems. The recovery success rate for those with depression who combine psychotherapy with medication to control symptoms is more than 80 percent, according to some studies. Although best in person, therapy is also provided on the phone, via e-mail, and online. Therapy can be held in one-on-one sessions, family or couple sessions, or in a group led by a trained counselor:

Family therapy or couples therapy

Family therapy includes discussion and problem-solving sessions with every member of the family. Some sessions are done as a group, in couples, or one on one. Family or couples therapy is helpful when one of the family member's physical or mental health is directly affecting family dynamics or the well-being of significant relationships. In therapy, interpersonal relationships shared among family members are examined and communication is strengthened. If a family member suffers from depression, the roles played by various family members in reinforcing the depression often are examined.

Group therapy

In group therapy, a small group of people meet regularly to discuss individual issues and help each other with problems with the guidance of a trained therapist.

DIFFERENT APPROACHES TO PSYCHOTHERAPY

Much psychotherapy is not limited to a particular type or technique. Many therapists are trained in several different approaches. They then combine techniques from these various approaches that fit their own style and personality and the needs of the patient. Medication may be used with psychotherapy. For many people, this is the best approach to treatment. People with moderate-to-severe depression typically do best with a combination of antidepressants and some form of psychotherapy. The following are the common types of therapy available:

Behavior therapy

Behavior therapy, also called behavior modification or behaviorism, sets up rewards and punishments to change thinking patterns and shape behavior. Behavioral therapy can involve relaxation training, stress management, biofeedback and desensitization of phobias. Behavioral therapists help patients learn how to get more satisfaction and rewards through their own actions and how to unlearn the behavioral patterns that contribute to, or result from, their problems.

Cognitive therapy

Cognitive therapy seeks to identify and correct thinking patterns that can lead to troublesome feelings and behaviors. Beliefs and expectations are explored to identify how they shape a person's experiences. If a thought or belief is too rigid and causes problems, the therapist helps the client to modify his or her belief so that it is less extreme.

Cognitive-behavioral therapy

Cognitive-behavioral therapy (CBT) helps a person to recognize his or her own negative thought patterns and behaviors and to replace them with positive ones. Used both with and without medication, cognitive-behavioral therapy is the most popular and commonly used therapy for the treatment of depression. A major aim of CBT is to reduce anxiety and depression by eliminating beliefs or behaviors that help to maintain problematic emotions. CBT generally lasts about 12 weeks and may be conducted individually or in a group. There is evidence that the beneficial effects of CBT last longer than those of medication for people with panic disorder, obsessive-compulsive disorder, posttraumatic stress syndrome and social phobia.

Interpersonal therapy

Interpersonal therapy (IPT) is a short-term therapy often used to treat depression. This treatment approach focuses on an individual's social relationships and how to improve social support. IPT therapy seeks to improve a person's relationship skills, working on communication more effectively, expressing emotions appropriately and being properly assertive in social and work situations. In depression, IPT helps patients learn how to deal more effectively with others to reduce conflict and gain support from family and friends. It is usually conducted, like cognitive-behavioral therapy, on an individual basis but also can be used in a group therapy setting.

Movement/dance/art/music therapy

These methods include the use of movement, art or music to express emotions. This type of therapy is effective for those who have difficulty expressing feelings.

Phototherapy (light therapy)

People who suffer from seasonal affective disorder (SAD), a form of depression that is related to the change of the seasons within their geographic location, may benefit from bright light phototherapy. Phototherapy uses special light bulbs, which are much brighter than ordinary lights and made for this purpose. A physician or therapist instructs the patient in how to use these high-intensity lights to improve symptoms of seasonal depression.

Psychoanalysis

Also called psychodynamic or psychoanalytic therapy, this type of treatment helps a person look inside himself or herself to discover and understand emotional conflicts that may be contributing to emotional problems. The therapist (psychoanalyst) helps the client "uncover" unconscious motivations, unresolved problems from childhood and early patterns to resolve issues and to become aware of how those motivations influence present actions and feelings. This is a lengthy process, typically taking several years.

There are different types of psychoanalysis, each with a different focus. Freudian psychoanalysis has been criticized because of its tendency to create long-term dependent relationships between the therapist and the client. Recent types of psychoanalytically oriented therapy have become popular, such as Jungian therapy. Jungian therapy sessions focus more on the immediate situation and life problems than on the root of the problem to help individuals develop greater self-realization.

COUNSELLOR-CLIENT RELATIONSHIP

As a general rule, counsellors working for the Service will not inform a third party of any details relating to your attendance for counselling. This includes any information that is disclosed within the counselling relationship as well as details about whether or not you have used the Service. Confidentiality is contained within the Counselling Service, so that certain client information may be discussed within the counselling staff team. Issues relating to clients are often discussed amongst the counsellors in an attempt to monitor and improve their work; where necessary, matters may be discussed in detail with the Head of Counselling Service.

The Director of Employability and Student Support may also be consulted in exceptional circumstances. In addition, each counsellor has regular contact with a supervisor in order to further monitor their work. However, there are certain circumstances where a counsellor may feel it necessary or be bound by law to break confidentiality with a client, liaising with an appropriate third party (other than their supervisor) outside the Counselling Service. It should be stressed that in such circumstances an attempt would usually be made to discuss the matter with the client first, hopefully working towards some kind of agreement that would not involve breaking confidentiality against the client's wishes. There are certain circumstances, however, where this may not be possible.

However, there are certain circumstances where a counsellor may feel it necessary or be bound by law to break confidentiality with a client, liaising with an appropriate third party (other than their supervisor) outside the Counselling Service. It should be stressed that in such circumstances an attempt would usually be made to discuss the matter with the client first, hopefully working towards some kind of agreement that would not involve breaking confidentiality against the client's wishes. There are certain circumstances, however, where this may not be possible. Where a client does agree that a counsellor may communicate certain information about them to a third party, wherever possible 'an agreement on the release of confidential information' form will be signed. This is in order to provide a record for both client and counsellor that such an agreement was made.

Working with self-harming and suicidal clients

The counsellors work with many clients who harm themselves through cutting or eating habits, or who are indeed suicidal or have attempted suicide. However, it is not the policy of the Counselling Service to break confidentiality as a matter of course when working with clients of this nature. Where such a client does not wish for a third party to be involved the client's wish will usually be respected. In any situation where there is client suicidal intent, however, the counsellor will ensure that the client is aware of other relevant sources of support, such as the Samaritans and their GP, in case they wish to access them.

When working with self-harming or suicidal clients, though, there are still circumstances (as with all clients) in which confidentiality may be broken, even if it goes against the client's wishes. In addition to these circumstances the Service has a clear policy where the client actually attempts to commit suicide in the presence of the counsellor (or another staff member of the Counselling Service), or informs the member of staff that they have taken an overdose of pills or some other substance that is intended to kill themselves.

In this situation the counsellor (or another staff member of the Counselling Service) will automatically call for an ambulance, letting the client know that they have done so. If there is any uncertainty as to whether the client's life is in danger, the member of staff will still call for an ambulance. The client will not be prevented from leaving the building if the client does not want to wait for an ambulance to arrive. Where the client telephones the Counselling Service and expresses a similar intent, an ambulance will be called if the client's location is known.

On first using the Counselling Service, you will be asked to complete a form giving basic details about how you can be contacted, your gender, date of birth, whether you are a part or full-time student, etc. Statistics are collected from the data on yours and other clients' forms and held anonymously (by reference number) on a database. This database also includes a list of the dates you came for counselling, the broad category of concern you were experiencing and the extent to which you were struggling with this concern (indicated by a number on an eight-point scale). The forms are kept securely at the Counselling Service and will be destroyed four academic years after the date you last attended counselling.

The counsellors working for the Counselling Service usually make notes about the counselling sessions they provide. These notes are identified by a reference number, do not contain your name and are kept securely, separate from your details form. Along with any correspondence relating to you having counselling here, these notes form a paper-based file.

The counsellors will provide a supporting statement on a client's extenuating circumstances form where this is appropriate. However, counsellors cannot comment on a student's wellbeing prior to meeting them. Counsellors can only confirm the dates of the student's sessions and that the student was experiencing difficulties during the period they had been attending counselling. Occasionally, where a student has submitted an extenuating circumstances claim form but it has not been seen or signed by a counsellor, the student's subject department contacts the Counselling Service requesting confirmation of the dates the student attended counselling. If possible, the Counselling Service will check with the student first that it is all right to confirm this information. But if the Service cannot reach the student, and where it is clear that they have indicated on the form they have been a counselling client, the Service will usually confirm their attendance.

Correspondence and telephone calls

Any correspondence that is sent to you by post in relation to your counselling will be clearly marked as private and confidential. The subject matter of any correspondence will be limited to the purpose of writing and will not include any unnecessary personal information. (Where a counsellor and their client have entered into a joint correspondence as part of their therapeutic relationship, there will obviously be much greater openness in what is written.) Correspondence by email will only be conducted if you have given your permission to be contacted this way on your form. This is due to the potential lack of security of the email system.

If you choose to discuss personal information over email, the counsellor cannot be held responsible for a breach in confidentiality if a third party gains unauthorised access to the email messages: this is a risk you accept responsibility for by choosing to discuss such matters over email. If the counsellor or Service receptionist ever need to telephone you, perhaps to confirm or rearrange an appointment time, they will not leave a message if you are unavailable unless you have specifically made it clear that it is all right to do so.

Audio-recording counselling sessions

Counsellors may periodically want to make audio recordings of their counselling sessions with clients. This may be in order to monitor their own work or because they are conducting some research or, in the case of a counsellor working for the Service on a training placement, because they are required to record counselling sessions as part of their training. Whenever a counsellor does wish to record sessions you will be given at least one week to decide whether or not you agree to such an arrangement.

The counsellor will make clear to you the purpose of the recording clarifying who, if anyone, would listen to the recording other than the counsellor. However, there is no obligation whatsoever for you to be recorded and should you prefer not to, your wish will be entirely respected. If you do agree to be recorded, though, a simple form will be signed by yourself and the counsellor to confirm your agreement on the matter. All recordings will be destroyed once they have been used for their intended purpose, unless you come to some other arrangement with the counsellor.

Role of the counseling personnel

One of the most important aspects of the chief petty officer's job is providing advice and counseling to subordinates. Counseling personnel who make themselves accessible to subordinates will find they are in great demand to provide information and to help in finding solutions to problems. A information and to help in finding solutions to problems. A point to remember is that counseling should not be meddlesome, and the extreme, of playing psychiatrist, should be avoided. But neither should counseling be reserved only for a subordinate that is having problems; you should also counsel subordinates for their achievements and outstanding performance.

Counseling of a subordinate who is doing a good job reinforces this type of job performance and ensures continued good work. Counseling of this type also provides an opening for you to point out ways that a subordinate might improve an already good job performance. Counseling the subordinate who is doing a good job is relatively easy, but a different type of counseling is required for a subordinate whose performance does not meet set standards.

Ending the counsellor-client relationship

It is hoped that the counselling provided by the Service will facilitate each client in their attempt to live a more satisfying and fulfilling life. The counselling offered will, however, have to stop at some point. This may be because the client is no longer a student, which may feel like an enforced ending for the client, or because either the client and/or the counsellor decide to end the counselling relationship.

Wherever possible, the counsellor will endeavour to work towards an ending of the counselling relationship that is respectful of the client. You have the right to discontinue your counselling at any time.

There may be circumstances, however, where the counsellor feels that offering counselling to a particular client is not appropriate and therefore will end the counselling relationship. In this type of situation, the client will usually have the opportunity to see another counsellor within the Counselling Service: However, in exceptional circumstances this will not be possible and a referral to other support agencies will be made.

COUNSELING DYNAMICS

Counselors can facilitate movement through the phases that are described above by using a combination of good communication skills and structured activities. Skills such as paraphrasing, clarifying, empathy, information giving, open-ended questioning, and summarizing are helpful in the initial phases. There is also a role for reframing and for constructive critical reflection. Thus, skills such as immediacy; self disclosure; advanced, accurate empathy; supporting; limiting; and confrontation (strength-challenge, in most instances) can be helpful.

A wide variety of other structured activities can be applied to both information gathering and reframing. The strategies focus on different time orientations and facilitate the development of new perspectives. Activities which focus on the past address normalization and the careful scrutiny of past accomplishments. Within a present-time focus there is the emphasis upon positive affirmation, limiting negative thinking, externalizing the problem, decision making, and information giving. In terms of the future, there is a focus on hypothetical solutions, behavior rehearsal, focusing, and new cycles of activity. All of these activities involve the client in a structured sequence of events which lead to greater personal awareness.

Movement through the various phases is not always sequential; what is occurring throughout is movement from expansion to contraction and then to further expansion. The need for expansion at the action planning phase is often overlooked because of the need for closure. While it can be comforting for clients and counselors to develop one plan of action, in today's labor market more options and greater flexibility are necessary.

2

PRINCIPLES AND TYPES OF GUIDANCE AND COUNSELLING

ETHICAL PRINCIPLES OF COUNSELLING

The following principles are expressions of these core values in action. They form the foundation for ethical practice.

Counsellors shall:

— Act with care and respect for individual and cultural differences and the diversity of human experience.

— Avoid doing harm in all their professional work.

— Actively support the principles embodied in the Treaty of Waitangi.

— Respect the confidences with which they are entrusted.

— Promote the safety and well-being of individuals, families, communities, whanau, hapu and iwi.

— Seek to increase the range of choices and opportunities for clients.

— Be honest and trustworthy in all their professional relationships.

— Practice within the scope of their competence.

— Treat colleagues and other professionals with respect

The Counselling Relationship

Safety

(a) Counsellors shall take all reasonable steps to protect clients from harm.

(b) Counsellors shall, in their professional practice, take responsible action to challenge violence and abuse of power.

(c) Counsellors shall take all reasonable steps to protect themselves from actual or potential danger.

(d) Counsellors shall warn third parties and appropriate authorities in the event of an imminent threat of serious harm to that third party from the client

Respecting diversity and promoting social justice

(a) Counsellors shall take account of their own cultural identity and biases, and seek to limit any harmful impact of these in their work with clients.

(b) Counsellors should work towards bi-cultural competence.

(c) Counsellors shall learn about and take account of the diverse cultural contexts and practices of the clients with whom they work.

(d) Counsellors shall avoid discriminating against clients on the basis of their race, colour, disability, ethnic group, culture, gender, sexual orientation, social class, age, religious or political beliefs or on any other basis.

(e) Counsellors shall work with clients in ways that are meaningful in the context of, and respectful towards, the clients' cultural communities.

(f) Counsellors shall support their clients to challenge the injustices they experience.

(g) Counsellors shall be committed to the equitable provision of counselling services to all individuals and social groups.

(h) Counsellors shall promote social justice through advocacy and empowerment.

Appropriateness/suitability of counsellor

Counsellors shall determine, in consultation with the client, whether they are appropriate to provide the counselling. Where necessary and feasible, counsellors shall refer clients to other counsellors who would be more appropriate by reason of their skills, gender or culture or for any other reason indicated by the clients' needs.

Clear contracts

(a) The terms on which counselling is provided shall be clear and reasonable. Contracts negotiated between counsellors and clients may include matters to do with availability, fees, cancelled appointments, the degree of confidentiality offered, handling of documentation, complaint procedures and other significant matters.

(b) Counsellors shall establish with clients the aims or purposes of counselling and renegotiate them as necessary.

Informed consent

(a) Counsellors shall provide services to clients in the context of free and informed consent. Informed implies understanding and free consent implies a lack of pressure. Counsellors shall respect clients' rights to refuse or withdraw consent at any time.

(b) Counsellors shall use clear and understandable language to discuss with clients the purposes, risks, limits and costs of the counselling.

(c) Counsellors shall take all reasonable steps to safeguard the interests and rights of clients with limited or diminished capacity to give informed consent. Where relevant, this needs to be done in partnership with caregivers.

(d) Counsellors should respect the rights of children: to receive age appropriate information and to give consent on their own behalf, commensurate with their capacity to do so.

(e) Counsellors shall inform clients, where relevant, of the availability of government funding for counselling services.

Fees

(a) Counsellors shall clarify fees and methods of payments with clients at the beginning of a counselling relationship.

(b) Counsellors shall ensure that fees are reasonable and commensurate with the service provided.

(c) Counsellors should be cautious about accepting goods or services from clients in lieu of payment. Counsellors who do accept goods or services from clients as payment for professional services are responsible for demonstrating that this arrangement will not be detrimental to the client or to the professional relationship.

Documentation of counselling

"Documentation" in this code refers to all material about the client or about the counselling, recorded in any form (electronic, audio, visual and text). Documentation includes material collected for the purposes of: enhancing counselling practice; and meeting the requirements of research, accountability, appraisal, audit and evaluation.

(a) Counsellors shall maintain records in sufficient detail to track the sequence and nature of professional services provided. Such records shall be maintained in a manner consistent with ethical practice taking into account statutory, regulatory, agency or institutional requirements.

(b) Counsellors shall obtain informed consent from clients when writing reports for third parties.

(c) Counsellors shall keep records and notes secure. They shall create, maintain, transfer and arrange to destroy them in a manner compliant with the requirements of the confidentiality sections of this code.

(d) Counsellors shall inform clients of their right to access their documentation, to know how this information is being kept and to know who has access to it.

(e) Counsellors shall take all reasonable steps to ensure that documentation remains retrievable as long as is professionally prudent, or as is required by law.

(f) Counsellors are encouraged to ensure policies are in place for the safe and confidential storage and eventual destruction of client notes, in the event of the counsellor ceasing to practice, leaving the employing agency, or the counsellor dying.

Respectful language

(a) Counsellors shall use appropriate and respectful language in all communications, verbal and written, to and about clients.

(b) Counsellors should avoid using diagnostic labelling in any way which is likely to cause harm to their clients.

Maintaining competent practice

(a) Counsellors shall maintain their competence through regular supervision.

(b) Counsellors shall undertake appropriate professional development activities.

(c) Counsellors shall work within the limits of their knowledge, training and experience.

Fitness to practice

(a) Counsellors, together with their supervisors, shall monitor and maintain their fitness to practice at a level that enables them to provide an effective service.

(b) Counsellors shall withdraw from part or all of their counselling practice while their emotional, mental or physical health is significantly impaired.

Multiple relationships

(a) Counsellors assume full responsibility for setting and monitoring the boundaries between a counselling relationship with a client and any other kind of relationship with that client and for making such boundaries as clear as possible to the client.

(b) Counsellors should consult with their supervisor(s) when dual or multiple relationships arise.

(c) When dealing with more than one party, counsellors should be even handed when responding to the needs, concerns and interests of each party.

(d) When counsellors agree to provide counselling to two or more persons who have a relationship, counsellors shall clarify which person or persons are clients and the nature of the relationship the counsellors will have with each person.

(e) Counsellors should declare any previous acquaintance with a client or any other circumstances that may prejudice the counselling.

(f) If conflicting roles with clients emerge during counselling, counsellors must clarify, adjust or withdraw from these roles by an appropriate process.

Exploitation

(a) Counsellors shall not exploit clients for purposes of personal, professional, political, or financial gain.

(b) Counsellors shall not solicit testimonials from current or former clients.

Sexual relationships with clients

(a) Counsellors shall not engage in sexual or romantic activity with their clients.

(b) Counsellors shall not exploit the potential for intimacy made possible in the counselling relationship, even after the counselling has ended.

(c) Counsellors shall not sexually harass their clients.

(d) Counsellors shall not provide counselling to persons with whom they have had a sexual or romantic relationship.

Referral

(a) Counsellors shall refer clients on, where possible, when other specialised knowledge is needed, or when the counselling is not being useful.

(b) Counsellors shall obtain clients' consent before making referrals to colleagues and other services and before disclosing information to accompany such referrals.

(c) Counsellors shall be responsible, as far as possible, for verifying the competence and integrity of persons to whom clients are referred.

(d) Counsellors shall not ask for or accept referral fees.

Interruption of services

Counsellors should make reasonable efforts to plan for alternative care in the event that counselling services are interrupted by a significant change in circumstances, such as the counsellor becoming unavailable, ill or dying.

Ending counselling

Counsellors shall work with clients to end counselling when clients have received the help they sought, or when it is apparent that counselling is no longer helpful.

Confidentiality

Extent of confidentiality

(a) Counsellors shall treat all communication between counsellor and client as confidential and privileged information, unless the client gives consent to particular information being disclosed.

(b) Counsellors may discuss, in supervision, information received in counselling as part of the normal management of confidentiality.

(c) Counsellors should take all reasonable steps to communicate clearly the extent and limits of the confidentiality they offer clients. Any agreement between the counsellor and client about confidentiality may be reviewed and changed by joint negotiation.

(d) Counsellors shall protect clients' identities when information gained from counselling relationships is used for purposes such as counsellor training, research or audit.

(e) Counsellors shall respect confidences about the clients of colleagues.

(f) Counsellors should establish procedures to ensure the ongoing management of client confidentiality in the event of the counsellor's death.

Exceptions to confidentiality

(a) Counsellors shall only make exceptions to confidentiality in order to reduce risk.

(b) When counsellors need to pass on confidential information, they should provide only the minimum of information necessary and only then to those people to whom it is absolutely necessary.

(c) Exceptions to confidentiality occur when:

— there is serious danger in the immediate or foreseeable future to the client or others,

— the client's competence to make a decision is impaired,

— legal requirements demand that confidential material be revealed,

— responding to a complaint about counselling practice.

(d) Wherever possible, the decision to make an exception to confidentiality is made:

— after seeking the client's co-operation, unless doing so would further compromise the safety of the client or others,

— after consultation with a supervisor.

Confidentiality and the law

(a) Counsellors are encouraged to seek legal advice about their rights and obligations under the law, when the counsellor's work with clients involves contact with the legal system.

(b) When issued with a search warrant or subpoena to give evidence in Court, or other legal processes, counsellors should pursue the status of privileged communication, in accordance with the client's wishes, until all legal avenues have been exhausted.

Responsibility To Colleagues and The Profession

Responsibility to Colleagues

(a) Counsellors should treat colleagues with respect, fairness and honesty.

(b) Counsellors shall not solicit clients away from other counsellors.

(c) Counsellors shall avoid establishing a professional relationship with clients of other counsellors without appropriate communication with the counsellor or agency concerned.

Responsibility to the profession

(a) Counsellors shall uphold and foster the values, integrity and ethics of the profession.

(b) Counsellors should participate in the activities of the profession.

(c) Counsellors are encouraged to devote a proportion of their professional activity to services for which there is little or no financial return.

(d) Counsellors shall represent honestly and accurately their membership status, qualifications, training and competencies.

(e) Counsellors shall not use their position within an organisation to recruit clients for their own private practice.

Collaboration with counselling colleagues and other professions

(a) Counsellors should endeavour to achieve good working relationships and communication with other professionals in order to enhance services to clients.

(b) Counsellors should be respectful and mindful of confidentiality in all communications with other professionals about clients.

(c) Counsellors should negotiate to work collaboratively with other professionals working with the same client.

(d) Counsellors working in a team with other professionals should seek respect for counselling ethics from the team.

Counsellors and the law

(a) Counsellors shall work within the law.

(b) Counsellors shall notify the Association when they are convicted of a serious offence (being either any offence under the Crimes Act or an offence under any other statute that carries a potential sentence of six months imprisonment or more).

Relationship with employers and third party funders

(a) Counsellors should adhere to and uphold the ethics of the profession and should avoid compromising them in the face of institutional requirements.

(b) Counsellors shall be honest and trustworthy in dealings with employers and third party funders.

(c) Counsellors shall endeavour to build healthy working relationships and systems of communication with employers and third party funders in order to enhance services to clients.

(d) Counsellors are encouraged to contribute to policy development and seek to maintain and improve the quality of service in their work setting.

(e) Counsellors should promote equal employment opportunity policies in their work settings.

Supervision

The purpose of professional supervision is for counsellors to reflect on and develop effective and ethical practice. It also has a monitoring purpose with regard to counsellors' work. Supervision includes personal support, mentoring professional identity development and reflection upon the relationships between persons, theories, practices, work contexts and cultural perspectives. Professional supervision is a partnership. It is a contractual, collaborative and confidential process, based upon informed consent. Professional supervision may take a number of forms, including individual or group supervision and may involve telephone, email and letters. It may be live or may be based on personal recall, notes, videotapes, audiotapes, transcripts or client's creative works.

Professional supervision arrangements

(a) Counsellors shall arrange for regular and ongoing supervision with competent supervisors, who should be either NZAC members, or members of another professional body with a Code of Ethics acceptable to the NZAC National Executive.

(b) The frequency of supervision shall be in relation to workload and relative to the experience of the counsellor. The recommended guideline is that while working full-time, the counsellor averages one hour of supervision per fortnight.

(c) Counsellors should seek supervision from a person who is not in a position of authority over them.

(d) Counsellors should seek cultural consultation to support their work with persons who have different cultural backgrounds from their own.

(e) Counsellors and supervisors shall be jointly responsible for establishing a supervision contract, which should be regularly reviewed and time-limited.

Responsibilities in professional supervision

(a) Counsellors shall be responsible for:

— selecting and taking to supervision relevant aspects of their work and their personal functioning.

(b) Supervisors shall be responsible for:

— assisting counsellors to explore and address their professional practice,

— helping counsellors to monitor their competence, safety and fitness to practice.

— disclosing concerns about the counsellor's work to the counsellor, before taking further action.

— maintaining the boundaries between supervision and other relationships the supervisor may have with the counsellor.

(c) Counsellors and supervisors are jointly responsible for:

— distinguishing between supervision relationships and other professional or personal relationships.

— identifying when the counsellor needs to seek counselling for personal concerns.

Competence in professional supervision

(a) Supervisors should actively participate in professional education in supervision.

(b) Supervisors should participate in ongoing professional development.

(c) Supervisors should obtain supervision for their work as supervisors.

(d) Supervisors should take into account limitations to their competence and suggest consultations and referrals when appropriate.

TYPES OF COUNSELLING

Counseling should be looked upon in terms of the amount of direction that the counselor gives the counselee. This direction ranges from full direction (directive counseling) to no direction (nondirective counseling).

Directive Counselling

Directive counseling is the process of listening to a member's problem, deciding with the member what should be done, and then encouraging and motivating the person to do it. This type of counseling accomplishes the function of advice; but it may also reassure; give emotional release; and, to a minor extent, clarify thinking. Most everyone likes to give advice, counselors included, and it is easy to do. But is it effective? Does the counselor really understand the member's problem? Does the counselor have the technical knowledge of human behavior and the judgment to make the "right" decision? If the decision is right, will the member follow it? The answer to these questions is often no, and that is why advice- giving is sometimes an unwise act in counseling.

Although advice-giving is of questionable value, some of the other functions achieved by directive counseling are worthwhile. If the counselor is a good listener, then the member should experience some emotional release. As the result of the emotional release, plus ideas that the counselor imparts, the member may also clarify thinking. Both advice and reassurance may be worthwhile if they give the member more courage to take a workable course of action that the member supports.

Nondirective counseling

Nondirective, or client-centered, counseling is the process of skillfully listening to a counselee, encouraging the person to explain bothersome problems, and helping him or her to understand those problems and determine courses of action. This type of counseling focuses on the member, rather than on the counselor as a judge and advisor; hence, it is "client-centered." This type of counseling is used by professional counselors, but nonprofessionals may use its techniques to work more effectively with service members. The unique advantage of nondirective counseling is its ability to cause the member's reorientation. It stresses changing the person, instead of dealing only with the immediate problem in the usual manner of directive counseling.

The counselor attempts to ask discerning questions, restate ideas, clarify feelings, and attempts to understand why these feelings exist. Professional counselors treat each counselee as a social and organizational equal. They primarily listen and try to help their client discover and follow improved courses of action. They especially "listen between the lines" to learn the full meaning of their client's feelings. They look for assumptions underlying the counselee's statements and for the events the counselee may, at first, have avoided talking about. A person's feelings can be likened to an iceberg. The counselor will usually only see the revealed feelings and emotions. Underlying these surface indications is the true problem that the member is almost always initially reluctant to reveal.

Personal counseling

All personal problems should not be referred to a specialist. Your first duty as a chief is to recognize whether the problem is beyond your ability to help or not. Many times you can solve personal problems with a telephone call. If the problem is beyond your ability to solve, then give the division officer a chance to solve the problem. Stay informed of the progress made toward solving the problem. If the problem requires assistance from outside the command, you can smooth the process by making appointments and ensuring the counselee gets help. Keep informed of progress and follow-up! As a CPO, you may encounter situations in which persons being counseled must be referred to other sources for assistance. There will be times when a person will have special problems that will require special help. These problems should be handled by such specialists as the chaplain, legal officer, and medical officer.

The effective CPO should be able to recognize situations in which referral is necessary and to assist the counselee in obtaining maximum benefit from these referrals. Examples of situations in which referral would be appropriate include drug and alcohol abuse, psychological problems or behavioral disorders, medical problems, personal limitations, such as a personality conflict with the counselor and the inability of the counselor to relate to or comprehend a counselee's problem. In each instance, the key to successful referral lies not in the ability to diagnose a problem but rather in the ability to recognize those signs or symptoms that indicate referral to appropriate sources. To assist CPOs in fulfilling their advising and counseling responsibilities with regard to referral, the Navy has developed an impressive array of helping resources.

Professional, performance, and enlisted evaluation counseling all have several things in common. Standards should be set; standards should be clear and understood by the counselee; targets should be set for each individual; and both good and poor performance of subor- dinates should be documented and the subor- dinates counseled. Professional and performance counseling takes place throughout the year. Enlisted evaluation counseling should take place once a quarter to allow personnel a chance to improve before receiving the formal evaluation. A good place to start is at the end of the formal evaluation period. You can outline the minimum required performance you expect from each paygrade and rating within the work center or division. This is setting a clear standard of performance. Professional and performance counseling will be based on these standards.

Ensure each subordinate understands the required level of performance you expect from him or her. Set performance targets for each individual. People are different and have different capabilities. By setting performance targets above the required minimum, you will be able to maximize subor- dinate output. Setting a standard target of performance could discourage less capable performers or cause more capable performers to become bored. Remember to individualize the target performance.

CONSTRUCTIVIST CAREER COUNSELING

Counseling as a profession has developed in a social context.

The advance of science and technology, the rise of mass consumerism, the deterioration of families, neighborhoods, and small communities, and the increasing irrelevance of traditional authority, all create problems for people trying to cope with everyday living. At the same time the modernist ideas of progress, productivity, and perfectibility, buttressed by the belief that objective rationality would eventually "cure all," carry people into more complex and disturbing life circumstances. In this modernist context, counseling took on the trappings of Technical Rationality (e.g., objectivity, neutrality, expertness, behavioral reductionism, quantification, measurement) and aspects of instrumental reason (e.g., efficiency, effectiveness, and accountability)—all of which belong more to economists than to counselors.

These social transformations have enormous implications for career counseling. Client lives are increasingly characterized by ambiguity, uncertainty, and conflict. Globalization and the undercutting of traditional customs radically alters the nature of day-to-day social life and affects most personal experience. In certain ways the 1990s are better than previous decades (for some) and in other ways the 90s are simply awful (for many). To quote Dorothy, "We're not in Kansas anymore, Toto." In order to help individuals navigate these changing contexts, counseling is in need of revision and re-formation. Counselors must comprehend both the scope and the effect of these transformations and how they intertwine with each individual and therefore with the self.

In general, this means that issues such as "self-construction" instead of "self-presentation," "self-as-narrative" instead of "self-as-traits," and "life-planning" instead of "career choice," become of paramount importance to career counselors. The author has begun to outline a constructivist career counseling perspective which is designed to be appropriate to the post-industrial/post-modern context. The main concepts and practical career-counseling procedures from this perspective are outlined below.

Constructivist Concepts

Constructivist thought has its roots in philosophy, psychology, science, and cultural studies. Some constructivist concepts which can be applied to counseling include the following:

1. There is no single "God's eye" view of reality—rather, there are multiple realities. Although there is no "one right way" to think, feel, or do, some ways are better than others. One of the challenges for constructivists is to devise ways of ascertaining better and worse ways of thinking, acting, and being, usually by considering more vigorously the consequences of our thinking and acting; examining the assumptions and beliefs underlying our alternatives; and taking individual choice more seriously.

2. Humans are "self-organizing" entities, not a set of traits or repertory of behaviors. Each person's life is a story, or set of stories-an evolving biographical narrative under continuous revision.

3. Individuals "construct" their own selves through the interpretations they make and the actions they take. Increasingly, societal conditions call for individuals to be active and reflective selves, aware of the contexts in which they live, and capable of becoming agentic—at times resistive—and creative in relationships and work.

4. A self is "polyphonic"; it has several voices. Four important voices are voice of health and well-being: voice of intimacy: voice of work life and learning ; and voice of spirituality.

5. People are "meaning-makers" and word-munchers. They use language and action to make meaning out of daily activities. The most important personal meanings are relational. They are constructed through interactions with others and with aspects of the surrounding world.

6. To exist as an empowered person requires reflection and examination of the assumptions underlying daily decisions and actions. Critical reflection enables the building of a world-view which includes the following elements:

— A wholistic rather than reductive psychology of people.

— The moral idea that self-fulfillment is "good"-one should strive to become what one is capable of being.

— A tripartite concept of personal freedom. First, one is responsible for one's own thinking and actions. Second, personal freedom is dependent on the quality of relationships which one builds and maintains. Third, personal freedom is influenced by the kind and quality of one's engagement in meaning beyond one's own ego (transcendent meaning) in such phenomena as nature, society, art, hobbies, God, compassionate action on behalf of others, and work.

Practical Counseling Consideration

Constructivist career counseling is a general method of life planning. It is a philosophical and psychological framework from which to work, rather than a set of techniques. However, certain counseling interventions are clearly constructivist.

— *Collaboration*: The counselor and client are allies, with each making significant contributions to counseling. The counselor is an expert on the counseling process and the client is an expert on his or her own life experience.

— *Receptive Inquiry*: The counselor promotes inquiry into the client's life-world within a context where the client feels simultaneously safe and challenged. Receptive inquiry tools include meaning-generating questions, metaphorical transformations, the use of artwork and objects to create meaning, autobiographical writing, visualization, and dialogical discussion.

— *Pattern Recognition*: The counselor and client try to identify "patterns of influence" which are shaping the client's thinking and acting, especially influential relationships. Relationships, informal relations with peers and family, and mediated relationships such as those generated by media, often are more influential in career development and job-getting than traditional psychometrically-oriented career counseling activities.

— *Primacy of Life Experience*: The counselor and client work directly with the client's life experience (i.e., with perceptions and personal meanings as revealed through narrative, journaling, interview dialogue, concept-mapping, artwork, and other self-revelatory activities). Counseling is not so much a matter of "initiating" change as it is a matter of influencing change already underway—influencing the direction of an "evolving self.) Client resistance or reluctance is a concept not used by constructivist counselors. The constructivist assumption is that whatever a client is doing or thinking is necessary for the client's coping or survival, given the client's immediate frame of reference.

— *Mindfulness*: The constructivist career counselor regards mindfulness as a desirable goal for both clients and counselors. The essential elements of mindfulness are:

a) the creation of new categories of constructs to help interpret experience,

b) expanding openness and receptivity to new information, both internal and external, and

c) the awareness of more than one perspective on any aspect of one's life-world, including career. Critical reflection is a key tool in developing mindfulness.

— *Creating Meaning Through Activity*: It is involvement in activities such as work experience, cooperative education placement, job shadowing, volunteering, work-site visitation, and work simulation, which can provide the basis for personal meaning. The usefulness of such activities to clients is greatly enhanced through "reflection-on-activity" and "discussion and dialogue" with a counselor. Activity provides the raw materials (experiences), but it is reflection and counseling activities such as interview dialogue, group discussion, journaling, concept-mapping, dependable strengths analysis, and metaphorizing of experience and self, which influence both the evolving self and career decision-making.

Constructivist Approaches for Career Counselors

Constructivist theory offers alternative approaches to career development and counseling. Based on holistic approach, constructivism emphasizes the self-organizing principles underlying human experience. The decision to use a constructivist framework for career counseling resulted from the observation that youth often were not lacking career information; instead, they did not feel empowered or motivated to put the information to use. In a number of cases, feelings ranging from disempowerment to apathy were due to a lack of knowledge about self in relation to the world of work. Consequently, a counseling approach, which empowers clients to adopt proactive, mindful stances about their worklife, needed to be developed. Constructivist framework several core counseling approaches were identified as important for career counselors. The more essential ones will be summarized below.

Meaning-Making

One of the basic tenets of a constructivist approach is that people are meaning-makers. Terms such as "autopoesis," "sense-making," "self-organizing," and "meaning-making" have been researched and described by numerous constructivist writers and include specific references to how people interpret the events of their lives in the pursuit of meaning. A constructivist premise is that career information is enhanced significantly when personal meanings become the central task of the counseling session. These meaning-making processes take on a variety of forms that promote client self-awareness of the processes underlying meaningful career decisions.

Perhaps the most ubiquitous meaning-making opportunity is that which exists while clients are relating important events in their lives. Counselors can significantly enhance their understanding of client self-organizing processes by listening carefully to the words and phrases used when clients relate an event or story. Although this appears to be rather obvious, professionals often overlook the positive impact of using clients' own interpretations as evidence of their meaning systems.

Meaning-making occurs when counselors assist clients in becoming aware of the latter's meaning structures connect to create an overall life story and how the client interprets events in order to author a story that has sense, cohesion, and viability. Furthermore, collaborating with clients to create stories featuring possible, future selves greatly increases the likelihood of client growth and change. Counselors therefore need to be able to work effectively with client narratives in the following ways:

1. Listening closely to unique phrases and words used by the client.
2. Recognizing that client interpretations are unique and can be viewed as either viable or not viable rather than valid or not valid.
3. Assisting clients in moving beyond rational explanations of experiences to deeper underlying beliefs, values, and assumptions.

Metaphors: Metaphorical language is a valuable meaning-making opportunity often missed in counseling interactions. Although the benefit of working with client metaphors is beginning to be more widely accepted, counselors often overlook opportunities to use them effectively. In everyday language, metaphors help transfer one idea or concept to another. When simple verbal descriptions fall short of describing experiences, metaphors provide a bridge towards deeper understandings. Working with metaphors within the counseling session is not an easy task. Perhaps one of the most difficult challenges facing counselors is to refrain from imposing their own metaphors onto the clients' experiences.

Asking descriptive and contrast questions helps to elicit metaphors from the client. For example, one client described her alienation from her friends when she returned to the workforce as no longer being the "hub" of a tight network of friends. She mourned this loss. After asking descriptive questions which helped her articulate, and "connect with," her experience of now being more like a "spoke of the wheel," the counselor was able to help her re-define her role as a friend and the overall meaning of friendship. Now perceiving herself as an integral part of the network, but not necessarily the center, she felt more secure in knowing that she did not have to abandon important relationships in order to pursue her career. Consequently, this new version of her metaphor, explicated through effective questioning by the counselor, provided a visual reminder of a newly defined aspect of self which subsequently had a positive impact on her career goals.

Critical Reflection. Helping clients become more cognizant of their beliefs, values, and assumptions is a central component of meaning-making. Without a certain degree of self-awareness, people tend to lead mindless, haphazard lives where important decisions are often left to chance. A constructivist perspective promotes an "examined life" and encourages the critical reflection of values, beliefs, and assumptions. Once beliefs, values, and assumptions have been explicated, clients are more likely to:

(a) deepen their understanding of their own world views and how these views influence their worklives;

(b) gain insight into the origin of these world views; and

(c) determine the viability of maintaining or perhaps revising their views.

Enhancing self-knowledge enables a person to assess life positions; in doing so, an individual can determine the extent to which these positions may either constrain or support growth in various aspects of employment. Counselors act as a mirror or a lens, enabling the client to gain more knowledge of self and the world. Through the process of explication, leading to either re-vision or re-affirmation, the final stage of empowerment occurs when the client realizes that choices can be made from different vantage points. Outdated, non-viable, beliefs and values can be modified and re-worked into broader, more inclusive structures of meaning.

Counselors need to become aware of the ways in which they either empower or disempower clients through their counseling approaches. A traditional "test them and tell them" approach to counseling, for example, can disempower the client when the counselor assumes an expert position regarding the client's personhood. It is, therefore, important for career counselors to begin by clarifying expectations, roles, and tasks of both the client and the counselor. One client complained about a counselor who was not helpful because she refused to tell him what he should be. This highlights the importance of clarifying anticipated outcomes and processes as soon as possible. By doing so, clients can assume a proactive stance during the initial session.

Often counselors inadvertently disempower clients by asking questions that fail to promote critical reflection. Instead, they begin dispersing information that clients themselves could gather. While information is a necessary part of career counseling, how it is shared and received directly influences client motivation. Career counselors can significantly enhance their practice by re-defining their roles as "empowerment promoters" rather than information providers.

DISTANCE DELIVERY IN CAREER COUNSELING

Generations of rural people have relied on resource industries for their livelihoods. In many areas, these career opportunities have been eroded by changing trade policies, technology, and the depletion of renewable resources. Career education and counseling are more important in modern rural societies than ever before, but providing services to a dispersed population by conventional means is costly and, in many cases, impractical. Modern technologies now allow career counselors to deliver their services from afar.

Distance Career Counseling

Distance education grew out of efforts to provide academic courses in schools that could not afford conventional methods of teaching. However, Pelton emphasized the need for sensitivity to geographic and cultural differences to avoid using communication technologies for "mindless megatraining". In distance career counseling, four factors must be considered.

1. *Community Characteristics*: Most career counseling theory is rooted in an urban-industrial environment and value system. For example, job-search skills include some forceful techniques that make sense in a competitive labor market where employers do not know one applicant from another. However, the more informal hiring practices in many rural communities make it improper to use tactics such as follow-up telephone calls for making oneself more visible. However, there are differences between rural communities in terms of location, history, transportation links, and economic base. Some communities embrace a set of values and practices that approximate those of urban society; others have very different customs. Where communities lie on the rural-urban continuum has a major influence on the career education needs of residents.
2. *Nature of the Labor Market*: Conventional career development theory assumes a diverse, specialized labor market. Most rural communities have a narrower range of occupational opportunities and are more generalist, with people engaging in multiple activities in both formal and informal labor markets. Because rural communities are not smaller versions of urban society, career paths and career values are significantly different. In fact, rural Canadians likely have more in common with rural people in other nations than they have with urban Canadians.

3. *Rural Communities in Transition*: Rural labor markets are changing. Non-traditional businesses and occupations are emerging, but the process of economic diversification is uneven. Some communities are quick to seize opportunities while others avoid the risk and uncertainty of change. Communities have a significant influence on people's occupational goals and expectations, propensity for risk-taking, approaches to problem-solving, and self-concept, all of which are important to career development.

4. *Rural Culture*: Environment shapes language. People develop a sense of the meaning of words from personal experience. Shared language is fundamental to any teaching. Experiences with career education programs show that it is important to understand the implications of even a simple word such as "work." When most people think about going to work, they envisage working for an employer in exchange for money and fringe benefits. In non-industrialized areas, work entails not only wage-earning labor but any activity that contributes to the standard of living of the household. Rural careers involve a wide range of non-market activities. Distance career counselors must develop sensitivity to the differences between their own culturally-derived assumptions and those of their clients, and use language that the client finds meaningful.

Distance career counselors use a variety of communication technologies to deliver programs. Each technology has strengths and weaknesses and the choice depends on the task, the availability of equipment, and the cost. An effective means of distance counseling is audio-teleconferencing: it is accessible, affordable, and a comfortable medium for discussion. The author's programs generally incorporate 8-12 teleconferences of 90-120 minutes each. Most clients use temporary sites fitted with portable equipment which has been shipped to host communities before the program begins. Any facility that has regular telephone service is viable: hospitals, schools, and community organization offices. Each site has a microphone and speaker box which are linked to other sites, allowing participants to speak and listen to each other.

The system ensures confidentiality, which is important to promoting free and open discussion of personal matters. It also allows counselors to use guest speakers. Young, rural women have been introduced to nontraditional occupations via role models in teleconference sessions; others have been provided information on rural-development initiatives through their interaction with a panel of community and government representatives. Guests participate from their homes or offices, making it convenient to engage competent resource people. The widespread use of video-cassette players allows counselors to demonstrate skills and to stimulate discussion of sensitive issues using video. Video cassettes have been produced to give parents ideas for helping their children explore career options, to encourage young women and teen-aged mothers, to help career drifters examine their lives and their feelings, and to teach peer and lay counselors to aid others.

Print materials are also integrated into programs. Workbooks explain career development issues and strategies and provide clients with a record of their experiences. Supplementary materials give information on the local labor market. Counselor handbooks offer detailed suggestions for delivering the programs. By adding their own supplementary materials, counselors can adapt the programs to any locality. In developing and delivering distance career counseling programs, several factors will enhance success:

1. *Partnerships*: Community-based partners, whose mandate and/or activities agree with the program, must be actively involved throughout. Possible partners include schools, community colleges, co-operatives, development associations, business organizations, farm associations, unions, rural women's associations, youth groups, and native organizations.

2. *Program Content*: Variations among rural communities demand that programs remain flexible and adaptable.

Within a general framework, local considerations may require career counselors to add, drop, or modify program content.

3. *Program Delivery*: Many community associations are willing to volunteer their facilities. In one program, participants used fax machines to introduce themselves and handle information requests during the program. A local coordinator received bulky materials and distributed them to participants as needed.
4. *Program Administration*: Many administrative tasks can be simplified with local on-site coordinators. Local knowledge can help avoid problems.

THREE-TIERED MODEL OF CAREER COUNSELING SERVICES

The increasing probability that the average person will have many jobs over a lifetime is accompanied by a growing recognition of the need for lifelong career development services. To provide a coherent and articulated system for career and employment counseling, it has been suggested that counseling services for adults should be organized in a three-tiered structure. The argument for using such a structure is to ensure that individuals have access to a counselor in accordance with the individuals' level of need. Identifying needs and offering targeted assistance is at the foundation of a tiered organizational structure.

First Tier —Career Exploration

The focus of the first tier of service would be on self-exploration and career assessment. There would be a guided self-serve information system to meet the widespread need for occupational, educational, and labor market information. It would be the first stop for almost all clients who currently go to varied agencies for this type of information; such clinics presently strain existing resources which provide this service, mostly via individual counseling. Some of the occupational, educational, training, and labor market information that is required can be obtained on a self-serve basis.

— *Coached Self-Help*: There are people who are not served properly by "self-serve" systems, and frequently the most needy clients are confused and intimidated by this kind of service. Therefore, it is important to have a coach to ensure that visitors can define what they want and then find it.

— *Computer Assistance*: Many people who have little difficulty in working with a computer, prefer this mode of help. This is particularly true for clients who have developed a distrust of people in the helping professions or who have difficulty rising to the demands of interpersonal counseling. A computer system can undertake the role of performing "needs determination" interviews with clients. At the present time, Human Resources Development Canada has under development an Automated Service Kiosk (ASK) which will allow clients to explore four employability dimensions (occupational goal, training, job search and job maintenance). This methodology has great promise for first line delivery systems, and can provide a good alternative to the person who is reticent about talking with a counselor and who prefers to get started with a machine.

— *Needs Determination Interview*: Fundamental to the first tier of service is the inclusion of a career needs determination interview. By assessing needs "up front," false starts and unnecessary steps are avoided. The needs determination will help the client to recognize the services available from or through the Career Service Center and to identify what steps need to be taken next. The career needs determination interview could be conducted by a counselor or by an "expert" computer system.

— *Group Seminars*: Few clients receive group counseling, yet brief group career serninars or workshops may satisfy the needs of perhaps 75% of people seeking help. Group sessions cover the exploration of one's talents, the formulation of occupational goals, the examination of educational alternatives, the development of a plan, the learning of appropriate skills, or as a lead in to computer-assisted career guidance systems. There would be extensive use of group information and self-help sessions in the first tier of service.

— *Special Needs Clients*: Special needs clients must be connected with the right agency at the outset of service delivery. In tier one, information on entitlements for income support, housing, day care, and the like would be available from the center "coach" or from the computerized information kiosks.

Second Tier Self-Exploration

In the second tier, more in-depth assistance would be available. A great many people want and need more than information about education, training, and the labor market. They need to clarify their ideas about their interests, aptitudes, and personality, and how these relate to education, training, and work. Conger, Hiebert, and Hong-Farrell found that many clients, who initially requested career information, quickly acknowledged the need to take control of their lives and overcome their self-defeating thoughts and behaviors, to learn to cope with the "hassles" of trying to improve themselves, and to believe that they really can achieve something. Assistance may be given in small group training sessions.

In some cases, guided group exploration might be appropriate. The small group work should focus on the development of skills necessary to sustain group members' motivation and overcome their self-defeating thoughts. Clients need actual skill training (demonstration, practice, and feedback, in addition to the discussion) if they are to learn how to implement the skills in their lives. The second tier would also house entitlement officers who could handle inquiries and claims for unemployment insurance and social assistance, as well as information on other entitlements. There would be other specialized staff available to arrange testing or other diagnostic services, and to assist clients in getting placed in training programs. Some rehabilitation counseling could also be provided in the second tier of service.

Third Tier — Reaching out

The third tier would include individual counseling where the client clarifies his or her inability to do what needs to be done; evaluates career strengths and barriers; examines assumptions which color thoughts and actions; lists ways of overcoming barriers and of using strengths; evaluates the alternative resolution against strengths, barriers, and values; and, states a specific counseling goal or action plan to which the client is committed and which focuses on a relevant career concern.

Another important feature in this tier of service would include an active intervention with third parties, and the mentoring and coaching of clients. Many people at risk do not have a friend who can help them through the difficult steps of actually managing their own careers. Few counselors reach out of their offices on behalf of a client to speak with family members, educators, agency officials, and employers. Counselors who have gone an "extra mile" for their clients by intervening with third parties have often found it to be the most effective and most satisfying counseling task that they have done.

COUNSELING AND GUIDANCE SOFTWARE

Computer-enhanced counseling programs offer exciting possibilities in this age of the Information Revolution. While technology continues to leap forward, research literature indicates a gap in resources addressing counselors' computer-relevant needs. One critical need is for information about counseling software that is appropriate to the needs of clients and that performs as advertised.

To begin to address this need, the Counseling Software Guide was developed. The Guide is a collaborative product of two years and three organizations that continue to provide significant leadership in promoting the use of computers in counseling and human services: the Career/Vocational Education and Guidance Department of the Santa Clara County, California, Office of Education; the ERIC Clearinghouse on Counseling and Personnel Services; and, the American Association for Counseling and Development. The wealth of information contained in this 492-page major reference includes:

(l) general information about the use of computers in counseling,

(2) practical guidelines on what to look for in software,

(3) an overview of trends and developments in the availability and use of software,

(4) an overview of the range of software programs available on a particular topic, and

(5) information on specific software programs.

The Guide includes these other unique features:

— Factual and up-to-date descriptions of over 500 counseling-relevant software programs.

— A large number of intensive software reviews.

— A thorough discussion of how far we have come in the use of computers in counseling and what paths and options the future holds.

Resources in the Appendices include: a complete contact and program address list, a program list with user level and computer compatibility, a software evaluation checklist, and an index of reviewers and programs. Software program topics include software for:

(1) personal counseling,

(2) career counseling,

(3) academic advising,

(4) testing, and

(5) administration.

Characteristics of Ideal Couinseling Software

Some of the most important characteristics of high quality programs include:

1. Detailed, accurate advice about hardware requirements (e.g., capacity, printer support, type of monitor) and clear instructions on how to install and/or start the program.
2. Compatibility with both IBM PC and the Apple series of computers.
3. Trial use and/or rental options.
4. Frequent revisions and updates provided at no, or minimal, cost to the purchaser.
5. Ability to complete the program, or at least stand-alone segments of it, within a 50-minute time period.
6. Attractive graphics (images and colors).
7. Features that capitalize on the interactive and user-involvement potential of the computer.
8. Ability to back up and change answers and move between sections.
9. Option for printed feedback and the ability to save information.
10. Minimal consequences of errors.

One of the many ideas suggested in the Guide for selecting software is a simplified three-step process called the SEP Approach. See the software for a cursory visual assessment to determine if further consideration is warranted; Evaluate the purpose, usefulness, appeal, and cost of the program for your clients; and Plan how the software can be incorporated into your program of services. If the software passes the SEP test, a professional trial/assessment of the contents is critical, with both counselors and clients.

Price generally parallels complexity and quality of programs; however, check on the company's return policy. If possible, preview the product through exhibitors at professional conventions. Consider also whether it is generative (i.e., allows the client to expand their consciousness to trigger growth) or limited and "canned." Will it enhance the quality of the counseling relationship, or will it interfere with research-proven qualities of counseling effectiveness?

Trends and Development

Research: As need and implementation increase, further research will be needed on procedures and outcomes. Many program topics (e.g., personal counseling) need further development, matching technique with:

(1) medium of presentation,

(2) skills of the counselor constructing the materials,

(3) training of counselors using the software, and

(4) research on specific use of programs.

Quality: The extreme differences in both quality and potential effectiveness demands that the user be alert. Quality factors to signal include theoretical orientation, user manual and support, training needed, research, client interaction, technical problems and which need careful scrutiny by the potential user.

Ethical Standards: The integration of computer technology into counseling raises many potential problem areas and ethical issues. The revised AACD Ethical Standards provides ten guidelines for acceptable professional training and service delivery. Counselor educators and practicing counselors should examine their "boundaries of competence" to use computer technology ethically in their services to clients.

Innovations: A significant new development is the proliferation of software programs that are easily understood (e.g., Hypercard, which allows the counselor to focus on needs, not the program language). Voice activation programming will further enhance the trend toward user-friendliness, and with wider acceptance, the price will become more affordable.

Holistic, multidisciplinary computer applications will refine and interrelate the current domains of self-reporting, performance, and psycho-physiological measuring by the computer. If counselors are to use computers effectively they will need a systematic strategy and comprehensive model for implementing computer applications in counseling and human development service delivery systems. Progress toward interconnectivity, with all programs running on all machines, makes startling improvements each year, but is yet to be fully realized. Counselor generated programming is an important future step.

Counselors will creatively adapt marketed software to meet client needs. Compact Disk-Read Only Memory (CD-ROM) players and touch screens are looming on the periphery of counseling software, and many counselors now have access to the hardware necessary to run the programs. Vertical markets (programs scaled for various levels of competencies) for special groups (e.g., at-risk youth, adult career-changers, the outplaced) will increase.

Future Trends

1. Greater attention will be paid to careful and systematic planning for the use of computers in counseling.
2. Various counseling functions will become increasingly interrelated as a result of the use of computers.
3. Counselors will increasingly demonstrate more imaginative and innovative uses of computers in counseling.
4. Counselors will make regular use of a centralized source of review and evaluation of counseling-relevant software.

MULTIMEDIA CAREER INTERVENTIONS

It is estimated that over one-third of Canada's high-school

students will drop out of school.. This is devastating when one considers that two-thirds of the new jobs created between now and the year 2000 will require qualifications beyond high school. One of the great challenges to career development professionals is how to motivate this massive "at-risk" youth population

(a) to persist with education & training through high school and beyond, and

(b) to take responsibility for, and action toward, their own career development. The advent of multimedia computer technology has increased the potential for "high impact" career interventions. This can be particularly effective for at-risk youth, a population with extremely low motivation to use print-based materials.

Knowledge for Youth About Careers (KYAC) is one such interactive, multimedia career program. Pilot-tests with youths aged 13-19 years suggest that it can improve motivation and can instill knowledge of (and skills in) career decision-making, information interviewing, networking, and career planning. KYAC is based on Weiner's attribution change theory and Bandura's self-efficacy theory. The video scenes model career development skills like information interviewing, networking, mentorships, and seeking assistance with learning disabilities. Concerns such as persistence with math and science courses; women in technology, trades, and management occupations; and minority representation in all of the above, are also addressed.

In addition to the videodisc, CD-ROM disc, and computer diskettes, program materials include a Facilitator Manual and Participant Workbook (photocopy master) with 32 hours of classroom & workshop activities, a Research & Development Handbook, and a Facilitator Guide to Scene Playback. The program operates on IBM PS2s and 486 DOS-based ISA computers In KYAC, students select one of two main characters, (each character then ages from 17 to 28 years), by touching their chosen character's face on the computer screen (decisions can also be made using a mouse, but at-risk youth prefer touch-screen technology). One character is a young man who has dropped out of high school and is now working as a janitor.

The other is a young woman (multiracial black/white) who is having learning difficulties at school and is working part time as a waitress. A "grabber" scene (with rock music) introduces the two characters and the "future" orientation of the program. The next scene to appear is a conversation between the selected character and his or her future self. It was found that at-risk youth much prefer this approach to the standard parent/teacher/counselor/'career expert' giving advice. Such conversations occur several times throughout the program. At the conclusion of each scene are two decision choices, represented by animated graphics. Users touch the screen (or click the mouse) to make their selections, and the computer plays an "outcome" scene, many of which have time-delays (e.g., 1 1/2 years later) built into them.

In some cases, the computer selects outcome scenes based on probabilities; this allows the program to be more consistent with real life since a given decision can have a variety of outcomes. During scenes, the action "freezes" at key points, and small graphic "thought-balloons" appear on the screen. These are used

(a) to enhance user identification with characters in the scenes,

(b) to illustrate ineffective beliefs and attitudes, and

(c) to model effective, empowering career beliefs and attitudes.

If users touch these thought-balloons within 2 seconds of when they appear, they will hear what the character is thinking. If users do not respond within 2 seconds, the icon fades and the video continues. In this way, users actively seek the information in the thought-balloons and therefore anticipate and attend to the information. This same principle applies to all of the character decision sequences users request the outcomes of their own decisions, so they are more alert when the information is presented or when skills are modeled.

Approximately 2 1/2 hours of interaction time is available in the main character decision sequences described above, although users can interrupt their interaction at any time and pick it up on another occasion. In addition, 32 hours of classroom & workshop activities reinforce and provide more personal application of the skills, knowledge, and attitudes presented in the video scenes.

AN ACTION APPROACH TO CAREER COUNSELING

Although counselors have implicitly understood and used a number of its tenets for some time, an action-theoretical approach is a relatively recent development in career counseling. It is based on the premise that the subject of career counseling is the goal-directed and intentional action of the client. Action theory sees clients as agents who steer and direct their activities. As applied to career counseling, it represents an integration of constructionist, contextual, and narrative approaches that have recently received attention in counseling, psychology, and the social sciences.

Counselors frequently base their practice on how clients construct and resolve problems in their daily lives. Career and counseling theories and research have not always been able to remain close to this understanding of practice. In an effort to remedy this situation, action theory offers a conceptual framework and language for understanding career development and career counseling that is close to human experience.

Much of career counseling has either been based on the measurement of client interests and personality or aimed at the remediation of socialization effects. Action theory's perspective is based on a constructionist epistemology which highlights the importance of the way we organize our knowledge in our daily lives. Essentially, constructionists suggest that people use a variety of concepts and frameworks to organize and explain their own and other people's behavior. Moreover, the meaning of people's experience is reflected in their construct system. Action and career are two important and interrelated constructs in the lives of many people. People frequently think of themselves and other people as purposive, proactive, and self-organizing. For the most part, their behavior is goal-directed and intentional. Action refers to short-term behavior of this kind, but other constructs are needed for sequences of interrelated actions over the long term.

Career is one construct that many people use to understand goal-directed and intentional action over the long term. For example, completing an examination has meaning in the short-term; it provides a sense of closure, or perhaps accomplishment. When joined with other actions, it can also have long-term meaning, such as qualification for further study or job entry. Action theory provides a conceptual framework and language useful to our understanding of career and career counseling. Some of the relevant propositions are

1. Action can be seen from three perspectives:
   - the manifest behavior of the actors
   - the conscious cognitions (thoughts and feelings) that accompany, steer, and direct the manifest behavior as it occurs
   - the social meaning in which the action is embedded.

   All three perspectives are critical to understanding action and career. Some theories approach career from one of the perspectives and emphasize behavior, cognition, or social meaning almost exclusively. The action-theoretical approach integrates all perspectives.

2. The construction of career occurs, at least in part, through social discourse between counselor and client. However, the action pertinent to career occurs both outside of and within counseling.

3. Most counselors recognize that career profoundly involves the emotions of their clients. For example, long-term plans and goals are intimately related to happiness. Moreover,

career is concerned with practical action, that is, balancing between what must be done in the short term and what can be done in one's life. As clients take action regarding these expectations and possibilities, emotions are likely involved.

4. There is also joint action, which is a third kind of activity which lies between individual activity and external events. This is in contrast to theories that place the locus of career within the person. Career is not solely a matter of individual action, but heretofore counseling has not had a language to describe persons acting together in the social and dynamic nature of career. Nevertheless, this is what counselors and clients do. As they engage in counseling, they actually construct action and career. By virtue of this and other joint actions, the client comes to construct the career she or he will have.

5. The term career itself may not be critical to clients. What is critical is to identify the constructs that clients use to represent long-term, goal-directed, intentional action. For example, "project" may be a construct that represents a sequence of goal-directed action which may be useful to clients.

One primary value of an action-theoretical approach to career counseling is its ability to link theory and practice. Counselors want a conceptual framework that is close to human experience. Among the specific practice implications are the following:

1. *Interpretation is emphasized*: Clients are seen as engaged in the process of making sense of their action—they are interpreters. Intentionality and goal-directedness are two constructs they use to interpret their actions. Actions are also interpreted in light of long-term constructs, such as career. In addition, career involves the interpretation and reinterpretation of past and future (possible) actions in terms of present action. For example, a young woman interprets her decision to quit school as goal-directed: "I needed to get away from a boring and frustrating place." She may

also have some understanding of the long-term implications of her action, such as, "Lots of people quit high school, I'll go to evening classes when I need to." Later in life she may reinterpret these actions in light of subsequent events.

2. Counselors recognize that interpretation occurs in social settings, that is, between clients, their peers, families, employers, or teachers. Thus, career counseling also addresses interpersonal relationships and their meaning for the client.
3. A self-confrontation method can be used to access the conscious cognitions that accompany career-related actions. This method helps clients see themselves in action, aids them as they process their cognitions, and enables them to receive feedback. It integrates cognition, emotion, and action in a conceptual and practical manner. It also uses everyday constructs related to the meaning and experience of clients.

To date, work has largely focused on describing the features of action theory and how it can be applied to career theory and counseling, and research. Young et al.'s method for studying the career conversations of parents and adolescents involved the action of the conversation, the conscious cognitions as the participants steer and direct the conversation, and the social meaning attributed to the conversation by the participants.

CENTRIC CAREER COUNSELING MODEL

Four developmental phases are used to describe movement within the centric model. Although these phases usually develop in a sequential fashion, counselors should expect considerable back and forth movement.

— Readiness (Establishing the Working Alliance).

The initial relationship between counselor and client is critical and sets the foundation for further counseling. Counselors need to create a "mattering" climate where the client feels acknowledged, respected, and valued. Creating this type of climate requires attention to both physical environment and interpersonal dynamics. Within the positive relationship there is the need to assess readiness with respect to expectations, the fulfillment of basic needs, and self-esteem. For many clients there is little point in proceeding to the second phase until some basic issues are resolved. Many unemployed clients, for example, need to normalize their experiences with unemployment before beginning any form of assessment. Also, some clients have misperceptions about the nature of career counseling and should discuss the process with their counselors prior to engaging in further activities. Whatever the issue, counselors must pay particular attention to pacing and only move forward once readiness has been attained.

— Career Exploration and Assessment.

Here the focus is on two different domains: the personal and the external. The personal factors include interests, values, strengths (skills), limitations, and personal style. Clients are encouraged to develop information on the various personal factors through qualitative and quantitative assessments. The information can come from a consideration of each area separately, or in a more comprehensive fashion through the exploration of experiences. The external domain includes significant others, work/leisure experiences, educational background, and labor market options. Obtaining information in these areas requires research, contact with others, and careful consideration of past experiences.

— Evaluation, Compromise, and Integration.

Following exploration and assessment, there is a need to draw the information together and evaluate the viability of various options. Compromises may be necessary, which may facilitate a new integration. It is important in this phase that clients recognize the uncertainty associated with career choice. Some common myths which may need to be addressed are as follows:

- Once you make a career choice you are committed for life.

— The choice you make should be totally fulfilling.

— If you choose correctly you will be guaranteed a successful future.

— Commitment, Action Planning, And Follow Through

This last phase is based on the assumption that clients are ready to move forward with their plans. They are willing to make a commitment to the process and then select and pursue a few basic issues. To assist this process, Walter & Peller use the following criteria in goal setting:

(a) be positive;

(b) use action verbs (ending with "ing");

(c) focus on the present;

(d) be specific and think through the details;

(e) consider only goals which are within the client's control; and

(f) use the client's language.

As clients move forward with their goals and overall action plans, there will be consequences. A need then arises for follow-up to check the viability of plans and to maintain client motivation. This final step leaves room for "fine tuning" and is critically important to long term counseling effectiveness.

ELEMENTARY SCHOOL COUNSELLING

Elementary school counselors face changing demands as education and society move rapidly toward a new century. Counselors must set clear priorities in the face of changing expectations. Our society faces challenges in accepting and benefiting from cultural diversity. Problems emanating from racism exist despite efforts aimed at educational reform.

Elementary school counselors must be aware of transmitting their own cultural values to children and of drawing erroneous conclusions about children's emotional and social well-being based on cultural differences. Moreover, because counseling theories and techniques are not always applicable across cultures, counselors must often look to new and creative ways to work effectively in multicultural settings. Elementary school counselors should advocate for educational programs that include counselors, teachers, parents, and students working together for increased cultural understanding through role playing and other awareness activities.

The so-called traditional family has virtually disappeared in America. Divorce and single-parent homes are a fact of life confronting children. Elementary school counselors must understand the effects of changing family structures and find ways to promote child growth and development within the context of family change. These ways will include divorce groups, training groups for single parents, guidance for latchkey children, and a variety of other important strategies. Elementary school counselors need to develop innovative approaches to help children and parents develop in a healthy fashion in spite of the ambiguity created by divorce and single-parent families. Counselors should assume a proactive stance by collaborating with teachers in developing and implementing family education programs.

Students often begin to experiment with drugs in elementary school and early experimentation frequently leads to abuse and addiction in adolescence. Moreover, educators are aware of problems coming from families made dysfunctional by alcoholism and drug addiction. Elementary school counselors must understand the scope and implications of substance abuse and implement drug education programs that are designed to prevent drug abuse and to help children overcome the effects of substance abuse in their families. Elementary school counselors also need to recognize the serious effects of parents' alcoholism on children's development and implement compassionate approaches to helping these young victims receive help whether or not their parents are willing to accept help.

Child abuse and neglect are rampant in our society. Elementary school counselors can build a positive school environment for youngsters who suffer from abuse and neglect by implementing such programs as parent support groups to prevent physical abuse of children, programs that help identify potential child abusers, and preventive sexual abuse programs. Elementary school counselors cannot work alone in preventing and treating child abuse. They need to develop close working relationships with social services and other community agencies that frequently advocate for victims of abuse and neglect.

Counselors also need to work closely with teachers to help them thoroughly understand signs of abuse and to acquaint them with correct referral procedures. The elementary school classroom may be the most stable setting neglected and abused children experience and may provide the empathy and positive regard needed to help children cope with their ordeal. Elementary school counselors must, therefore, become increasingly sensitive to the victims of abuse and to the need for effective counseling programs in this troublesome area.

Many children in our schools are labeled exceptional and find it difficult to accept that they are "simply human." These children need to feel accepted and to use their exceptional characteristics in extraordinary ways. Children who are not so labeled need to learn ways of benefiting from those who are exceptional. The parents and teachers of exceptional children also need to find ways to understand and assist these youngsters. Elementary school counselors should work to build a supportive learning environment for exceptional children. There is a need for strong ties between counseling and special education.

Counselors should develop programs for parents of exceptional children. Parents of gifted youngsters, for example, have unique needs resulting from misunderstandings created by myths, stereotypes, and the small number of gifted children in the population. Counselors should also develop strategies to help teachers work more effectively with parents of handicapped children because the teacher is in a position to develop an active, ongoing relationship with parents but may lack the training to provide effective counseling support.

Technological advances have changed education, work, and leisure in our society. Although most people experience the benefits of these advances, most also know the anxiety and frustration that accompany rapid technological change as well as the alienation generated by impersonal aspects of technology. Elementary school counselors need to help children develop emotionally and socially in the context of rapid technological change. Counselors often need to deal first with their own concerns about technology before helping children understand the benefits and limitations of technology. Elementary school counselors especially need to acquire competencies with computers, to overcome anxieties about using the technology, and to integrate computer technology into counseling programs.

Elementary school counselors face major challenges as they work with parents and teachers to introduce children to an ever-changing world of work. The emphasis on career education, however, seems to have diminished from its peak in the 1970s when the United States Office of Education demanded high visibility for career education programs in schools. This decline in career education at the elementary school level is unfortunate because economic, political, and social changes have brought women and minorities into the work force in large numbers and have altered how children must be prepared to enter the world of work. Elementary school counselors need to enhance children's career awareness, prevent sex-role stereotyping through career exploration programs, and use role models to expand children's occupational aspirations.

American society has placed increasing emphasis on the need for children to learn basic academic skills. Parents throughout the country complain that children are not learning to read, write, and perform basic mathematics. Governmental and private commissions have studied the poor academic achievement of children and are asking educators to account for the failure of our schools in this important area. If elementary school counselors are to fulfill their mission in schools, they must collaborate with teachers, parents, and school administrators in an effort to improve children's achievement. Elementary school counselors can positively effect children's achievement. Counselors, for example, can implement and evaluate a ten-session program called "Succeeding in School".

Counselors can also consult with parents on matters related to children's academic progress, implement classroom programs that improve the work habits of children who procrastinate with school work, and use group counseling as a means of motivating children to attend school. Children's behavior, both in and out of school, is an important concern of parents and educators. The popular media has documented seemingly widespread school absenteeism and delinquency among our nation's youth.

How to change children's misbehavior and to foster productive behavior are concerns of elementary school counselors. The techniques available to parents, teachers, and elementary school counselors for managing children's behavior are numerous and include modeling, positive reinforcement, behavior contracting, and desensitization. These behavioral change procedures have been thoroughly tested.

Although the application of these methods is often difficult, the collaborative efforts of elementary school counselors, teachers, and parents in applying behavioral techniques eases some of the difficulties and increases the chances of success. Counseling interventions to improve behavior include classroom guidance sessions, small group counseling sessions, and consultation with teachers. Students who receive a combination of these treatment procedures are likely to behave well in the classroom and elsewhere. Children need to support each other in a world filled with conflict. They must learn and practice the interpersonal skills necessary for their present lives and also for the demands of peer pressure in adolescence.

Elementary school counselors must find ways both to challenge and support youngsters in the area of human relations. Counselors can build positive relationships among children and between children and adults through affective education programs in the classroom and through innovative approaches to peer counseling. Elementary school counselors play a major part in developing and maintaining a healthy social climate for children. This aspect of counselors' work is important in part because children's relations with teachers, peers, and family affect learning and achievement. In addition, counselors who strive to improve children's interpersonal skills are helping to ensure that the 1990s and beyond will be years in which society will move forward on the basis of cooperative efforts among the nation's citizens. Finally, the work of elementary school counselors in this area will likely help to produce citizens who strive for productive relations across cultures and nations.

SECONDARY SCHOOL COUNSELLING

Several influences have impacted what has been referred to as "the role" of secondary school counselors. Among the influences are state certification standards; counselor education training programs; the nature of school systems; professional organizations; principals and other administrators' beliefs about counselors; and the counselors themselves. Principals have had a major influence on counselors' roles. In many situations, principals have dictated "the role" by assigning the counselor "duties"—often administrative or quasi-administrative duties (e.g., counting credits, keeping track of attendance, discipline) that have little to do with the actual role of school counselors or the needs of students.

School counselors appear to be reluctant or unable to convince principals that they should perform the duties for which they have been trained. This must change if school counselors are to have any influence in the restructured schools of the future. In this complex and troubled society, school counselors are being asked to assume a greater role in the lives of their students and the students' families. The challenges facing counselors and demands on their time will continue to grow during the next decade. School counselors must choose carefully where they spend their time and energy. But, given the challenges faced by today's students, school counselors must focus on students' personal/social, educational, and career needs. In order to do so, counselors need to move from a services-oriented approach (orientation, information, assessment, counseling, placement, and follow-up) to a school counseling program approach. They must be clear about their "scope of practice"—the responsibilities for which they are trained—and not allow themselves to become assistant principals, attendance officers, substitute teachers, and clerks.

School counselors can exert more control over their scope of practice if they commit themselves to designing and implementing developmental school counseling programs. While crisis and remedial counseling will always be a part of the school counselor's responsibilities, counselors must provide assistance to as many students as possible. Emphasizing developmental counseling programs permits counselors to be seen as contributing to the growth of all students and not just working with those "in trouble." Developmental counseling programs focus on meeting students' needs and lead to activities and structured group experiences for all students. They are proactive rather than reactive and when counselors are busy implementing their program, they are unavailable for unrelated administrative and clerical duties.

Developmental Counseling Programs include both "content" and "process" components. The content component of the program speaks to:

1. The rationale for the program (why the school and children need a counseling program);

2. The personal-social, educational, and career development skills or competencies needed by children and youth; and
3. The management plan or blueprint intended to guide counselors' management of the counseling program.

The process component includes:

1. The activities counselors will use to help students achieve the designated skills or competencies;
2. The counseling strategies they intend to employ, e.g., individual counseling, group counseling, classroom guidance, and/or consultation; and
3. Methods to be used to evaluate their program and improve their effectiveness with students, staff, and parents.

Counseling Programs

In a comprehensive developmental school counseling program, the counselor has the following scope of practice (the responsibilities for which a school counselor is trained and qualified):

Design: Counselors design the content of the program. Gysbers, refers to this content as a "guidance curriculum." The content of the program is designed to help students gain skills or competencies in personal-social, educational, and career domains. Following is a list of skills/competencies that one might expect to see in the content of a developmental counseling program.

1. Personal-Social Skills: Students will:
   (a) gain self-awareness and improve self-esteem;
   (b) make healthy choices and effective decisions;
   (c) assume responsibility for their own behavior;
   (d) respect individual differences and cooperate; and
   (e) learn to resolve conflicts.

2. Educational Skills: Students will:
   (a) acquire study and test-taking skills;
   (b) seek and use educational information;
   (c) set educational goals; and
   (d) make appropriate educational choices.
3. Career Development Skills. Students will:
   (a) analyze interests, aptitudes, and skills;
   (b) recognize effects of career stereotyping;
   (c) form a career identity; and
   (d) plan for their future careers.

Delivery: Counselors must be involved in the delivery of this developmental program content or curriculum that they have developed. They must allocate significant amounts of time to facilitate or team teach developmental learning activities in the classrooms. Also, they will need to set up inservices for teachers to enable them to assist in the facilitation of the activities. Counselors need to deliver their program content in small and large group sessions. Large group sessions may be appropriate for the information about and discussion of post-secondary or vocational education options and financial aid. Small groups may be more appropriate for interests or aptitude test interpretations.

Counsel: Counselors must counsel students both individually and in small groups. Counselors must not forget their unique counseling skills. While schools are not appropriate cites for "caseloads of clients," counselors must always allot time for counseling students with personal-social problems, both individually and in small groups. In order to be as effective as possible in a limited number of sessions, counselors should utilize newer theoretical approaches such as brief therapy.

Consult: Counselors must consult with parents, teachers, other educators, and various community agencies to help students deal with more serious personal and educational problems, both individually and in small groups. In order to be as effective as possible, in a limited number of sessions, counselors should utilize newer theoretical approaches such as brief therapy.

Coordinate: Counselors must coordinate or collaborate with others who may be offering mental health-oriented programs, e.g., substance abuse. Counselors report that more and more community-based programs are operating in the schools. The school counselors should either coordinate the efforts of these programs or collaborate in their delivery. Testing programs are often coordinated by school counselors. In these days of accountability, counselors must be careful not to permit this responsibility to consume too much of their time. While counselors should understand thoroughly all relevant interest, aptitude, and achievement tests and should be able to offer inservices to teachers on their interpretation and use, they should not be spending their time in direct administration of tests.

Manage: Counselors must manage the school counseling program. Directors of guidance are a dying breed. Many counselors find themselves supervised by individuals who have more responsibilities than they can handle. Counselors must take charge of their own programs and encourage interaction and regular meetings of the counselors in their district in order to assure program progress. Managing a school counseling program includes developing an active staff/community public relations program. Counselors should orient staff and community to the counseling program through newsletters, local media, and school and community presentations. Managing also involves pulling together advisory committees of parents and community members to gather input related to student needs. The management function is critical to the success of a school counseling program.

Evaluate: Counselors need to evaluate their efforts with students, staff, and community. Counselors can gather evaluation data from several sources. One source of information is "general evaluation" data which includes number of students seen in individual or crisis counseling, number of small group counseling sessions, number of large group information sessions, number of conferences with parents, and number of phone calls to parents and community agencies. While this kind of general evaluation does not speak to the quality of counselor contacts, it does provide the school board and administration information about the scope or breadth of the counseling program. "Specific evaluation" data takes more counselor planning time.

Counselors need to plan to evaluate their work with students (particularly the delivery of the guidance activities in classrooms). Ratings scales to be completed by teachers and/or students and short surveys to determine what students gained from the guidance activities are two additional methods that can be used to evaluate the counseling program. Program evaluation is one of the weakest areas in school counseling. Many counselors will need to seek assistance from nearby counselor educators in setting up their evaluation process.

Certainly school counselors being trained today have the advantage of graduating from more rigorous counselor education programs than those of the past. However, counselors, particularly those who were trained over a decade ago, must participate in inservice training (designed for counselors not teachers), attend professional meetings, and read professional journals if they intend to meet student needs in this complex society.

3

Counselling Skills

Counselling is a relationship between counsellor and client(s). Counselling can be on a one to one basis, with families or several people. While counsellors offer a variety of helping skills, ultimately it is the client who determines the content, the methods and the success of counselling

The role of the counsellor is to assist people to grow and solve their own problems. Most people who need help have within themselves some resources for coping which counsellors can bring out.

The counsellor needs to be able to show the following qualities:

— sincerity warmth empathy

— flexibility acceptance of others open-mindedness

— genuineness respect for others

Empathy: Empathy involves seeing the world of another through their eyes. Empathy is not sympathy.

Each person needs to examine their own motives for wanting to counsel others. Are you:

(a) avoiding dealing with your own problems?

(b) looking for status and/or control?

(c) looking for close contact with others?

(d) do you believe that you have the answers to life?

Or do you

(e) counsel out of a sincere wish to help others?

The counsellor's credibility and effectiveness will be enhanced by their awareness of these reasons. Motives will be quickly perceived by clients. Ask yourself:

— What are your strengths and weaknesses as a counsellor.

— What you need most from people?

— What can you give to people?

Counsellor Values

The basic qualities of acceptance and concern for others, recognition of the worth of each individual, honesty, truthfulness, self awareness, tolerance, goodwill and caring are desirable counsellor traits. The counsellor may find themselves at variance in values and lifestyle with some of their clients and with sections of the community, particularly on controversial issues such as sexual behaviour, contraception, abortion, drug use, and racial issues. How a counsellor copes with the value conflicts will be an inevitable part of their work.

Basic principles in counselling

1. The counsellor cannot divorce him/herself from their own social, moral, and spiritual values. They have a right to them. But they must recognise them and be honest to themselves about them.
2. The counsellor does not have the right to impose their own values on the client.
3. The counsellor's position is not that of judge; their function is not to assign guilt or innocence but to encourage objective evaluation of attitudes, standards and actions.

4. Many clients have an expectation and fear of being judged. They already feel guilty because of having contravened their own, their family's or society's moral code. It does not help to deny the reality of this conflict by suggesting that there is no need to regard their behaviour as deviant.
5. If there is any place for judgement it should be actions rather than persons that are judged.
6. A counsellor does not operate in isolation. They are expected to work within the law and basic values of society. Each counsellor should place themselves under the supervision of another more experienced counsellor. Accountability of the counsellor and his/her work to a peer or senior is important for both the counsellors and their clients.

Counselling occurs in a reciprocal relationship. A warm trusting relationship between the counsellor and client needs to be built up if change is going to take place. The client will look for empathy, respect and sensitivity from the counsellor. They will want to feel that the counsellor has the ability to see the situation as they do. The client may wonder whether they are free to express their real concerns.

There are some fundamental issues that need to be taken into consideration as much as possible before you actually begin to talk. The physical setting, the way the client is greeted, gestures and tone of voice all convey messages to the client. She/he will react to the length and delay of the counsellor's responses, interruptions, amount of talk and voice quality. A counsellor who talks too much discourages the client. If the counsellor delays responses there is an increased chance that the client will talk more.

Surroundings

— Counselling needs to be in a private and relatively informal setting

— No noise or distractions.

— Seats need comfortable and well placed

— The counsellor and client need to be comfortably apart

— Be aware of your own non-verbal posture.

— Sit slightly angled

— Leaning towards client

— Open stance on your part

Eye contact

— Look at the client when they are talking

— Use glances that express interest and acceptance.

Getting the client to talk is important in the initial stages. If the client is invited to talk freely instead of being subjected to a series of questions they are more likely to talk. An opening question or statement can be made to make the client feel welcome. For example: 'How can I help you?'

Open-ended questions

Open-ended questions or statements invite the client to continue talking by suggesting that she/he gives more details about a topic she has introduced. Beginning questions with: what? when? how? where? why? is a useful way of making them open. In contrast, closed questions tend to shut off conversation by inviting a 'Yes' or 'No' answer. A series of such questions or statements can sound like an interrogation. Gestures such as nods, single words or noises, body postures or repetitions of key words indicate that the counsellor is interested and are effective in keeping the client talking.

The use of silence

The counsellors are often afraid of, or embarrassed by silences during conversations. To use silence effectively the counsellor needs to accept its worth, to feel confident about allowing it to continue, and to be sensitive to timing.

Engaging reluctant clients

Counsellors should remember that they do not have the right to persist in efforts to engage unwilling clients to talk. Counsellors can choose to accept the reluctance of a client as a refusal of help. Alternately, they can sensitively attempt to engage the client so that the real meaning of the reluctance may become clear. Many reluctant clients may need only to find genuineness, reassurance, and the right invitation from the counsellor to begin the relationship. When working with clients it is essential to allow them time to feel comfortable and develop trust. Clients can be encouraged to express thoughts through writing or drawing or physically by acting, miming, or posturing.

The counsellor's ability to respond effectively depends on her/his being able to follow leads the client presents. All conversations contain: the content and feelings.

1. Content - the story
2. Feelings - emotions

The counsellor needs to be able to respond to both the feelings and the content of what the client is saying. When someone perceives our feelings accurately we usually respond positively or the counsellor may ask the client questions such as: How does that make you feel? What are you feeling right now? Reflecting on the content of what the client is saying and their feelings conveys to the client that the counsellor is trying to understand what has been said.

The counsellor might respond by saying:

Is what you're saying... You seem to be saying...

Let me see if I understood correctly... Correct me if I'm wrong...

In the early stages of counselling the client leads the session. When the counsellor has enough information the counsellor assumes more responsibility for the discussion. However, leading responses used too soon and too frequently may irritate or seem insensitive to the client.

Advice: Advice should be given as little as possible; only when requested and only after careful listening and thorough discussion of all the facts. It is a skill that is easily misused. It can be open to game playing in that it places the counsellor in the role of expert (and all experts are sooner or later proved wrong). Also, it may be a manoeuvre by the client to avoid taking responsibility for him/herself.

Support and Encouragement: Used skilfully, support and encouragement of the client as a person who is accepted and capable of coping can be extremely reassuring and energising. The counsellor should affirm the whole person rather than judge particular beliefs, attitudes and behaviour.

Confrontation: Confronting should be used carefully. If used successfully it can help overcome a block or barrier and can be challenging and helpful to the client.

Summarising: Summarising brings together the main points clarifying what has been accomplished and what remains to be done.

For example: Counsellor: Let's see if we can pull all of this together. On the one hand you feel lonely and isolated, especially with groups of people. On the other hand, you say that you find it hard to mix with others even on a one-to-one basis. So even though you want to get to know others there is no easy way to begin. Is that it?

Points to be aware of:

1. Be aware of your attitude. How do you feel about the client and how are those feelings influencing your perceptions of him/her?

2. Be attentive both to what is being said (content) and what is implied or hinted at (unstated or emotional message/ feelings).
3. Focus on what the other person is trying to tell you, not on what you might say in response.
4. Do not hesitate to say that you do not fully understand. Also, do not assume anything about your client.

Practical Tools to Changing Behaviour

Setting Goals

Some clients express their goals in vague terms. Some people's goals are too broad or far reaching and may need to be broken into smaller more manageable ones. The client may need help with planning practical steps toward the desired goal. It is best if the client choose their own goals for they are then more likely to work hard to achieve it. However, the counsellor can assist in offering suggestions. Goals need to be realistic and ones into which the client is prepared to put time and effort. The client might be encouraged to write down their goal(s) to discuss with the counsellor. Clients might choose something rewarding that they enjoy doing after they have achieved some of their desired goal. e.g. have a cup of coffee, visit a friend.

Role Playing

Role playing and role reversal are practical skills for counsellors to use in helping clients to change. These skills would be appropriate for example, if a young girl wanted to talk to her mother about something which she was afraid to. The counsellor and client might take turns at being the mother and daughter, according to the instructions of the client. By acting out feelings and hunches be able to anticipate more accurately how her mother might respond to the different approaches.

Tools: A useful tool may be to teach the client how to relax. This may be particularly useful if the client is to face a stressful situation. Physical activity may also be a way to reduce stress. Hobbies, listening to music, and other things that the client enjoys doing may also be looked at in counselling.

Theories and Treatment

There are three major models today:

1. The biochemical model holds that mental illness is an illness of the body.
2. The environmentalist model includes the *behavioural* and *cognitive* approaches. The *behavioural* approach holds that we learn to be abnormal through conditioning and as such can be unlearned. And the *cognitive* approach holds that abnormality springs from disordered conscious thought about oneself and the world.
3. The psychodynamic model holds that abnormal behaviour is driven by hidden conflicts within our personality (self theory and existential theory, which deals with questions of life's meaning, human potential, responsibility and will).

It is dangerous to follow one particular model of abnormality. For example, one might spend years looking into the childhood of a person to find that it might turn out to be a biochemical defect. The biochemical model defines psychological disorders as an illness. The result of biological or anatomical abnormalities. Usually a drug, will be used to alleviate the symptoms.

Studies that show that psychiatric illness is more likely to run in families and is transmitted genetically are supported by studies of twins. For examples, studies show that if one twin is schizophrenic then the likelihood of the other twin being schizophrenic is higher than the general population. After examining about 400 pairs of identical twins, fifty percent showed a concordant rate for schizophrenia. Fraternal twins, on the other hand, showed a concordant rate of about 10 percent while the general population was as low as about one percent. The biochemical malfunctioning of the brain is the most common cause of mental illness according to the biomedical view. The brain is corrected by changing its biochemistry with drugs. Drugs have been used to help alleviate disorders such as schizophrenia, depression, panic attacks, anxiety and phobia. But these drugs may also have serious side effects.

How much of our behaviour is heredity (nature) and how much is caused by our environment (nurture)? The environmentalist model claims that our behaviours are the product of our environment. This model falls into two classes; behavioural (learning) and cognitive (thoughts) theory. The behavioural model sees behaviour as being learned from past experience and behaviour can be changed by learning new ways. Behaviour is learned and what is learned can be unlearned. E.g. If we are rewarded for what we do we are more likely to do it again and vice versa. To the behavioural psychologist two basic learning processes exist: Classical and operant conditioning.

Classical, named after Ivan Pavlov, a Russian psychologist who when studying the digestive system of dogs, specifically the salivary reflex when he noticed that dogs begun to salivate when he walked into the room. Thus, his appearance became associated with 'food'. Similar when a cat hears the fridge door open it comes meowing for food. Or an alcoholic who when he drives past a hotel begins to experience craving for alcohol. Behaviour is learned through past association with an event. Operant therapies are based on Skinner's assumption that people learn behaviours through reinforcement or rewards and punishment. e.g. we reward and punish our children in order to increase certain behaviours and stop others.

Treatments

Aversive therapy

Aversive therapy aims to rid the client of the undesirable

behaviour by pairing the behaviour with aversive consequences. e..g. If alcohol is paired with a nausea-inducing drug, or a sexually deviant impulse is paired with electric shock, the expected results is that the client will avoid the undesired behaviour. Merely thinking about alcohol makes the person feel nauseated. However, this method does not always last as upon withdrawing the drug or electric shock the old behaviour may returns.

Systematic desensitisation

Systematic desensitisation introduced by Joseph Wolpe in 1958, is used mainly to treat phobias and specific anxieties. The client is fgradually exposed to the feared object or situation. Over time the panic induced by the feared object will disappear.

Flooding

Flooding treats anxiety in quite the opposite manner. The phobic patient is immersed in the phobic situation and are encouraged to experience the full force of the anxiety storm. For example, someone who is agoraphobic and afraid to leave home would be encouraged to spend an hour in the park and thus be flooded with anxiety. Gradually the anxiety would disappear.

Cognitive Psychology

Cognitive psychologists content that behaviour is influenced by far more than just a direct relationship between environment and response. Rather cognitive psychologists believe that what a person thinks, believes, expects, influences how he or she behaves. Therapy consists of changing negative thoughts. A.T.Beck argues that specific emotions are always preceded by our thoughts. Depressed individuals frequently have more negative thoughts than non-depressed. Sadness is preceded by the thought "something of value is lost." Anxiety is preceded by the thought "a threat of harm exists," and anger is preceded by the thought "my personal domain is being trespassed against." Thus for the cognitive therapist, modifying these thoughts will alter the emotion.

Rational emotive therapy

Albert Ellis, the founder of rational-emotive therapy (R.E.T.) argues that psychological disorders are the result of irrational beliefs. The therapist directly attacks the client's irrational beliefs arguing that they are irrational and illogical in attempt to get the client to change them.

Cognitive-behavioural therapy

Cognitive therapists believe that distorted thinking causes disordered behaviour and that correcting the distorted thinking will alleviate or cure the disordered behaviour. Behaviour therapists, in contrast, view distorted behaviour as learned from past experience and attempt to alleviate the disorders by learning new, more adaptive ones. However many therapists combine both techniques which is called cognitive-behavioural therapy.

The psychodynamic theories are concerned with those forces that influence the mind, both conscious and subconscious. Psychodynamic approaches of human development began with the work of Sigmund Freud and have been greatly revised by others over the years. Feud stated that from birth people move through five psychosexual stages of development. If certain tasks are not resolved at each stage problems develop later in life. Those who do resolve these tasks at each stage go on to live fulfilled lives.

The Three Processes of Personality

Freud divided the personality into three kinds of processes: id, ego, and superego. The *id* is concerned with sexual and aggressive desires and is dominated by the pleasure principle. The *ego* is concerned with the individual's safety, allows desire to be expressed only when aversive consequences from other sources are minimal, and is dominated by the reality principle. The *superego* consists of the individual's conscious and ideals and regardless of what reality permits it either forbids from expressing desires, or urges them toward the achievement of higher goals.

Levels of consciousness

Freud also proposed three levels of consciousness. The first is perceptual consciousness, consisting of the very small number of mental events to which the individual is presently attending. The second is pre-consciousness. It consists of information and impulses that are not at the center of attention but that can be retrieved more or less easily. The large mass of memory, experience and impulse lies at the third level of consciousness: the unconscious, which includes forgotten and repressed memories. Repressed memories live on because they are not subject to rational control; they are the dominant forces in personality. Freud proposed that individual's use coping or defense-mechanisms, such as, denial, repression, rationalisation and so on, to prevent from becoming consciously aware of and to cope with threatening feelings, thought and impulses.

Faults of early psychoanalytic theory

Freud's theories were not able to be subjected to any kind of scientific test and therefore were not able to be varified. He had spent little time with children and his theories are considered to have been no more than speculation.

Existential theories

Existential theorists have identified three issues that contribute to human growth or abnormality: fear of dying, personal responsibility and will. They stress the importance of freedom of choice. Clients are encouraged to view their problems as being of their own making and are encouraged to take responsibility for their own behaviour and feelings. As a result they become more aware of the choices open to them.

Psychodynamic treatments

Just as there are a vast number of pscyhodynamic theories so there are numerous and varied treatments. Pychodynamic therapies seek to make conscious that which is unconscious through encouraging the client to speak what is on their mind bringing out what was formally repressed to consciousness and examining dreams, resistances and the transference that occurs between the client and therapist. Thoughts feelings and emotions that have been repressed since childhood come to light. Encounter groups, where clients are encouraged to express their feelings have grown out of this movement.

Client-centered therapy

Client centered therapy developed by Carl Rogers emphasis unconditional positive regard and empathy. Unconditional positive regard is the belief that people are fundamentally good even when they are doing bad things. Empathy is the therapists ability to see the clients world as they do which is important for the client to overcome their defenseness and to begin to clarify and accept their own experiences.

DIFFERENT COUNSELLING TECHNIQUES

There are many different approaches to helping to sort out issues or manage mental health difficulties. Counsellors, psychologists, social workers and psychiatrists are likely to specialize in a particular approach, or they may use a number of approaches depending on their training and your needs. For more information about what a counsellor, social worker, psychologist or psychiatrist does you may want to check out the Finding Help section of the site. There are many different techniques that can be broadly split into 3 groups. These include:

— *Insight therapies* - This type of therapy is often known as "talk therapy". Talking about your experiences will help get an understanding of the difficulties you may face and sort through the possible solutions. The more common types of insight therapy are psychoanalysis, psychodynamic approaches, client centred approaches and cognitive therapy. For more information about these and you may want to ask your counsellor, psychologist or psychiatrist. A common form of insight therapy is Cognitive Behavioural Therapy. This therapy looks at changing negative thought patterns and maladaptive beliefs. Maladaptive beliefs are beliefs that a person has about them self that may not be correct, but are having a negative effect on the person. Cognitive Behavioural Therapy (CBT) is one of the most common forms of counselling.

— *Behaviour therapies*- Behaviour therapies focus on the changing behaviour patterns. Behaviour therapists will often use some of principles of learning, such as providing punishments for bad behaviour and rewards for good behaviour. This type of therapy may be used to change compulsive behaviours, to help with learning problems, or to modify avoidance behaviours. With this type of therapy it is assumed that the behaviours are a product of learning and what has been learnt can be unlearnt.

— *Biomedical therapies* - This involves the use of drugs to help to manage mental health difficulties. Drugs may be used to treat anxiety, psychosis or depression. It is a good idea to talk to your psychiatrist or doctor about the type and dosage of the drugs you are having. Everyone is different and it is possible that you may experience side effects. It is not unusual for these approaches to overlap or for your social worker, counsellor, psychologist or psychiatrist to use a combination of approaches to help you. If you are seeing someone it may help to talk about the approaches that they are using and why they are using them.

Everyone is different and it may be that while one approach is good for one person it may not suit someone else. It is a good idea to talk to your counsellor, social worker, psychologist or psychiatrist about which approach they are trained in. It is possible that they may use a mixture of techniques to help you. If you are not finding a particular approach helpful, it may be useful to look at the other options.

Characteristics of an Effective Counselling

There are hundreds of counselling courses available now, and any of those being presented by recognised educational establishments should be alright. The usual route to becoming a counsellor is via a counselling college, but some quite experienced counsellors have received substantial training and obtained substantial experience in other ways. Some have entered the 'profession' by volunteering to become a counsellor with one or more of the many counselling charities such as 'Relate' or 'Cruse'. They will sometimes offer their own training to suitable volunteers, and over a period of time (with supervision and ongoing training) it is possible to achieve a high level of competence in your 'spare' time whilst holding another unrelated job down.

In addition to the major national counselling charities there are numerous local charities and voluntary groups that use volunteers and which sometimes offer their own 'in house' training. Sometimes, over a substantial period of time, the training offered and the experience gained may equal, and in some cases exceed, that offered by some colleges. Others have entered counselling via other professions. Ministers of religion, nurses, care assistants, social workers, teachers, occupational health managers, or occupational therapists for example, may all be taught some basic counselling skills as part and parcel of their training. Usually these are topped up from time to time with further seminars or short courses.

Sometimes, however, members of these professions develop an increasing counselling based practice and aquire considerable counselling experience. Sometimes, almost by default, the counselling may become their full time work (Nurses in paliative counselling units, social workers becoming youth counsellors, occupational health managers becoming occupational counsellors for example). The qualities you need to have as a counsellor include personal integrity, genuineness, warmth and responsiveness. You should be a member of a professional body such as 'Counselling', should be able to explain the code of practice that they work to, the limits of your confidentiality, and the range of your counselling training and experience. It should be obvious that age and maturity are prerequisites for a counsellor.

The main items to be considered, therefore, when becoming a counsellor are;

— Do you have the necessary experience and personal qualities that your clients would want from a counsellor?

— Do you adhere to a recognised professional code of conduct?

— Is there a complaints procedure or system of redress for your clients if you break that code?

— Do you have recognised academic qualifications in counselling?

As regards question four, it should be noted that qualifications come in a variety of forms. The usual progression for a counsellor is a counselling skills-certificate, counselling certificate, counselling diploma, counselling degree. However, all is not always as it seems. Some diploma courses last over three years and involve many hours of supervised practice. Some Diplomas, however, can be obtained by mail order, as can some degree level courses. This is not to say that they are not equally valid, the Open University for example works to a high standard, but standards do vary. This applies equally to all types of training. For example many two and three year college diploma courses comprise only one day per week actual tuition, and a one year certificate course may contain a similar amount of tuition.

List of Personal Qualities of the Counsellor

1. Counsellors are vitally intersted in helping their clients and energetically work to fulfil this interest.
2. They unconditionally accept their clients as people.
3. They are confident of their own therapeutic ability.
4. They have a wide knowledge of therapeutic theories and practices and are flexible, undogmatic and consequently open to the acquiring of new skills and to experimenting with them.
5. They are able to cope with and ameliorate their own disturbances and consequently are not inordinately anxious, depressed, hostile, self-downing, self-pitying or undisciplined.
6. They are patient, persistent and hard-working in their therapeutic endeavours.
7. They are ethical and responsible, and use counseling almost entirely for the benefit of the clients and not for personal indulgence.

People Who Offer Counselling Counsellors

People with many different backgrounds work as counsellors. The name is not used to refer to any one type of training or qualification. There are many training courses in counselling skills.

— *Psychotherapists*: Psychotherapists have a variety of qualifications. They have usually been in counselling or psychotherapy themselves and can work on personal change at a deeper level.

— *Community Health Nurses*: They are qualified nurses who have completed extra training in community health which includes some counselling skills.

— *Family Therapists*: They have a variety of qualifications. Members of the Victorian Association of Family Therapists (VAFT) have at least two years additional training in working with individuals and families.

— *Feminist Counsellors*: There is no specific qualification in Victoria in feminist counselling. They have an awareness of the specific experiences and pressures on women. You need to ask each individual what she means by feminist counselling.

— *Financial Counsellors*: They are trained to help sort out finances and renegotiate contracts and other financial obligations.

— *Social Workers*: Social workers have a degree in social work. Some of them do counselling and they use a variety of approaches.

— *Psychiatrists*: They are medical doctors with extra training in psychiatry. They deal with the diagnosis and treatment of mental illness. They can prescribe drugs. Some of them use other approaches as well.

— *Psychologists*: They have university qualifications in psychology. Some with extra training are registered psychologists. They counsel people in a variety of settings using a range of techniques. They do not prescribe drugs.

— *Psychoanalysts*: They can train in several ways which are regulated by the Psychoanalysts Association. Some are medical doctors. They use a specific process to explore buried feelings from childhood. It can involve several sessions per week and take many years.

'Support groups are good later on, particularly with incest the secrecy means that it is incredibly threatening to start doing that in a group it's very exposing. Later on it's great and what you get is understanding and not feeling isolated and validating your own experiences.' 'I was on medication prescribed by a psychiatrist, but another doctor said that it was bad for me and took me off it.'

Valuing Diversity in the Schools: The Counselor's Role

The valuing of diversity in the schools is no longer merely a social goal. With the make-up of the student body changing so rapidly, school counselors, teachers and administrators realize that they are now required to learn new techniques and skills for understanding, motivating, teaching, and empowering each individual student regardless of race, gender, religion or creed. We are a nation of diverse populations and groups. The future of our society depends upon our ability to effectively talk with one another, to reach mutual understanding, and to realize that in diversity there is strength.

By the year 2056, the "average" U.S. citizen will trace his or her descent to Africa, Asia, the Hispanic countries, the Pacific Islands—almost anywhere but white Europe. Obviously, the United States is changing significantly. By the year 2000 the population of the U.S. will be 43% people of color. In 1990, over 30% of the public school students were either African-American or Hispanic. The statistical meaning of the word minority is quickly losing its significance, especially in America's classrooms. And by the year 2075, African Americans, Alaskan Natives, American Natives, Hispanic Americans, and Asian Americans will be the statistical majority in the United States. School counselors can serve as catalysts to insure that teachers, students and others learn how to value diversity. That is, the valuing of diversity can be taught to others and should be a major part of any school's comprehensive guidance program.

The "A" in ASK stands for Awareness of self and others. Self and other awareness is a must if cultural diversity is to be appreciated in our schools and elsewhere. The "S" in ASK refers to both Sensitivity and Skills. Sensitivity to others as well as new, innovative, communication. Skills are needed by students and others if we are to learn to value diversity and intercultural communication is to improve. The "K" stands for Knowledge of cultures different from our own. Culture influences feelings, thoughts, non-verbal behaviors, ideas and perceptions and "cognitive empathy" (knowledge) of another's culture is needed to improve intercultural relationships.

Awareness of Self and Others

Self-aware individuals avoid a condescending attitude and do not patronize culturally different persons. To patronize implies the belief that we hold a superior position to them—we come across to them as being "better" than they. And members of other cultural groups view this as disrespectful. Relatedly, some Anglo Americans seem to have a characteristic that could best be described as "assumed similarity." That is, they assume that people either ought to be like them or want to be like them! Self-aware individuals do not hold such assumptions. Students of all ages can be taught, through various guidance and counseling activities, to be more aware of self and others.

Our sensitivity toward and willingness to understand others is a major key to effective communication with the culturally different. Counsellors need to be aware of others' thoughts and feelings, regardless of their race, creed or cultural background. Effective, multicultural communicators are aware of other persons' frames of reference, their views of the world. And, they understand that worldviews are influenced by culture. We can learn communication skills that will assist us in understanding how others view their worlds and react to them, as opposed to telling them how they should react and behave toward their own worlds! Their worldviews may be very different from ours, but they are based on their perceptions—which are their "realities." And, their reality determines how they feel, think and behave.

How sensitive are you to your own views of those who are different? Do you view other cultures as equally valuable to yours? Is your cultural group superior to another? Are you culturally sensitive to your own heritage and the possibility that you were taught (perhaps unconsciously) to be prejudiced as a part of your upbringing? Do you value and respect differences? Are you aware of your own values and biases and how they affect those who are culturally different? Do you avoid stereotyping and labeling? Do you monitor your own assumptions about those different from you? Are you willing to accept someone of a different race into your organization, i.e., your sorority, your fraternity, your church?

It is important that each of us examine ourselves concerning these questions if we hope to become culturally skilled communicators. The emerging sense of worth of members of culturally distinct populations can no longer be neglected. Learning about their different values, attitudes, desires, aspirations, and beliefs is necessary because it affects all of us. Learning skills to help us communicate effectively with people from different cultures will speed up this necessary learning process.

Feelings, thoughts, nonverbal behaviors, and ideas are important in interpersonal communication and are culturally influenced and learned. As noted, empathy, interest in others, caring, personal awareness, sensitivity and understanding are stressed as important to effective interpersonal communication and to learning to value diversity. However, having these core conditions present is not always enough for effective communication with a person from another race or culture. We also need "cognitive" empathy. That is, knowledge of that person's culture, or knowing "where that person is coming from" is also extremely important.

Students of all ages can be taught to be culturally skilled. A culturally skilled communicator is willing to gain cognitive knowledge about different cultures, i.e., their history, cultural values, current problems and lifestyles and how this impacts on their respective worldview. This may be the most important thing we can do in becoming more effective intercultural communicators. It is important that we approach different cultural members with understanding over and above our feelings. That is, having strong feelings of support for a particular culture and its participants is necessary. However, it is not enough to truly communicate with participants from that cultural group. If we are ignorant of the values and ways of participants from cultural groups different from ours, we will certainly be less effective communicators than we would be if we operated with accurate, cognitive understanding of them. The teaching of the values and ways of other cultural groups can, and should be, central to any comprehensive school guidance program.

Role of Schhol Counselors

The professional school counselor possesses many excellent communication skills that can, and should be, shared and taught to teachers, administrators, students, and others. The "cognitive knowledge" aspect of the above described model can easily be generalized to the school setting. There are many effective ways that students can obtain knowledge about others' cultures, e.g., outside speakers from different cultural backgrounds, culturally distinct student panels, field trips, etc. Learning about other cultures should be a major component of any guidance curriculum, regardless of the school level. In addition, self awareness, awareness of others and sensitivity to self and others in regard to diversity can and should be a major component of any comprehensive school guidance program.

Many guidance activities can be developed and delivered by various modes with these themes in mind. School counselors know how to communicate effectively with others regardless of their or the other person's cultural background. They are skilled in how to "tune in to" the feelings of others, how to put the speaker at ease by clarifying the content of what was just said, how to show interest in others through the use of open-ended questions, etc. And the research is clear, these skills can be taught to students of all ages, i.e., there is considerable evidence that peers can become very effective in helping other peers. And, through structured guidance and counseling approaches all students and teachers can be taught these facilitative communication skills.

A condemning finger is being pointed at the country's public school system. Industry leaders claim that postsecondary students are not graduating with the "basic skills" needed for success at work, at home, and in further education. What are these basic skills? The contemporary list goes far beyond the traditional Three R's to include the attitudes, knowledge, and behaviors needed to function in an increasingly self directed, interpersonal, and technological workplace.

In addition to reading, writing, and computing, these skills include: learning to learn; effective verbal and nonverbal communication; adaptability (including creative thinking and problem solving); personal management (including self esteem, goal setting/motivation, and personal/career development); group effectiveness (including personal skills, negotiation, and teamwork); influence (including organizational effectiveness and leadership); the ability to understand technology; the ability to apply scientific knowledge to work situations; and the ability to balance and manage family and work.

Schools are being challenged to integrate these new basic skills across their curricula. This presents school counselors with an opportunity: if they can prove their effectiveness in helping students plan for and acquire the basic skills and prepare for life after high school, they can trade their traditionally services oriented, possibly expendable positions in schools for positions of influence in matters such as school reform and restructuring. Currently, the most promising models for helping school counselors take this active role are "comprehensive counseling and guidance programs."

Comprehensive counseling and guidance programs are the "umbrella programs" of the 1990s, designed to provide all students with life competencies through personal, social, and career counseling. Abandoning the traditionally passive, service approach to counseling, comprehensive counseling and guidance programs employ four interactive components that take the vagueness out of the school counselor's role:

1. *The Guidance Curriculum*: counselors provide structured, competency based activities in the classroom or in group situations, using this focused time with students to focus on content areas such as self knowledge, educational and occupational exploration, and career planning.
2. *Individual Planning*: Counselors help students think ahead and think for themselves, teaching them how to plan rigorous and coherent sequences of courses, as well as monitor and manage their lives.
3. *Responsive Services*: Counselors meet the immediate needs of students confronting personal or educational challenges.
4. *System Support*: Counselors work to sustain and enhance the implementation of comprehensive counseling and guidance programs.

An essential part of the effort to equip students with the basic skills is the integration of academic and vocational instruction. Basic competencies in these areas are prerequisites for lifetime learning. Additionally, as technology continues to become more sophisticated, the competencies with which students graduate are rapidly becoming requirements for landing and keeping good jobs with growth potential. Conversely, college-bound students can benefit from vocational methods of instruction and experiences connecting school to work. By using academic theory in real life settings, they can acquire skills needed outside the classroom. Schools emphasizing acquisition of the basic skills recognize the critical role counselors can play in helping students plan a demanding sequence of academic and vocational courses that will prepare them both for employment and postsecondary education.

School counselors promote the idea that vocational education is better supported when vocational and academic education are seen as complementary strategies for student success, not as competing programs of study. An example: a Pittsburgh, Pennsylvania, school district has discontinued its general education track. Students must now make specific curriculum choices early on. It is therefore necessary for guidance professionals to contact all students earlier and stay in contact with them. To receive a diploma, each student must plan and complete a focused curriculum leading to an academic or an applied technology and career development certificate, or both.

To inform the community about the methods the district is using to infuse career education into curriculum, the district sends letters to parents of all eighth graders, and requires all tenth graders to view a video explaining graduation and certificate requirements within a group guidance class. Counselors now find it much easier to promote the merits of Pittsburgh's 40 vocational options and their relation to graduation, the workplace, and postsecondary education. This action, along with other initiatives, has significantly reduced dropout rates.

Without a comprehensive counseling and guidance program to address the needs of all students, developmental needs are overlooked and students unable to state their needs fall through the cracks. Due to the large student to counselor ratios, many students end up selecting courses based on availability, instructor popularity, or other criteria that may have nothing to do with career plans, learning styles or basic skill needs. Traditionally, counselors have been rewarded for attending to students who already know their career needs and their principal's priorities. Little attention has been given to what has been called the "forgotten half". Part of this stems from the nebulous role of school counselors.

Counselors are expected to perform roles as varied as the schools within which they work. Some are advocates for students confronting severe family and social change, while others are saddled with large amounts of "administrivia." Many confront substance abuse, suicide, and teen pregnancy as regular parts of their day. Comprehensive counseling and guidance programs call for counselors' reduced involvement in administrative and clerical work. They place counselors in fewer one-on-one counseling situations. At the same time, they strengthen counselors' accountability for effectively helping all students prepare for the world beyond high school. Unfortunately, implementing comprehensive counseling and guidance programs has been a low priority in the school reform movement. This could be due to

(a) hesitancy of school counselors to vocalize their positions,

(b) school counselors' traditional isolation from schools' mainstream instructional programs, or

(c) school counselors' limited involvement in reform.

Implementing comprehensive counseling and guidance programs on a large scale requires the revamping and greater standardization of school counselors' education. Preservice school counselors need a more specific, focused program that arms them with the essentials of professional renewal. School counselor education should be built on a foundation of educational developmental theory and practice as well as psychological theory. Preservice school counselors need training in several areas:

1) helping students plan their coursework and futures;

2) promoting curricula and instructional methods which integrate academic and vocational education; and

3) implementing comprehensive counseling and guidance programs.

Strategies for Contributing to the National Education Goals

Achievement of the six National Education Goals adopted by

President Bush and the nation's governors will require changes in our present educational system, change in how our communities respond to education, and especially change on how education is visualized. More than anything else it requires a new level of collaboration by significant individuals and groups and a full commitment by the community. What is needed is "...an education revolution," a basic change in how education is envisaged and the manner in which it is delivered.

Counselors have always played important roles in ushering in new educational goals and priorities. Whether helping students at risk to acquire the insights and skills supportive to their staying in school or assisting all students to make appropriate career choices and plans which are important to both the students' and the country's future, counselors have played a significant role in providing support for educational priorities. To participate in the achievement of the six National Education Goals, counselors are shifting their efforts to focus on student learning and achievement to a higher degree than ever before.

An effective guidance program, perhaps more than any other educational component, has the capacity to make major contributions to all six National Education Goals. School administrators, guidance directors, and others who are in a position to help determine the goals and content of their guidance programs can significantly enhance this capacity by encouraging the implementation of the following strategies:

1. Adopt a "comprehensive guidance" program model. This model provides for the systematic delivery of guidance as a curriculum organized around a sound theoretical framework, rather than a set of loosely related services. Features of the model that are particularly relevant to the National Goals include:

   (a) a focus on student behavior outcomes;

   (b) delivery of coordinated guidance services K-12;

(c) attention to all students' developmental guidance needs; and

(d) program evaluation and accountability.

2. Reach out to the community to involve parents and other community members in both the determination of guidance priorities and the delivery of counseling and guidance services. Meeting the guidance needs of all students in a school cannot be done by two or three counselors. However, counselors who play a "brokering" role by coordinating the many valuable contributions that others can make can significantly extend and enhance the guidance services that students receive.

3. Encourage collaboration and teamwork among the various education specialties. If teachers, counselors, psychologists, social workers, and other education specialists can be freed from a concern about "turf" issues, they can devote more time and energy to a concerted effort to achieving the National Education Goals.

4. Emphasize the mission of a guidance program to be the facilitation of better student adjustment as an intermediate outcome that enables students to achieve better academic performance rather than better student adjustment as an end in itself.

Counselor Interventions

As individuals, counselors have the opportunities and skills to contribute to each of the National Education Goals in many different ways. The following examples provide an illustration of how counselors can and do contribute to each Goal.

1. All children in America will start school ready to learn.

Counselors can:

— Assist in the selection of appropriate kindergarten screening instruments.

— Provide staff consultation on the interpretation of test results.

— Coordinate the kindergarten screening process.

— Interpret test results to parents.

— Provide information and support to parents.

— Work with Head Start and other pre-school programs to provide a smooth transition for students entering kindergarten.

2. The high school graduation rate will increase to at least 90 percent.

Counselors can:

— Help each student establish meaningful education and career goals.

— Identify and work with potential dropouts, individually and in small groups, at an early stage.

— Work with teachers, parents, and students to insure that individual students are able to stay at grade level.

— Address student attendance problems at an early stage.

— Interface school and community dropout prevention resources.

— Provide a caring and mentoring environment for students.

— Provide counseling to students whose personal and family problems interfere with their school performance.

— Help students whose parents do not value education to develop an understanding of the importance of a high school diploma in today's competitive job market.

— Assist schools to use alternative approaches to assessment that, through meaningful feedback to students, motivate them to learn.

3. American students will be competent in the core subjects.

Counselors can:

- — Assist students to develop effective study skills and habits.
- — Help students to assess and make use of their individual learning styles.
- — Establish programs that respect and reward student achievement in the core subjects.
- — Provide consultation and/or individualized student assessment to help teachers diagnose specific learning problems of students.
- — Work collaboratively with teachers to develop individualized study plans for students experiencing difficulty.
- — Collaborate with teachers to undertake action research studies that compare the effectiveness of various education and counseling interventions.
- — Help students overcome performance blocks due to test anxiety.

4. U.S. students will be first in the world in science and mathematics achievement.

Counselors can:

- — Emphasize the importance of math and science in the workplace.
- — Encourage students to enroll in math and science courses.
- — Help students explore career opportunities in math and science.
- — Encourage girls and minorities to enroll in math and science courses.

— Help students who have had difficulty in math and science in the past improve their study skills or develop new study strategies specifically for math and science.

— Assist students to examine and discard fears or negative attitudes towards preparation for careers in science and mathematics.

5. Every adult American will be literate and possess the skills necessary to compete in a world economy.

Counselors can:

— Work with dropouts and potential dropouts to get them involved in adult education programs.

— Provide career guidance that informs students of the basic skills necessary to compete in today's job market.

— Encourage students to view learning as a lifelong process.

6. Every school will be safe and free of drugs.

Counselors can:

— Help parents and teachers recognize the signs of early drug use by students.

— Work collaboratively with special counselors employed in drug prevention programs.

— Help students learn how to overcome peer pressure.

— Work with administrators and teachers to develop and implement effective group guidance programs for preventing crime and violence in schools.

— Provide counseling to victims of violence.

CHALLENGES TO AND CENSORSHIP OF SCHOOL GUIDANCE MATERIALS

Right to Challenge/Right to Respond

Textbook controversies are not new. Throughout the history of public education in the United States there have been well-intentioned groups that thought they had detected a conspiracy to subvert the nation's children. However, specific challenges to school guidance materials are rather recent phenomena—occurring primarily after 1960. This can partly be attributed to the fact that many schools simply had no counselors prior to that time. However, developmental guidance materials have been discovered and they are being challenged.

A challenge should not be equated with censorship. Some parents, for personal reasons, may request a school to provide alternative guidance materials or to have their children excused from certain guidance activities. Many schools will accommodate these requests. Censorship, however, is a main tactic of some national organizations that want to change the way schools select and use educational materials. Censorship, as defined by the American Library Association's Intellectual Freedom Committee, is the removal of material from open access by government authority. Censors try to impose their views by deciding what others should not read, see, or hear.

Special interests groups are trying to force many school systems to remove or alter developmental guidance materials and practices. The freedom of these groups to speak and write is guaranteed by the First Amendment; however, some of these groups are unwilling to grant such freedom to those who hold opposing views. Special interests groups are an essential ingredient in a democracy and contribute to the formation of public policy, but they can also be a negative and restrictive force. Few challenges by special interests groups reach the courts, but self-censorship happens. A group makes itself known and a counselor silently retreats from the use of established materials and practices. The special interests group goes away and so do some developmentally-appropriate guidance materials.

Each year, People for the American Way, an organization that is opposed to censorship, compiles a list of challenges to school textbooks and materials. This annual compilation includes attempts to remove guidance materials, library books, textbooks, films, and other instructional materials. A review of the four most recent annual reports indicates that a wide array of guidance materials have been challenged in various school districts throughout the United States. It is important to note that in the vast majority of cases where challenges have occurred, school boards have elected to retain and use the challenged materials.

An analysis of recent challenges which occurred in 1988-1991 reveals that the following reasons were those most frequently cited by challengers:

— "New Age" concerns—hypnotism, self-hypnosis, meditation, Far East religions, guided fantasy, visualization

— Undermining parental authority/family values and teaching children they can handle problems on their own

— Promoting secular humanism

Other reasons, "having teachers and untrained persons act as therapists," "having children harmed in some way because of exposure to certain material or practice," and "using materials unproven by research" seem to be emerging as three that challengers are citing more frequently.

Pivotal Issues

The challengers have the right to challenge. If that opportunity does not exist, there is little reason for the First Amendment to exist. When public schools are involved, however, a number of pivotal issues become apparent. Items deemed by the state to be in the best interest of all students are not always acceptable to certain parents and special interests groups. Even after thorough adherence to materials selection policies, a school district that adopts a set of materials for counselors to use in helping build self-esteem may find itself the subject of charges by selected parents and, in some cases, well-financed special interests groups. How can the rights of the many be protected and the rights of the minority be accommodated?

Parental and community involvement should be encouraged. At issue, here, is the notion that a small, vocal minority, often well-organized and well-financed by legal defense funds, can make it appear as though it represents the community as a whole. Group guidance and health education activities related to sex education and AIDS education have been opposed in certain communities. In some cases a small group of parents has requested the removal of a state- or locally-developed sex-education curriculum and requested that one which meets their criteria be substituted for the "offending" curriculum. Should materials that have been selected on the basis of carefully-designed procedures and policies be altered, removed, or replaced when opposition by a few emerges? Not only has the use of certain developmental guidance materials been challenged, but the freedom to counsel in both individual and group settings has been questioned on occasion. Sometimes it is the use of materials which has caused certain groups to call for the removal of school counselors.

During the 1989-90 school year the Armstrong County Taxpayers League of Armstrong, Pennsylvania objected to some developmental guidance materials. In addition to requesting the removal of guidance materials, the League campaigned to remove all guidance counselors. Counselors must assess whether they are functioning in an environment where the school board has a commitment to free expression or whether it is a board which placates a vocal minority. In some cases, counselors may find themselves working with board members who have been elected with the support of special interests groups whose agendas include forcing their viewpoint on materials selection and curriculum practices.

To what extent are counselors free to use certain materials that support the goals of the school without fear of retribution and, at the same time, to what extent do counselors have support for designing alternative programs to meet unique student and parental needs? Counselors have sought ways to encourage students to sort out their own values. However, such activities become troublesome to certain parents who confuse values education with morality education. Many school personnel choose to avoid private morality topics, which they believe are better left to the home and church.

Some parents believe that religious beliefs and private morality issues should have a place in the school curriculum. The stated goal of several special interests groups is to bring public education under the control of Christians. The absence of references to religion by guidance materials and textbooks authors, counselors, and teachers have brought accusations that the schools are in fact practicing religion—the religion of secular humanism. To what extent should private morality be addressed in the nation's public schools? The pivotal issues surrounding challenges to school guidance materials and programs can be further reduced to two very important questions that must be addressed if schools are to deal effectively with challenges to developmental guidance materials:

(1) Who determines what school guidance materials are used in public schools? and

(2) Is the role of schools seen primarily as a place where diverse ideas should be presented and explored or is the role of schools to be primarily that of transmitting community values?

Peterson and Poppen have developed a 16-item "Actions to Prevent Problems Checklist" which outlines steps that school districts and counselors can take to prevent the likelihood that challenges will result in censorship. The 16 actions are not arranged in order of importance, but four may be of high priority for many counselors:

— Base developmental guidance programing on sound educational practices which are appropriate for the age and maturity level of students.

— Relate developmental guidance goals and activities to district and state educational goals and to student educational needs.

— Ask the Board of Education to act on materials selection and materials reconsideration policies and procedures.

— Read "The School Counselor and Censorship," the position statement of the American School Counselor Association.

If challenges happen, responsible actions are needed by school counselors:

— Listen carefully to those who express special concerns.

— Avoid debate, but do state the basis for current practices.

— Handle complaints with carefully constructed procedures and accurate records of all contact and actions.

— Keep the focus of the complaint on the material rather than on the program.

— Ask for assistance from other district personnel, publishers (several publishers of "challenged" guidance materials have excellent printed materials for use in "challenge" situations), and professional associations.

ASSESSMENT SKILLS FOR SCHOOL COUNSELORS

Perhaps the most controversial area within counselor education is that of assessment. Following Shertzer and Linden, assessment is used here to mean methods or procedures that are employed to obtain information that describes human behavior. Knowledge needed by counselors to obtain evidence, evaluate its usefulness, and interpret its meaning have long been and continue to be debated. According to Minor and Minor, that debate arose, in part, from the adoption of a humanistic perspective by many counselors and counselor educators, leading to a de-emphasis of models of counseling that entail quantitative assessment. In the 1960's, tests were viewed positively and were used primarily to identify students of outstanding abilities. However, in the early 1970's, Goldman suggested, using a well-known metaphor, that the marriage between tests and counseling had failed. At about that time, courts prohibited some established tests for certain purposes and legislatures passed bills to regulate aspects of the use of standardized tests.

The validity and practical utility of all testing and appraisal techniques were questioned and negative consequences of "labeling" were emphasized. Yet assessment remained commonplace in schools. Consider these findings in a survey by Engen, Lamb, and Prediger and reported by Zytowski: 93% of secondary schools administered at least one test to all students; 76% administered achievement test batteries; 66% administered academic aptitude or intelligent tests; and 16% administered inventories of school or social adjustment or personality tests. By the 1980's, vocational guidance, according to Zytowski, had become a unifying force between counseling and testing.

Zytowski described several changes that had been made in tests, themselves, and in their uses in counseling. One of these was an erosion of reliance on predictive validity and an accompanying emphasis on convergent and discriminant validity, along with construct validity. He also described the value of an assessment in terms of its ability to guide and motivate a professional toward seeking additional information for decision making. De-formalizing assessment, another change, included increased use of one-item measures, informed self estimates, and card sorts or inventories in which quantified outcomes are less important than is the process the client engages in. Computers had become more instrumental in testing, from primarily scoring and score reporting to actual test administration and providing immediate feedback. Availability and interest in computer testing have clearly increased in the decade since Zytowski's summary appeared.

The counseling community has become more aware of ethical issues in testing. An American Counseling Association

(ACA) statement titled Responsibilities of Users of Standardized Tests (RUST), published in 1978 and revised in 1989, urges awareness of differing purposes for testing and reminds us to consider the limitations of tests for any purpose and to evaluate the costs of not testing or using alternative methods of gathering the information needed.

In their study of skills needed by school counselors, Schafer and Mufson reviewed job analyses conducted by five school districts in five different states. They found a natural division of the job role expectations of school counselors into six areas: counseling (individual and group), pupil assessment, consultation, information officer, school program facilitator, and research and evaluation. There are assessment-intensive aspects of each of these. The counselor's major function in the school is to counsel students individually and whenever practical in small or large groups. The counselor also is responsible for identifying students with special needs. These activities include interpreting test scores and non-test data.

Pupil assessment includes scheduling and preparing for testing, scoring them or sending them out for scoring, recording results, and scheduling for interpretation. Counselors are also responsible for assisting students in evaluating their aptitudes and abilities through interpreting standardized tests. They may be expected to advise teachers who need to understand psychological evaluations and who are interested in improving their content-referenced testing skills. The third function is that of a consultant. The counselor consults with and advises teachers, parents, and administrators in guidance matters and test score interpretation. In some schools the counselor helps teachers with psychological evaluations and content-referenced testing and advises school committees in selection of tests.

The function of information officer includes informing parents, teachers, and staff about counseling services, informing employers and colleges about students according to school policy, and ensuring two-way communication between school and home. Many of these activities involve test interpretation.

The fifth function is administrative, including school administration and counseling administration. Within school administration, the counselor is responsible for administering tests. Within counseling administrative functions, the counselor is expected to analyze guidance services. Also, the counselor is often asked to participate in decisions about the instructional curriculum.

The sixth function is research and evaluation. The counselor may be responsible for evaluating the school guidance program. The counselor is also expected to read and interpret literature to apply research findings to everyday counselees' situations and to improve his or her skills continuously through evaluation of counseling techniques. The counselor responsibilities identified by Schafer and Mufson would likely be found in the large majority of school districts across the nation. Within the area of assessment, roles include test interpreter, test developer, evaluator of programs, consultant, and researcher. Several studies reviewed by Schafer and Mufson were supportive of these roles.

The roles that have been identified imply that counselors should have certain skills related to assessment. Schafer and Mufson organized these into three areas: doing pupil assessment, doing program evaluation, and using basic research. Doing pupil assessment includes: types of assessment; assessment systems and programs; test administration and scoring; test reporting and interpretation; test evaluation and selection; design, analysis, and improvement in instrument development; formal and informal methods of assessment; methods for using assessment in counseling; administrative uses of assessment; computer-based applications; and ethics of using assessments.

Doing program evaluation includes: needs assessment; formative and summative evaluation; sources of evaluation research invalidity (instrumental, internal, and external); choosing evaluation designs; choices of and computational methods for descriptive and inferential statistics; writing evaluation proposals and reports; disseminating information; and research ethics. Using basic research includes: locating and obtaining relevant research reports; reading and summarizing research reports; evaluating validity of instruments and research designs; and purpose and assumptions of common inferential statistical procedures.

School Counselors Collaborating for Student Success

Living and working in a world class society with information age technology at their finger tips, all educators are challenged to improve their communication and collaboration skills. Current trends and issues in education, and specifically in school counseling, indicate the importance of collaborating for student success. A diminishing economic base in education, coupled with increased societal problems reflected in student needs and an era of educational reform, have challenged school counselors to maximize their effectiveness through improved counseling and guidance programs. In May of 1993 the American Counseling Association (ACA) with a grant from the ACA Counseling and Human Development Foundation sponsored an invitational Think Tank on the Crisis in School Counseling.

Representatives from ACA divisions, regions, committees, and affiliates came together dedicated to exploring and defining the needs of school counseling and the roles of the school counselors in educational reform. From the discussion during the Think Tank it was evident that primary concerns included achieving a clearer understanding of the school counselor's role in reform initiatives and improving counselor communication and collaboration within the school and in the community. Inter-association and/or interagency dialogue and collaboration were also stressed as components of an effective comprehensive developmental counseling and guidance program.

From a business and industry perspective Total Quality Management principles are being applied to educational reform. The concept of inclusion of all major publics in school improvement planning has led to the development of strong linkages between internal and external stakeholders. Support networks at the regional and local levels are being formed to foster system improvement and facilitate optimum student learning. Many educators believe that the school should be a community of both adult and more youthful learners. An essential ingredient in the development of such a community is the quality of interpersonal relationships. Those relationships need to be collegial, cooperative, and interdependent.

School improvement requires efforts both from within and from outside the school in order to develop a community of learners. Collaboration for student success is an integral part of educational reform. School counselors have often been perceived as being apart from, or separate from, the mainstream of education. Over the last 15 years well known national education reports, such as "A Nation At Risk", have had a conspicuous absence of references to school counseling. In the current educational reform literature a specific role for the school counselor has not yet been defined. School counselors themselves must define their part in educational reform.

Characteristics of Collaboration

Collaboration is the process whereby two individuals or groups work together for a common goal, a mutual benefit, or a desired outcome. Trust, respect, openness, active listening, clear communication, and risk taking are fundamental requirements for collaborative efforts. In order for collaboration to happen participants must share a common vision and agree on a common mission. The motivation for a common mission may be the need to identify or solve a problem, to focus on the issues, or to achieve consensus. Initiating and maintaining collaborative efforts is an appropriate role of the school counselor in educational reform.

Many barriers prevent educators from establishing and maintaining collaborative efforts. Effective collaboration is built on the strong personal characteristics of the collaborator, a clearly defined system, and administrative support for a change within the organization. Personal requirements needed to foster collaborative relationships include risk-taking, an ability to work well in a group process interaction, a cooperative leadership style, conflict resolution skills, knowledge of agency structure and terminology, an ability to develop rapport with collaborators, and flexibility in adjusting to change.

An unencumbered system has clear lines of authority, flexibility in the allocation of funds, clear mandates, and distinct policies and procedures which will facilitate collaborative efforts. An organizational structure which encourages collaborative efforts will demonstrate evidence of: administrative support for shared-decision-making; an organizational philosophy which encourages integrated or multi-disciplinary efforts; leaders ready to restructure with enthusiasm for change; recognition of the interdependence of organizations in society; a past history which is collegial; availability of financial support and time for skill training; and opportunities to develop collaborative efforts.

There are numerous benefits to be gained by collaboration. School counselors will gain increased visibility and viability by involvement in collaborative programs. Collaborative efforts reduce competition for diminishing resources, eliminate duplication of services, and provide a diversified approach to solving the problems and providing the services needed by students. Most grants for educational purposes require collaborative efforts, a history of collaboration, and the demonstration of cost effective methods for accomplishing goals. Acquiring additional funds for a special project or expansion of services may necessitate the pooling of resources through a collaborative grant. Integrated services models, in which several providers such as school counselors, school psychologists, and school social workers work together, as in the Education Development Center project on "Integrating Pupil Services Personnel into Comprehensive School Health and HIV Prevention" enhance the possibility for student success.

In working with the "whole" student through a comprehensive developmental counseling and guidance program it makes sense for the school counselor to coordinate the delivery of school-linked and community-linked services. The school counselor is the site-based professional best positioned and trained to coordinate comprehensive health and career programs for students. Collaborative efforts provide a diversity in services and approaches, a cost effective method of program and service delivery, an integrated approach to the "whole" student in the community of learners, enhanced expertise from a varied bank of resources, and improved programs and services. In defining the role of the school counselor in educational reform, the American School Counselor Association (ASCA) has provided bold and visionary leadership through the development of a pamphlet on "The Professional School Counselor's Role in Educational Reform".

During the 1994 National School Counseling Week an ASCA Summit was held in Washington, D.C. During the Summit significant collaborative efforts were initiated with a number of agencies and associations in government, education and business. At that time ASCA proactively announced the school counselor's role as facilitator and change agent in the local school community. Collaborating with the Goals 2000 Panel, ASCA is working to make that change agent role known across the country. It is now the responsibility of each school counselor to adopt the Summit model, implement their role, and begin collaborative efforts in their local school. A paradigm shift is needed in both school counselor role and school counselor function. To demonstrate their role change, school counselors must move out of the counseling offices into the community.

The school counselor is the most appropriate educator to facilitate "a culture of collaboration" in the local school community. As a human relations specialist, a facilitator of team building, a resource broker of services, an information processor, and a promoter of positive student outcomes, the school counselor as change agent develops and nurtures collaborative relationships by facilitating change through programs of prevention and intervention for all students. Developing a culture of collaboration at the local school will unite students, faculty, staff, and the community in a common vision and mission to prepare each student to be successful in school and to acquire the essential skills for successful employment, responsible citizenship, and lifelong learning. Many opportunities are available for school counselors to collaborate for student success.

Collaborative efforts may begin at the local school site as school counselors work with teachers, administrators, and other health care professionals. Partnerships with business and industry for school-to-work transition programs are developing. School-based and school-linked integrated services models are growing. Local civic groups are seeking collaborations with effective education programs that make a difference. State and federal agencies, such as the National Occupational Information Coordinating Committee, provide opportunities for collaborative efforts. Private organizations such as the Lilly Endowment, Inc. and the DeWitt Wallace Reader's Digest Fund have collaborated on school counseling projects. Businesses such as McDonald's Corporation sponsor collaborative efforts for students. The initiative and imagination of the individual school counselor will determine the extent and variety of collaborative efforts that can be developed in the local school community.

4

GROUP GUIDANCE AND COUNSELLING

A small group of people, usually between 5 and 8 members, who get together to learn more about themselves and the way they relate to others. As people get to know and trust each other, with the support of the group facilitator, they can risk sharing confidential feelings in a way that is often not comfortable between friends or family members. You might want to boast of an achievement or talk about the anxiety of living in a competitive atmosphere all the time, 'or omplain about having to seem OK when actually you feel shaky and lacking in confidence. However you are feeling, the group can become a safe place to talk about it. A counselling group is an invaluable tool for self-learning and experimenting with different ways of being and behaving with others. If you have never dared to show the vulnerable side of yourself, for example, or the outgoing side, this may be the time to start !

Following are aims:

— To develop emotional awareness.

— To help you feel clearer about yourself as an individual.

— To give you the strength to be more open and assertive with other people.

— To enable you to feel stronger and more confident.

As well as the benefits listed above, groups have many other less obvious and long-term benefits. You will probably find that the conversations you take part in within the group enrich your social friendships. You may find yourself daring to broach topics that you would previously have been too shy to mention. You may start feeling you are a more outgoing individual than before. Because counsellors make the assumption that how you feel about yourself and your life is very important, they encourage you to spend time exploring your feelings about the important relationships in your life. They also invite you to be aware of your feelings about the other people in the group.

Sometimes it is necessary to dip back into the past to understand how the past still lives on in the present. The more you give to the group in terms of talking and listening, the more you will find you get out of it. The group is a place where you can experiment with different ways of behaving. For example you may want to try talking a lot more than you normally do, or being a lot quieter than you normally are. You may find yourself wanting to disagree with people in the group on certain points, and that your opinions start to become more clearly defined. The more risks you take in daring to be different, the freer and more confident you will feel as a result.

As you listen to other people's experiences,you will have a chance to compare them with yours. You will be able to find out how other people react to your experiences. As trust in the group deepens, you may want to ask for feedback from others about the impact you make on them. Finally, in a group you have the chance to say things you would probably never dream of coming out with to friends or family!

You can participate in a counselling group for up to a whole academic year (although the group will not meet during vacation periods) if you find the experience helpful, you may choose to join a new counselling group the following academic year. Students tell us that they find the continuity of support and the deepening of relationships over time very helpful.

Take some responsibility for the group itself. Make a commitment to attending the first few sessions. Groups sometimes get off to a sticky start and take a little while to settle down and become comfortable. Commit to being on time for meetings. If you are going to be late or absent for a meeting, please either inform the group beforehand or phone and leave a message.

Agree to keep all information disclosed in the group confidential, as well as the identities of the people in it. Agree not to purposely meet outside the group, as social meetings can undermine trust and honesty while the group is meeting regularly. What you do after the group has ended is, of course, your business! One final tip - the more scared you are of joining a group and the more you face you fear and join it anyway, the more you will benefit from it !

LARGE GROUP GUIDANCE

Large group guidance is the prevention component of the guidance program. The purpose of large group guidance is to teach all elementary students skills they will need to become responsible individuals who can contribute to society. Group counselling provides members with the opportunity to explore and develop personal goals, and to promote positive changes in an atmosphere of honest sharing and listening. Experiential activities are used to facilitate exploration and learning. Some of the focuses include:

— Personal Growth

— Relationship Building

— Intimacy

— Emotional Management

— Self Esteem

— Stress Management

Group Employment Counselling

Within the current economic context of rapidly changing labor market opportunities and structural unemployment, many people are faced with the prospect of not simply losing a job, but a way of life. The loss affects the core of being and can result in a series of emotional reactions that approximate loss reactions, namely denial, anger, bargaining, depression, and acceptance. Coupled with loss is confusion of setting a new career direction and stress associated with job search. The end result can be an emotional roller coaster which is difficult for the person, the family, and for professionals trying to offer assistance.

Amundson & Borgen identified several factors that helped or hindered during unemployment. Facilitating factors included support from family and friends, positive thinking, career changes and retraining, part-time or temporary work, job search support groups, vocational counselling, initial job search activities, making job contacts, and physical activity. Hindering factors were job rejections, financial pressures, contacts with government agencies, unknown or negative future, ineffective job search activities, negative thinking, and spouse or family problems. The hindering factors reflect the stress of job search, the re-definition of self associated with unemployment, and strained relationships. The facilitating factors focus on relationships and meaningful activities.

Impacts

Taken together, these factors pointed to the potential of group employment counselling. In a group context there are opportunities for support and meaningful exchange with others. In order to examine this further, investigated the experiences of people who had been involved in a variety of group employment counselling programs. Participants were contacted 3-5 months after the groups had finished. Group employment counselling resulted in a dramatic upswing that in some cases led to a job (48 %) and in other cases to sustained, independent job search activity (52 %). Timing of the group experience seemed particularly important. Some people tended to emotionally drift slowly downward after 2 months of being unemployed, while others maintained a positive outlook for up to 6 months, but then experienced rapid emotional decline. Participation in the group around 8-9 months after job loss seemed to produce an "emotional rebound" where people were able to maintain a more positive outlook whether or not a job was found.

When participants described their group involvement, they emphasized what they had learned, the support that they had received, and the ways in which their self-esteem had been enhanced. They appreciated the structured learning activity which was meaningful and enabled them to meet others facing similar experiences. For most people, their main regret was that they had not joined a group earlier.

Based on the information that task (i.e., structured learning activities) and social support aspects of groups were about equally helpful, a group employment counselling model was developed. The model has two emphases: acquisition of relevant skills and information (the "educative" element), and the development and maintenance of a constructive attitude (often impeded by emotions which must be recognized: anxiety, fear and depression). The group counselling model focuses on the development of knowledge, skills, and personal awareness. These three elements are important regardless of the purpose of the group: career exploration, career decision-making, job search, or coping with unemployment. Within the approach, participants have the opportunity to acquire relevant information, practice skills needed to be successful, and address any barriers that they may be facing.

The stages of group development provide a second dimension to the model and are consistent with Tuckman's overview of group development.

1. The "planning stage" provides a foundation for the group. Initial referral and screening are important to ensure member needs match group goals.
2. When group members first come together ("initial stage"), there is a need for members to feel part of the group (inclusion). In this stage it is important to focus on the integration of individual and group goals and the establishment of group norms.
3. As members become more aware of the needs of each other and the leader, the issue of control can become more central. This leads to a "transition stage" in which there is greater potential for reluctance and conflict.
4. Following this period of potential unrest, group members move into the "working stage," characterized by greater trust and an emphasis on commitment and productivity. The group functions with greater autonomy, and there is less reliance on the leader for support and direction.
5. As the group approaches the "termination stage" there is an opportunity to integrate what has been learned and plan for reaching goals. Emotionally, there may be feelings of loss which need to be acknowledged by the leader.
6. The "post-group" stage involves meeting after the group has finished to provide continued support and encouragement.

The model is fluid and dynamic. The five components of group development influence and are influenced by each other. They require the group leaders to be aware of group member needs and to modify activities and leadership approaches accordingly. In addition, the stages of group development do not proceed in a linear fashion. Members often return to earlier stages in their general progression through the group and leaders need to be aware of which stages group members may be in at any particular time and tailor their approach and skills accordingly.

GROUP AS THE THERAPIST

In a group, everyone and no-one is a therapist. In a group, analytic understanding the group is the therapist, which means that group analysis is a form of psychotherapy "by the group, of the group, including it's conductor". The primary psychological unit is the group, the primary biological unit is the individual. The process of existing is a process of communication in different, significant groups. Radically said: without communication we can't exist. In a group analytic understanding, the individual is seen as a nodal point in a network of group relations. Psychopathology of the individual expresses a blockage in the communication within significant groups. Only through analysis of the conflictual group relations, this disturbance in the communication process, called psychopathology, can be understood.

In a process of free-floating communication, analyzing is the task of the group, thus interpretation is not the privilege of the analyist. Through analyzing, the group creates meaning. Under the specific conditions of a group analytic setting which follows well-defined rules, the group analytic attitude – slowly adopted by all group members – promotes the development of an intermediate space with clear boundaries, in which the group members – including the conductor – develop the ability to communicate and listen to each other in a non-judgemental, free-floating, non-directive and non-manipulative way.

In this free-floating communication which provides a maximum of free speech, the unconscious relationship in the network of the group becomes the object of communication and analysis. Conflicts which develop in this dynamic network of group relations can then be understood as figures on the background of the unconscious transference and counter-transference processes. Transference and counter-transference form the link to the outside world. Each patient brings his or her world into the group. Communication becomes the aim in such a free-floating process: "In learning to communicate, the group can be compared with a child learning to speak."

Group Analytic Attitude

A group analytic attitude is not a moral aim, but describes the technique which opens a space for the group members to reach access to the unconscious process within the group and between groups. Group analysts are not able to deal better with day-to-day conflicts, but they have learned a very specific way of relating within a well-defined group analytic situation which opens the way to the understanding of unconscious conflicts, the social unconscious of the group. Identity is a process which develops through interaction in which the reciprocity of recognition becomes the basic exchange in communication. Individuality develops through the deviation from expectations and norms of these significant communicating groups.

With this group analytic attitude the group conductor deviates from the regressive need of the group for a leader. In this case of a hierarchical perception of the group dynamic in which dependency and power are created, a sight for mutual recognition starts with the danger that this ideal free-floating communication can deteriorate in two different ways: on the one hand, autonomy can become arbitrariness, a regression into a mass with an idealized leader, on the other hand individuality can become isolation. For being able to use such dangers as creative forces we need to work through dependency needs, destructive hate and splitting as a defence against a group analytic free-floating process. "The group... shows a need... for a leader in the image of an omnipotent, godlike father figure..."

When S.H. Foulkes gave a talk in New York 1949, he addressed the group analytic understanding of conducting a group. The term 'leader' is not only unsuitable because the word 'leader' had been deeply compromised by Hitler's and Musselini's dictatorships, but mainly due to the group analytic understanding of conducting a group. "In thus refraining from leading, he shows up, 'by default', as it were, what the group wants and expects from a leader". The group analyst has to accept the unconscious fantasy of the group which puts the therapist in the position of a premordial leader image, one who is omnipotent, and the group expects magical help from him. But instead of fulfilling this regressive need, the conductor uses it in the best interest of the group, which means that he has to change from a leader of the group to a leader in the group, replacing thereby in turn the leader's authority by that of the group.

Accordingly, Foulkes came to define the essential role of group analysis "to replace submission by co-operation on equal terms between equals". By working through this regressive need of a fusion with an omnipotent leader, the group develops the ability to communicate between equals.

In this basic law of group dynamics, S.H. Foulkes defined the healing effect of groups as follows: "The deepest reason why patients... can reinforce each other's normal reactions and wear down and correct each others's neurotic reactions, is that collectively they constitute the very norm from which, individually, they deviate." Groups are brought together by the need to belong. In order to make this cohesion very strong, which means to define "Us" from "Not-Us", all differences within the group have to be denied at first. Another possibility is the fusion with an omnipotent leader and his or her ideology. Individuality is denied.

To belong to a significant group and to be recognized by the group is a therapeutic force in itself, but it becomes very soon a resistance and a dangerous dynamic within and between groups. This is why in group analytic groups the conductor is through this group analytic attitude the stranger from the beginning. The frustration of dependency needs provokes very powerful emotional recations. The need to belong to a unified group, makes differences within the group unconscious, the so-called social unconscious of the group. Through the process of a free-floating association within the group, mainly established by the group analytic attitude of the conductor and the basic rule, that every spontaneous thought should be shared, an exchange between different views and experiences can start. This differentiation process goes along with a very painful and slow process of accepting the otherness of the other. It also goes along with destructive fantasies which, according to Winnicott, create the differentiation between the self and the other.

The central defence against listening is a fear of the stranger, of a different view of the world. Only if we let the stranger, the different view of the world in, listen to it, a therapeutic process can take place. "The fight into individuality is a defence mechanism that seeks to build fortification against the therapeutic process which, if allowed to enter, will inevitably transform." According to F. Dalal, "a functioning group could be seen as a communication process in which competing discourses come into conflict, with the aim to free each group member from being stuck in ones down discourse, ones own experience of the self and the world, and opens up the possibility of connecting with other discourses, other ways of being and experiencing to which one did not have previous access to."

Mirroring

In a free-floating communication, the group members learn to tolerate the ambiguity of communication, which means to understand that each group member tells more than what he or she says. This is one of the preconditions for being able to use other group members as mirrors. Like mirrors allow us to see ourselves from behind, the understand of the mirrored meaning of what a group member has said, allows the access to the unconscious meaning of what has been told. For the process of differentiation, the groups make use of mirroring. Mirroring combines empathy in the other and the notion of being different from the other in one emotional reaction to the perception of the otherness of the other.

Through mirroring, similarities and differences between group members are sorted out. The group could use this mirror reaction, the aggression towards a manipulative way to control the communication process, for analyzing the way how this member tries to disrupt the communication by this ritual, by his symptoms. The newcomer confronted the compulsive speaker with the fact that others have a place and a space too within this communication process. The mirrored, destructive fantasy to exclude somebody who tries to control the group gave way to a process of differentiation within the group: both views have a place.

The "anti-group"

Morris Nitsun describes destructive group forces in his book "The anti-group". The term "anti", similar to the term negative, implies a movement against something contrary to the term "pro" or "positive". But if we understand destructive attacks as a creative attempt itself, there is nothing negative in destructive fantasies. Real destruction is only acted out if the destructive fantasy can't be verbalised and if the environmental object seeks for retaliation and not the other way around. This means that in group analytic psychotherapy we have to find ways to protect the group analytic attitude, which helps the group and the acting out member to understand the creative potential of what is being staged.

There is not polarity: anti- and pro-group forces, but there is one developmental process in which the survival of destructive attacks and the working through of destructive fantasies sets in motion a process of differentiation between self and object. It is not a matter of transforming a destructive attack into something creative, but to understand the creative potential of destructive fantasies, which is to transform the object still under omnipotent control into the perception of an external subject in its own rights.

Social unconscious

While the libido brings and holds together the group, destructive fantasies create a differentiation process within the group and thus make the social unconscious conscious. The social unconscious of the group can be understood as a harbour of all denied heterogenity within the group. This process of differentiation within a group through which the social unconscious, the denied heterogenity within the group, becomes conscious, gives sight on the power relations within and between groups. Such an analysis of the group by the group sets in motion a developmental process from two poles: firstly from a fusion of a mass and an omnipotent leader to a network of equal group members, and secondly from an isolated individual to an attached and connected social subject, who develops in an on-going exchange between group members.

This can also be seen as a process in the direction of democratisation. The task of the conductor is to establish a group analytic situation in which a free-floating communication comes to life. He has to combine the group according to a maximum of heterogenity, different views of the world and according to a similar ego strength. The basic rule that everything can be said and be understood as a valuable communication, opens the space for a healthier development of each group member by mutual recognition of being different.

PERSONAL COACHING

The terms Executive Coaching, Life Coaching, Career Coaching and Personal Coaching all refer to a process of helping normal or high functioning people achieve to their full potential. Coaching may be applied to work related or personal goals and may be used with an individual or with a group of people working as a team.

Positive goals for improvement may be professional, career, education or work related. Goals may be to improve work performance or to expand upon or make changes in career or profession. Goals may also be personal, life style or quality of life related. Coaching is focused upon heightening ability to achieve potential, to promote optimal level of functioning and to enhance the effective application of motivation to achieve specific goals.

Coaching is a cooperative and interactive effort. The professional coach evaluates, clarifies, challenges and supports a client in actions to achieve performance goals and to achieve greater satisfaction in work related and/or personal related areas of life.

Evaluation:The coach will help you specify answers to these questions:

— Where are you now?

— What is your current level of performance?

— What are your strengths and weaknesses?

— What are your areas of skill and competence?

— How can you identify your values, purpose, principles and priorities?

— Are you ready for coaching?

Setting Direction: The coach will help you clarify your vision, priorities and goals. The coach will help you clearly define the objectives, results or outcomes desired by you.

Implementing a Defined Plan of Action: After helping you define the goals and challenges, the coach will help you establish an action plan and timetable, identify likely obstacles and remedies, and support your commitment to follow the timetable to achieve your goals.

Following Through: The coach will help you evaluate your progress realistically, give you feedback, and help you modify or enhance your plan of action as needed for greater effectiveness.

If we think about the role of a coach in sports it helps to clarify what a life coach may offer. A world-class athlete already has the talent and skill to compete in the top echelon of his or her sport. Why would such a supremely talented athlete need to have a coach? Because top athletes know a coach can help them identify certain training or performance actions that will help them achieve up to their maximum potential. The coach helps the athlete make full and efficient use of his or her talent and skills. A similar principle is involved in Executive Coaching, Life Coaching, Career Coaching or Personal Coaching.

Coaching and Psychotherapy

Psychotherapy is a method of treatment for symptoms of emotional disturbance, such as anxiety, depression, panic attacks, obsessions or compulsions. Treatment may be directed at the overt expression of the symptom or it may include exploring personal family and history information in order to determine the cause of the symptom. It involves dealing with mental or emotional suffering, or dysfunction, internal conflicts, and psychodynamics. It is usually conducted in face-to-face meetings in the office of a psychologist, typically for 45 minute weekly sessions. Treatment is directed at a diagnosable mental or emotional disturbance and is often covered as a benefit under a medical insurance plan. The basic assumption in coaching is that an achievement oriented person wants to function at a higher level, to be more effective and to make positive changes in his or her life.

Coaching is a way of helping a person expand upon his or her perception of new possibilities and thereby upon an awareness of freedom to make choices. The coach does not tell people what to do, but helps them define the changes they want to make and the goals they want to achieve. It helps them take the step from wishing, yearning and hoping to actually taking practical steps in a realistic, productive way. Coaching focuses upon future possibilities, not past mistakes. It enhances a new learning process and implements effective action through a deliberate process of observation, inquiry, dialog, and discovery. It helps a person recognize and draw upon their strengths and under-utilized psychological resources and to overcome limitations, frustration and disappointment.

In other words, a coach helps a client recognize options for becoming a more effective person. The coach facilitates experiential learning that results in positive, future-oriented action and helps the client clearly define and strengthen his or her commitment to making positive changes. Coaching is a collaborative, goal directed form of cooperative planning between the coach and a healthy achievement-oriented person.

Because the coach is dealing with someone who is psychologically healthy, there are practical options to face-to-face sessions. Coaching is often conducted with clients by means of telephone conferences. Because of the well defined and circumscribed nature of the goals and because of the cooperative interactive nature of the coaching procedure this process can be effective using periodic consultations of about twenty minutes duration.

GROUP PSYCHOTHERAPY

Group psychotherapy, like individual psychotherapy, is intended to help people who would like to improve their ability to cope with difficulties and problems in their lives. But, while in individual therapy the patient meets with only one person (the therapist), in group therapy the meeting is with a whole group and one or two therapists. Group therapy focuses on interpersonal interactions, so relationship problems are addressed well in groups. The aim of group psychotherapy is to help with solving the emotional difficulties and to encourage the personal development of the participants in the group. The therapist (called conductor, leader or facilitator) chooses as candidates for the group people who can benefit from this kind of therapy and those who may have a useful influence on other members in the group.

Members of the group share with others personal issues which they are facing. A participant can talk about events s/he was involved in during the week, her/his responses to these events, problems s/he had tackled, etc. The participant can share his/her feelings and thoughts about what happened in previous sessions, and relate to issues raised by other members or to the leader's words. Other participants can react to her/his words, give her/him feedback, encourage, give support or criticism, or share their thoughts and feelings following his/her words. The subjects for discussion are not determined by the leader but rise spontaneously from the group. The member in the group feels that (s)he is not alone with her/his problem and that there are others who feel the same.

The group can become a source of support and strength in times of stress for the participant. The feedback (s)he gets from others on her/his behavior in the group can make her/him become aware to maladaptive patterns of behavior, change her/his point of view and help him/her adopt more constructive and effective reactions. It can become a laboratory for practicing new behaviors. Frequently the people you meet in the group represent others in your past or current life with whom you have difficulty. In group therapy you have the opportunity to work through these situations.

Group psychotherapy is suitable for a large variety of problems and difficulties, beginning with people who would like to develop their interpersonal skills and ending with people with emotional problems like anxiety, depression, etc. There are support groups for people in the same situation or crisis (e.g. groups for bereaved parents, groups for sexually abused women), but usually the recommendation for the therapeutic group is to be as heterogeneous as possible and represent a micro-cosmos. For that reason in building the group, the leader will try to include men and women, young and old people, married and singles, etc.

The group is especially effective for people with interpersonal difficulties and problems in relations. Whether these difficulties are in social, working, couple or even sexual relations, the participant can benefit a lot in these areas. Groups are ideally suited to people who are struggling with relationship issues like intimacy, trust, self-esteem. The group interactions help the participants to identify, get feedback, and change the patterns that are sabotaging the relations. The great advantage of group psychotherapy is working on these patterns in the "here and now" - in a group situation more similar to reality and close to the interpersonal events.

Different Types of Group

There are many kinds of groups in the group-psychotherapy field. The techniques used in group therapy can be verbal, expressive, psychodramatic etc. The approaches can vary from psychoanalytic to behavioral, Gestalt or encounter groups. Groups vary from classic psychotherapy groups, where process is emphasized, to psychoeducational, which are closer to a class. Psychoeducational groups usually focus on the most common areas of concern, notably relationships, anger, stress-management etc. They are frequently more time-limited (10 to 15 sessions) and thus very appealing in a managed care environment. Each approach has its advantages and drawbacks, and the participant should consult the expert which technique matches her/his unique personality.

When choosing a group psychotherapist you should look for a well-trained, reliable, and ethical professional. If you are in individual therapy you should consult your therapist and be sure that your group and individual therapists can collaborate. Reputable group psychotherapists usually belong to professional associations. In the U.S.A, for example, membership in AGPA (the American Group Psychotherapy Association), and certification as a Group Psychotherapist by AGPA assures some degree of expertise. An experienced group therapist will usually interview you before your entering the group and will answer your questions about the group and his/her experience without being uneasy. You can also ask the prospective therapist how many years experience (s)he has in the particular modality and as a therapist generally. Make sure you clarify fees (including costs for missed sessions). Above all, trust your feelings: If you do not feel you can trust the therapist, find another.

The participant in the group is expected to be present each week and come on time. It is required that the information brought up by members of the group and their names be kept confidential by all the group members. In some groups, the participant is asked to commit for a specified length of time at the beginning of the group. The usual commitment is between 3 to 6 months. This facilitates getting a sense of how the group works. When participating in a group, you will not be required to talk, or reveal intimate issues when you do not want to. However, it is clear that the more you can participate, be open and talk about yourself, your feelings and thoughts - the more you can gain from this experience.

Usually, there are between 8 to 12 members in the group. Above 15 members, it is impossible to create a therapeutic atmosphere and have enough time for each member to work personally. The length of every session can be from an hour and a half to three hours (this does not include workshops and marathon groups). The frequency can be once to twice a week. The duration of the group depends on many components such as the severity of the problems and the targets sought. It can be from a few months to a few years. You should allow 4 to 6 months to pass in order to feel the effect of the group.

Developing a Group Psychotherapy Practice

It is vitally important that a clinician go into group therapy as a patient before beginning to implement group therapy into his or her practice. The general training of group psychotherapists, no matter how effective or efficient a professor(s) may be, is not sufficient to teach group dynamics in an academic setting nor is internship or practicum sites sufficient in creating truly effective group therapists. Only experience on "both sides of the desk" and life experience in general, in my personal opinion, creates a truly effective group therapist. Personal experience in group therapy and working through ones own interpersonal issues as a member, is perhaps the best route to go if you wish to truly learn about yourself and experience the process of group psychotherapy. There is an old psychoanalytic statement, stating, "We can only take a patient as far as we ourselves have gone."

In order for you to sell the process and you must sell the process, you too must wholeheartedly believe in it and one of the the best ways to do that is to experience it firsthand as a patient. Granted and accepted is the belief by many clinicians that there exists both positive and negative group experiences for a group member but that does not discount the effectiveness of learning as one can just as easily learn what not to do as to what to do. Their argument should also include that individual psychotherapy can include both positive and negative experiences but that does not seem to be the case when they give their opinions. There is also another opinion that really must be done away with and that is group therapy is a second rate modality which it is not.

It provides a very timely increase of affect and offers the wonderful opportunity of multiple transferences occurring thus permitting the patient to work on a number of interpersonal difficulties at the same time. In individual psychotherapy, the therapist must become the virtual surrogate of all those problematic people from the past in order for the patient to resolve these multiple historical interpersonal conflicts. Unfortunately, often through time or economic constraints and due to perhaps the nature and skill of the individual psychotherapist, this does not occur and the patient leaves therapy with an incomplete opportunity to work through as many interpersonal issues as possible within a shorter period of time.

Besides being a finer therapeutic advantage, this obviously is economically more feasible for the patient to have a longer therapeutic experience as it is less costly than individual psychotherapy and offers more to be gained for the patient who may or may not have insurance. With these obviously opinionated beliefs in my specialty, let us move tóward the more practical issues at hand. Psychotherapy is a business. It is the business of helping people. Those individuals who have a greater acumen in business will do better in generating income into their practices than those who find the concept of helping others and making a living mutually exclusive concepts. It is my belief that specialization is the direction to follow and group therapy is a specialization, which can have within it many other specializations.

Being a "jack of all trades and master of none," is probably the best route to go in one's developing practice in order to generate income in the beginning of a career but to remain as such creates restrictions on the capacity of the business to obtain economic growth and results. The specialization of group psychotherapy offers a therapist a route to proceed in which to generate more income in a shorter period of time besides providing an arena for a patient's timely growth. Group therapy cannot only be a tremendous psychological paradigm and experience for the patient but too a wonderful income producer for one's private practice. It is also seen that patients who belong to psychotherapy groups generally come on a more consistent basis than patients in individual psychotherapy thus providing a greater sense of economic security for the practitioner. Interestingly, the profession seems to elicit in many new clinicians a terrible conflict between money and care. If you charge for your services that in some way you have muddied the purity of the psychotherapeutic relationship. If you feel your service is worth nothing than it is worth nothing and will be seen by the patient as worth nothing.

Granted wanting to help out a struggling individual seek psychotherapy is a most honorable deed. Counselors occasionally do this but if you cannot afford to do this and continue setting the tone of your private practice as if it was a clinic, you are probably indicating a lower self-esteemed issue in your own personality as its correlates to your self-worth. The issue of money and charging for one's services is an amazing and very important issue in this profession.

The reality is couselors only have two things upon which they can charge and make a living:

1) knowledge and

2) time

The care we give is free as there cannot be placed a price on that commodity. We do not give a tangible product like a grocery store and if you feel your knowledge and your time is not worth anything of value then you will be having some salient problems in this profession unless you seek some sort of paid position. It truly doesn't matter how many lives you have saved that month. The utility companies that service your office aren't interested and if you can't pay your bills you will not have a roof over your head, electric, phone, etc. in which to practice your profession. Also, if you can't help yourself, how can you truly expect to help others help themselves? In returning to psychology as a business, it must be remembered that your office itself does not generate any income but only debt, i.e., rent, electric, malpractice, phone etc.

All revenues from one's office come from outside of the office in the form of patients, corporations, writing, etc. This indicates that the private practitioner must go outside of his or her office to generate income. What is meant by going outside of one's office is basically; you need to make yourself known in the community in which you practice. Foremost you must be cognizant of your community. Is psychotherapy a viable profession in the location of your choice? For example, it would be foolish to place a gourmet market in a lower socioeconomic environment, as it would be foolish to set up a practice in an area where there is a paucity of potential patients.

Sadly, many well-intentioned and often very bright clinicians are just not approachable. They seem to have taken the "distance therapist stance" from the office out into the real world. If you have difficulty giving talks and making yourself known then either work on getting over that or seek employment in a clinic setting in which you will only be required to do therapy and not required to seek out patients. For many people this is a more comfortable route to go but has its obvious economic limitations.

A relationship must be developed between the patient and therapist before he/she can make a positive transition into group therapy. It is important that the patient has an initial positive experience in his/her first group session. Group can be a highly anxiety creating stimulus for most people and if the first meeting has been aversive, the chances are he or she will not be coming back. In fact, that might definitely be a healthy response on the part of the patient, as we would not go back to a group that was initially an aversive experience.

5

Techniques and Procedures of Guidance

Nature guidance is an interesting offer for everyone who wants to know more about nature, culture history, the landscape and the condition of the environment. You do not need to know a lot about nature, as long as you are interested in exploring – both outside and inside the city boundary. The nature guides work in the forest districts, in the counties, in the municipalities, at nature schools, in museums and in outdoor life organisations. Here they organise the outings and activities which everybody can take part in. Many of the outings are arranged for families with children.

The nature guides show you where you can experience nature closely. They will explain you how culture history and nature are connected and how we influence on the environment and also how we can help to preserve it. Groups and organisations wishing an outing in a particular nature area or knowledge of a particular nature or environment subject can contact the nearest nature guide or the nature guide in the area you wish to visit.The nature school managers and many nature guides offer training for schools. Courses for teachers, educationalists etc. who wish to make use of nature together with the pupils. The nature guides offer lots of possibilities for the educationalists who want the children to replace the toys with nature experience. Furthermore, educationalists who work in other institutions can arrange agreements on outings and activities for the clients of the institutions.

Teachers can agree on a training course in a nature school or with a nature guide. They offer many different training courses or arrange courses together with you which will fit into your schedule at the home school. The nature guide does not only offer training courses in the nature subjects but also in e.g. history, woodwork, mathematics and domestic science and other subjects with a "green weft". Courses for teachers, educationalists etc. which wish to use nature together with the pupils. The nature guides can offer a lot to the educationalists who want the children to replace the toys with nature experience. Educationalists who work in other institutions can also have trips and activities arranged. Nature schools are usually free to use for schools and day care institutions in the municipalities that pay for the conduction of the nature schools. Other schools have to pay.

GROUPS

Groups that is, associations, institutions, organisations, interest groups etc. can apply to the nature guide and agree on an arrangement. In most cases an arrangement can be fit to the group in question. The group is also welcome to come up with special wishes in relation to content and place. Make always sure to state what kind of arrangement you wish and where to meet. There is no standard price on arrangements with a nature guide. Therefore do also agree on the price of the arrangement.

Most nature guides organise public trips and arrangements which everybody can join. Many counties publish folders with surveys of all the public trips and arrangements that take place within the borders of the county. In these folders arrangements which are implemented by nature guides are mentioned. These take place in counties, State forests, municipalities, museums, organisations etc. Furthermore a number of forest districts, municipalities, museums and organisations distribute folders with their own arrangements.

A number of counties show a survey of nature guide arrangements on their web site. Folders and brochures with information about trips and arrangements are available in libraries and tourist offices. Very often these arrangements are advertised and mentioned in local newspapers. Here you can read what the trip is about, where to meet and whether it costs something to join the arrangement etc. some trips and arrangements are free others cost a little. You are also welcome to call your nature guide and ask when the next public arrangement takes place.

Definition and purpose of nature guidance

Nature guidance is a complete description of an explanation of a landscape's or an area's characteristic elements and connections which through direct experience leads to a discovery of, knowledge of, understanding for, respect and care for nature and the environment.

The purpose is to communicate

— that nature is a whole of the landscape, ocean, climate, plants, animals, history and culture which the human being is a part of, dependent of and which it influences,

— that nature is both being protected and used,

— about subjects relating to the basis of nature, the nature jobs and the outdoor life,

— about the written and unwritten rules of activities and stay in the open country,

— about Danish and global environment relations and participation towards a fruit bearing lifestyle,

— about nature in the cities and connections between the city life and environments.

During the 1980s, when "A Nation At Risk" set the tone for public discourse on education and when politicians throughout the country were clamoring for educational reform, school districts came under great pressure to raise academic standards, lengthen the school day, implement state-mandated basic curricula, and otherwise become more accountable to taxpayers. But by and large, the advocates of "educational excellence" at that time paid virtually no attention to addressing the urgent personal or emotional needs of our students.

Fortunately, a new school of thought is emerging among educators and counselors. Unlike the reform movement of the past decade, this new movement takes full account of students' personal needs in formulating educational goals. Proponents of this school of thought recognize the close relationship between students' academic development and their personal growth; accordingly, they are seeking to place guidance at the heart of the educational process. The three exemplary guidance programs presented here represent three different, but compatible approaches to this goal.

Norm Gysbers' Comprehensive Guidance Program Model, and Robert Myrick's Teacher Advisor Program are both based on the idea that guidance is an integral part of a school's educational mission rather than an "ancillary" service peripheral to the curriculum. This idea in turn presupposes an enlightened humanistic conception of education, which recognizes and validates the intrinsic dignity of every student, and which attends empathetically to students' personal and developmental needs. This conception forms the basis of William Purkey's Invitational Learning Model, a new paradigm for schooling that seeks to reconstitute the entire school setting—people, places, policies, programs, and processes—so that every aspect of the school serves to "invite" students to learn by respecting them, encouraging them, and validating their unique importance and possibilities.

Since 1971, Norman C. Gysbers and his associates at the University of Missouri-Columbia have been developing, field-testing, refining, and implementing the Comprehensive Guidance Program Model, an innovative, program-based organizational plan that has been adopted by school districts throughout the nation. The foundation for the Model—the theoretical basis for identifying the guidance, knowledge, skills, and attitudes (competencies) that students need is called Life Career Development, defined as self-development over a person's life span through the integration of roles, settings, and events in a person's life. Accordingly, this Model emphasizes three domains of human growth and development:

— *Self-knowledge and interpersonal skills*: Helping students to develop awareness and acceptance of themselves and others, and to develop personal standards and a sense of purpose in life.

— *Life roles, settings, and events*: Emphasizing knowledge and understanding of the interrelatedness of various life roles.

— *Life career planning*: Appraising personal values as they relate to prospective life career plans and decisions.

The Comprehensive Guidance Program Model consists of three structural foundations and four interactive program components. The structural foundations—definition, rationale, and assumptions—emphasize the centrality of guidance to the total education program, and define the relationship between guidance and other aspects of the curriculum. The four program components delineate the major activities, and the roles and responsibilities of personnel involved in the guidance program:

— Guidance curriculum, or structured classroom activities, organized around the three domains of student competencies;

— Individual planning, including activities designed to assist students in monitoring and understanding their own growth and development;

— Responsive services, such as information seeking, crisis counseling, and teacher/parent/specialist consultation; and

— System support, activities geared toward program management and operations.

One principal rationale behind the Comprehensive Guidance Program Model is to enable counselors to regain control of their time on the job by allocating 100 percent of their time to the four program components discussed above—guidance curriculum, individual planning, responsive services, and system support. The Comprehensive Guidance Program Model is oriented above all toward student development; it is a programmatic framework which allows counselors to devote their primary attention to guidance activities and structured group experiences for all students.

Teacher Advisor Program (TAP)

The assumption behind Robert D. Myrick's Teacher Advisor Program (TAP) is that each student needs a friendly adult in the school who knows and cares about him or her in a personal way. The advisors help their advisees deal with the problems of growing up and getting the most out of school. A teacher-advisor is usually responsible for an advisee's cumulative folder, work folders, teacher-student conferences, parent conferences, group guidance experiences and follow-up on academic progress reports. Advisors also consult with other teachers, school counselors, and support personnel about their advisees.

TAP is designed to provide an opportunity for all the students in a school to participate in a small and cohesive group of 15 to 25 peers led by a sensitive and caring teacher who promotes and monitors individual students' educational and developmental experiences as they progress through school. Teacher-advisors meet with their advisees on a regular basis through a "homeroom" or "homebase" group. This becomes, in effect, the students' home within the school, where they have a supportive teacher and group of peers with whom they can explore personal interests, goals, and concerns.

The guidance curriculum varies from one school to another, but it generally addresses personal, social, and academic concerns. Some of the personal and social skills addressed include getting acquainted, self-esteem, and time management. Academic topics might include policies and procedures from the school handbook and computing grade point averages. Career and educational planning topics include career exploration and choices, employability skills and the job market. Since many high school teachers have never had a guidance course and many are unsure of how to lead a group discussion with adolescents, teachers may need special preparation in how to work with their students and how to build guidance units for their groups.

Counselors can therefore assist teachers in developing guidance units, or they can work together as a team in developing and delivering a guidance curriculum, with counselors taking over homebase groups on occasion. It is important, therefore, to establish a cooperative and supportive relationship between teachers and counselors so that they can define their respective roles and differentiate responsibilities. To enlist the support of a school's faculty for TAP and developmental guidance, it is essential that all teachers understand the philosophy of TAP and commit adequate time to it.

Counselors should therefore provide a developmental guidance curriculum guide to establish guidance objectives and provide activities, but allow teachers to choose or discard suggested activities according to their needs. Since most teachers need more training in how to help students solve personal problems or get them working cooperatively in small groups, counselors also may need to assist teachers in developing guidance and interpersonal skills. Administrative support and periodic evaluation are also essential.

Invitational Learning for Counseling and Development

The Invitational Learning concept, developed by William W.

Purkey, offers a blueprint of what counselors, teachers, principals, supervisors, superintendents, and others can do to enrich the physical and psychological environments of institutions and encourage the development of the people who live and work there. Invitational Learning is based on four value-based assumptions regarding the nature of people and their potential and the nature of professional helping:

— *Respect*: People are able, valuable, and responsible and should be treated accordingly;

— *Trust*: Education should be a collaborative, cooperative activity where process is as important as product;

— *Optimism*: People possess untapped potential in all areas of human endeavor; and

— *Intentionality*: Human potential can best be realized by places, policies, programs, and processes that are specifically designed to invite development, and by people who are intentionally inviting with themselves and others, personally and professionally.

In a school or any other organization, everything is connected to everything else. And so, in applying Invitational Learning, everything counts in creating an environment that invites individuals to reach their potential:

— *Places*: Creating an attractive and inviting physical setting is the easiest way to begin the process of incorporating the Invitational Learning concept into a school or other organization.

— *Policies*: Professional counselors can assist schools in developing policies that encourage student responsibility and participation rather than those that create pervasive anxiety, mistrust, and mindless conformity.

— *Programs*: Programs that incorporate the assumptions of Invitational Learning include incentive programs such as peer counseling for dropout prevention, faculty mentoring, and other collaborative programs where students, teachers, and counselors all gain by helping and encouraging one another.

— *Processes*: How we teach or counsel and how we act while doing these things are far more important in the long run than what students or clients learn. Educators and counselors in successful schools establish behavioral norms of collegiality, professional development, mutual assistance, and ongoing discussion of instruction and curricular improvements among themselves, and they cultivate attitudes of respect for all students and attention to their needs in all of their interactions.

— *People*: The daily interaction between teachers and students, counselors and clients, and professionals amongst themselves, ultimately determines the success or failure of Invitational Learning. Counselors and teachers who wish to employ Invitational Learning therefore need a sound knowledge of human development.

The goal of Invitational Learning is thus to provide an optimally inviting total environment, both for professional helpers themselves and for those with whom they work. In this respect, it is fully compatible with both the Comprehensive Guidance Program Model and the Teacher Advisor Program. All three approaches affirm the centrality of developmental guidance to the educational process, and all are predicated on mutual respect and human dignity—for counselors, teachers, and students alike.

SCHOOL GUIDANCE PROGRAMS

"As soon as the first teachers were given part-time assignments as school counselors in the early 1900s, discussion began about what should be the nature, structure, position, and leadership of guidance. What should be the focus of guidance? How should guidance be organized and where should it be placed organizationally in a building/district? Who should lead and manage the program? What titles would best identify guidance program leaders? How should supervision be provided to school counselors and other program staff? How should school counselors and other program staff be evaluated and helped to improve their performance?"

The questions that were asked about the nature, structure, position, and leadership of guidance in the early 1900s are still being asked today, almost 100 years later. However, given the evolution of guidance over the years from a position, to a set of services, to a program, we are now able to more clearly answer these questions. The program concept for guidance provides us with an overall framework, an organizational system that specifies building and district level guidance program leadership roles. As a result this digest first focuses on the fundamental beliefs and the organizational structure of comprehensive guidance programs. Then attention is given to guidance program leader roles, titles, and functions that we feel are necessary to lead and manage comprehensive school guidance programs.

A comprehensive school guidance program, in close collaboration with parents, serves all students pre-kindergarten through grade twelve. It helps all students gain competencies in the areas of personal/social, educational, and career development at all educational levels, competencies that underpin students' academic success. It serves equally all students, parents, teachers, and other recipients regardless of gender, race, ethnicity, cultural background, sexual orientation, disability, family structure and functionality, socioeconomic status, learning ability level, language, level of school involvement, or other special characteristics. A comprehensive school guidance program guarantees that all students have access to school counselors and school counselors have access to all students. It helps develop and protect students' individuality and provides them with skills to function effectively with others in school, home, and community. It is developmental and preventative as well as remedial in design and implementation and is continuously refined and enhanced through systematic planning, designing, implementing, and evaluating.

A comprehensive school guidance program features a content element consisting of student competencies. There is an organizational framework element that contains three structural components (definition, rationale, assumptions), four program components (guidance curriculum, individual planning, responsive services, system support), and time allocations for the work of school counselors. Finally, there is a resources element that includes the human, financial, and political resources required to develop and operate the program effectively and efficiently. A comprehensive school guidance program mandates that school counselors spend 100 percent of their time working in the program with non-guidance duties eliminated. It is put into operation through a five-stage change process of planning, designing, implementing, evaluating, and enhancing. It is evaluated through program, personnel, and results evaluation.

A comprehensive school guidance program is implemented through a team approach that uses all staff members in roles appropriate to their training and competence. It provides for the professional development of school counselors and other guidance program staff to ensure their competence to fully carry out their leadership as well as their implementation roles. It requires strong district and building leadership for program development, implementation, and advocacy and for school counselor and other guidance program staff professional development. District and building guidance program leaders fulfill four roles: administration, supervision, management, and professional leadership.

— *Administration*: In the administrative role, guidance program staff leaders have primary responsibility for and authority over the program and the staff. They establish systems for accountability of staff members, help them organize and implement the program, and evaluate the program's effectiveness and the quality of staff members' performance.

Not only do they ensure the implementation of the designed program, but they also ensure its appropriateness within the context of the school building and district.

— *Supervision*: In the supervision role, guidance program staff leaders assist their staff members to continuously learn new ways to improve their job performance, that is, their professional skills, the currency of their knowledge and information, and their work habits. Meaningful supervision is the result of firsthand observation and directly communicated feedback. It involves helping staff members increase their competence in carrying out their jobs in the guidance program by conducting supervision as outlined in a district's performance improvement system. It is carried out in ways that are comparable with supervision provided by other department leaders for the members of their professional staffs.

— *Management*: In the management role, guidance program staff leaders ensure the efficient use of the resources appropriated to the program. These resources include information provided through the administrative and other staff channels; materials, equipment, and budget appropriated to the department; and the talent and time of staff members. It includes governing and controlling other staff members to ensure that department goals and objectives are accomplished. In this role, guidance program leaders ensure the maintenance of the program and at least the minimum functioning of each staff member. They are the conduit for the school district, the school building, and the department.

— *Professional Leadership*: In the leadership role, guidance program staff leaders influence the behaviors of their staff members in such ways that enhance not only their competence but also their commitment to the program, to the school, and to their profession. As leaders in the profession, they conduct as well as apply the outcomes of research in school counseling, education, and school counseling supervision.

Leadership titles

Titles continue to vary in educational administrative structures. The definitive organizational pattern has yet to be found. Titles reflecting responsibilities vary from school district to school district. What is clear, however, is that whether they are in school district offices or in school buildings, guidance program staff leaders should have titles that reflect their administrative, management, supervisory, and professional leadership responsibilities and fit their placement in the organizational structure of the school system. Individuals with direct responsibility for the guidance program and direct contact with the school counseling staff should have guidance, counseling, or both in their titles (e.g., Assistant Superintendent for Guidance, Director of Guidance, Counselor Supervisor, Guidance Department Head, or Head Counselor).

There are six major leadership functions for district and building level guidance leaders to carry out in fulfilling their leadership roles. These functions are:

(a) empowering school counselors to carry out program roles and responsibilities;

(b) advocating for the guidance program and staff;

(c) defining school counselors' jobs within the guidance program and, thereby, promoting maximum use of their competencies;

(d) promoting professionalism of school counselors;

(e) supervising; and

(f) evaluating school counselors' performance.

These strategies are applied by building and district guidance program staff leaders as defined by job descriptions based on appropriate application of their power bases, roles and competencies in the contexts of comprehensive guidance programs, school counselor performance improvement systems, and school buildings and districts.

QUALITY CAREER COUNSELING SERVICES: A DEVELOPMENTAL TOOL FOR ORGANIZATIONAL ACCOUNTABILITY

Accountability in career counseling is receiving increased attention. The general public is becoming more informed about what to expect from career counseling service providers and, as a consequence, more critical. Funders also are becoming more insistent about accountability and quality assurance. These factors are increasing the pressure on counseling agencies to have policies, standards, and benchmarks for service which "customers" can understand so that they can make comparisons and judgments as to what services to select. However, very few organizations have any guidelines specific to the delivery of career counseling and very few practical tools exist to help organizations who want to pay attention to creating better standards in career counseling.

To fill this void, the idea emerged of creating a developmental procedure for organizations and/or individuals to "do it themselves." The vision was to develop a tool that would be sufficiently generic to be useful in many jurisdictions and, at the same time, sufficiently specific so that it would provide a structure for examining standards and quality of service for a range of career counseling services.

The "tool" which evolved is entitled "Quality Career Counselling Services—A Policy Workbook." The Workbook takes an innovative approach to policies and standards. The procedures recommended are developmental and they concentrate on supporting organizational and staff growth. Quality of service (a more user-friendly name for policies and standards) is portrayed as requiring input from all levels of an organization. It does not just come from "up there," where policy often is seen to reside. The spirit of the workbook is to demystify policy formulation and use policies and standards to support self-initiated processes for quality development and change.

Quality of service in career counseling presents the experiences of the consumers of career counseling services, as well as the experiences of the staff when attending to their own career development needs. Organizations are encouraged to consider that quality career counseling services are best delivered by staff who see their own careers as personally meaningful and important to the organization. It is in the organization's best interests to attend to both dimensions of service (consumer and staff).

The Workbook is designed in two parts: Part One addresses policy development and Part Two addresses staff development. Each part begins with a self-assessment. In areas where the assessments indicate room for improvement, staff are guided step-by-step through suggested procedures for decisions, defining outcome statements, and clarifying plans of action. It is suggested that the assessments and subsequent work be completed in full staff meetings or in time set aside for appropriate working groups. Times for each discussion range from 30-60 minutes and can be spread out over several weeks if necessary.

Part One focuses on policy development for the external delivery of services. An assumption in Part One is that consumers evaluate the services they receive on the basis of how satisfied they are, the degree to which their expectations are met, the reliability of the services over time, and the results they achieve. Organizations which have in place policies and standards in each of the eight areas covered in Part One have a foundation which supports clients who experience these conditions and who evaluate services positively.

Part Two focuses on human resource planning practices. Staff skills are the basis for quality service; therefore, staff career development and planning at all levels of the organization is the focus. Parts One and Two are connected in two important ways. First, conceptually and philosophically, the procedures and processes promote a respect for the career development of all players in an organization. Second, in Part One, users develop a series of policy statements and standards of practice; then in Part Two, they develop achievable action plans to equip staff to deliver service to the standards defined in Part One. The Workbook was field-tested in several jurisdictions, including education, guidance, professional associations, boards of directors, rehabilitation, social services, and the YMCA. Without exception, all reported that the Workbook assisted them in identifying areas in need of attention, and recognizing areas that already were solid.

ADULT CAREER COUNSELING IN A NEW AGE

The changing workplace—a by-now familiar litany of economic, demographic, organizational, and social changes—has made ambiguity the only certainty in work life. Many adults had little or no career education, guidance, or counseling when they were "in school" and often seek such help now, making job or career changes spurred by their personal stage of development or by the "postmodern" workplace. Although career development is a continuous lifelong process, "media and some scholars continue to dramatize crisis in midlife". Crises and transitions can occur at any period, however. Hoyt and Lester found that the career needs of adults aged 18-25 are particularly not being met. The issues and implications of career counseling for adults in the kaleidoscopic context of today's workplace are the focus of this Digest.

In this era of organizational restructuring and technological change, individuals can no longer plan on spending their entire working lives with one organization. Life no longer follows a linear path: schooling, work, retirement. Career paths, too, are no longer a linear rise up the ladder to the top. Some analysts proclaim the "new rules of work": everyone is self-employed and the concept of "job" is disappearing. Such fundamental changes mean that people need more help than ever with career issues. However, a recent survey of 1,046 adults showed that 40% would turn to family or friends first; 37% to counselors.

Only 30% had discussed career choices with school or college counselors; only 36% had made a conscious career choice or plan; and, for 47%, the primary sources of career information were television, magazines, and newspapers.

Unlike counselors of high school or traditional-age college students, adult career counselors deal with an extremely heterogeneous population who are at vastly different stages of life. Their clients' career issues are complicated by family responsibilities and work and life experiences that color their attitudes, values, and decisions. Some may already have made the decision to change, have a great deal of self-knowledge, and need information or assistance in coping with the new context of job search. Others may have drifted into their jobs with little planning or guidance, have difficulty making decisions, and lack awareness of their skills, abilities, and interests. Some may be self-directed learners who just need to be pointed in the right direction; others may want to be given the answer to their career conundrum in a structured way.

Clearly, counselors must be familiar with adult development and adult learning theories and need varied approaches for these different types of clients. They can guide adult clients in mining their life experiences as a source of career information. For experienced clients who already know what they don't want, traditional resources such as the Dictionary of Occupational Titles orOccupational Outlook Handbook may be of little help. Washington suggests broadening their occupational horizons by identifying the special knowledge and technical skills they already possess, using job families instead of traditional clusters (e.g., outdoor jobs, jobs with exotic locations, jobs that use certain skills), and writing results-oriented resumes that describe work projects and results.

Gender Issues and Dual Careers

Because careers are integral to identity in this culture, adult career counseling becomes an exploration of personal identity and meaning. These issues are different for men and women; in this culture, "having a career is a consequence of being male". Often, men make other life choices to accommodate career requirements, and job loss can be a blow to their identity. Despite recent social changes, women's career development remains entangled with family issues, role conflict, sex discrimination, and harassment. Counselors must recognize what is unique about women's career development and help them expand options, remembering that individual women differ from one another as well as from men.

Men's choices are also constricted by gender role restrictions. Counselors can help male clients examine their gender and career socialization and find other ways to validate their identity than traditional narrow definitions. The rise in the number of dual-career couples has given a new focus to counseling approaches. Traditional counseling had an individual focus; now, counseling is incomplete if it fails to take into account the link between work and family life for both men and women. Career assessment for couples must include evaluation of the influences of gender-role beliefs, consideration of the interaction between the partners, and recognition of social policies that still favor the separation of work and family and the gendered division of labor. In "conjoint" career counseling, the individual career stage of each partner and the family stage of the couple must be considered.

Counseling for the Third Age

Another trend affecting career counseling is the expansion of life choices for older adults. The phenomenon of early retirement, especially among white males, the recognition that many older adults still want to work, and longer life spans and better health that make them still able to work necessitate preparing for the "Third Age"—"that period of life beyond the career job and parenting which can last for anything up to 30 years". Midlife and older adults must deal with a number of concerns, such as skill obsolescence, age discrimination, and lack of experience with current technology. They may have to cope with feelings of loss and change, whether their job change or retirement is voluntary or involuntary.

Counselors can help them envision and plan for their future life style and keep them open to new opportunities. One strategy that has proven effective with mature job seekers is the job club. Rife and Belcher found that positive social support for the job search increased the intensity of the search for unemployed adults over 50; more important, the support of other unemployed friends had a more positive effect than that of family or employed friends. The job search club thus serves as an effective network of information exchange and social support for others adrift in the same boat of midlife transition.

Career Counseling and Diversity

Greater attention is finally being given to cross-cultural issues in career counseling. The life and work experiences of ethnic minorities, including immigrants, may have been quite different from the mainstream, and minorities (as do women) experience culture-specific constraints and barriers that affect career development. The meaning of work and career are social and cultural constructions, not universal concepts. Counseling diverse clients should take into account three factors: similarities across cultures, unique aspects of cultures that influence members, and individual characteristics. The application of Western career development theories and norms to non-Western persons may lead to erroneous assumptions and ineffective practice.

Marsella and Leong recommend locating the individual client on a continuum of ethnocultural identity, identifying the relative importance of personal or cultural characteristics to an individual. For example, for a fully acculturated person, personality may be more relevant to career development, whereas for a more traditional individual, the cultural dimension has more influence. Prince et al. offer some guidelines for working with multicultural clients:

(1) assess comfort/familiarity with counseling and how it is viewed in client culture;

(2) consider cultural attitudes toward authority;

(3) is the culture group or individually based?;

(4) how are people socialized toward gender, family, and work roles?; and

(5) be sensitive to such barriers as discrimination, lack of nontraditional role models, and limited information resources.

Just as adult educators must be cautious in selecting tests for adult learners, counselors must ensure that career assessment instruments used with adult clients are appropriate. Counseling of high school or college students typically concentrates on decision making and career choice. Although adults may be dealing with these issues, the new workplace context confronts them with the additional problems of career adaptation, and the focus of adult counseling is on identifying the problems and assessing coping responses. Career assessment often emphasizes quantitative measures that evaluate interests, abilities, and traits and objectively identify realistic occupational alternatives. With adults at transitional points in their lives that have caused them to seek counseling, counselors act as interpreters of "lives in progress rather than as actuaries who count interests and abilities".

Adding subjective information derived from examination of life themes takes into account adults' multiple, nonwork roles that are highly influential on and interdependent with career. Qualitative methods include autobiographies, early recollections, and structured interviews on vocational and educational experiences. Appropriate assessment also has gender and cultural dimensions. Many measures normed on high school students may not be appropriate for adults; similarly, those normed on whites only or white males only may be invalid for women and diverse populations. Studies are beginning to test the validity of such instruments as the Self-Directed Search and the Myers-Briggs Type Inventory across different groups.

Other considerations are the language of the instrument (some have been translated, but the validity of the translations must be evaluated) and test-taking response or attitude (is the client responding according to cultural norms or expectations?). Fouad and Spreda offer the following guidelines for using interest inventories with women and minorities:

(1) increase counselor self-knowledge to avoid interpretation bias;

(2) avoid making assumptions—there are individual variations in ethnic identity, acculturation, and worldview;

(3) include the client in interpretation;

(4) test clients in languages they know; and

(5) use multiple measures.

"One-stop career centers" being developed in 16 states with federal funding are intended to bring together comprehensive, integrated career services—such as information on job training, education programs, and financial assistance; local labor market information; skills assessment and counseling—in accessible locations such as libraries and malls. State-of-the-art technology, such as CD-ROMs and computer networks, is emphasized. Community outreach and technology are also important features of Oakland University's Adult Career Counseling Center, which provides free computer-assisted career guidance and counseling services using such tools as System of Interactive Guidance and Information Plus and DISCOVER for Adults.

Adult career counselors should be aware of the following:

— the new conditions of work and the impact of constant change and uncertainty

— family systems theory and the relationship between family and work

— adult development and adult learning

— different approaches for different client groups—dual career couples, older adults, women, ethnic groups

— selection and use of appropriate career assessment instruments

They should recognize that the "new career contract" signals a shift from organizational to individual careers and strive to help adults develop internal criteria for success that enable them to achieve self-fulfillment in any domain, paid or unpaid.

ADULT EDUCATION TEACHER'S ROLE IN CAREER PLANNING

According to Deems, adult career development is a process with specific phases or stages, often paralleling human development stages. Career development involves a number of career decisions which occur throughout a lifetime. This means that adults can plan and influence their own careers. However, self-concept as well as the extent to which an individual feels responsible for his or her own future strongly influence the career development process. Keierleber and Sundal-Hansen have identified three models of career and adult development that "relate most directly and practically to the issues adult students are concerned about: life roles, concepts of age, and transitions".

The life roles model refers to the need to develop priorities for balancing a variety of roles including those of student, child, parent, spouse, worker, and citizen. Decisions about careers are an integral part of the life roles model; in fact, some have come to equate the term "careers" with the ongoing development and integration of an adult's life roles. The concepts of age model affects career development because adults may feel that career decisions should be age-related and as a result, they may impose constraints on their own career development. For example, a 30-year-old male may think he should stay in his original career field rather than "start over" because he feels men should be established in their careers by their early thirties.

The transitions model refers to the fact that life events or changes, such as transitions, frequently trigger the need for career planning. Such events include unemployment, dissatisfaction with current job or career, promotions, lack of career mobility, and so forth. Given the heterogeneity of the adult population, the career development needs of adults cover a wide range. Those adults who have good self-knowledge, who are knowledgeable about employment situations, and who have good decision-making skills are likely only to need information in order to make career decisions. There are many adults, however, whose career development has been characterized as "late, delayed, or impaired," who have very different career development needs. These adults need to develop more positive self-images, to increase their knowledge of careers and career choices, to increase their ability to use resources, and to improve their decision-making skills before being able to engage in career planning activities.

Either through choice or necessity, more and more adults are seeking career assistance, and in order to address career or job concerns, are frequently enrolling in educational programs. Therefore, adults may come to rely on the adult education teacher or instructor for their career development needs. Through classroom interactions, adult students come to know and trust their instructors, and as a result feel comfortable discussing concerns or questions related to their careers. Instructors, likewise, acquire knowledge about their adult students that is helpful in providing career planning assistance. Some career development activities involve counseling and should be provided by a trained professional counselor.

Like teaching, counseling is a special skill that requires training and supervised experience. Counselors, for example, are trained to administer and interpret career assessment instruments. Although many career development activities should be carried out in conjunction with a counselor, teachers may also appropriately engage in activities that support or enhance adult career planning. These activities, though, must be related to or compatible with the teacher's major role as deliverer of instruction. Adult education teachers may appropriately support career planning activities through instructional activities and by serving as a source of information about other career development and planning services.

According to Herr and Cramer, teachers and instructors can provide "much of the attitudinal support and knowledge from which more motivated and informed career development may flow". In the area of instruction, this can be done by including information and experiences that link general educational activities to specific vocational or occupational tasks. Some suggestions on how to do this are:

— Include concrete examples of relevant theoretical ideas from occupational settings.

— Help students to acquire and apply appropriate vocabulary.

— Support attitudes of personal mastery or competence among students.

— Reinforce the importance of formulating positive attitudes toward work and acquiring information about a variety of occupations.

— Discuss concepts related to life in organizations. Such concepts include authority relationships, routine and variety, teamwork, patterns of mobility, and promotions and demotions.

In vocational or skill-centered curricula, instructors of adults may support career planning efforts in the following ways:

— Provide current and accurate information about their specific occupational field, including opportunities for contacts with workers and work settings.

— Assist students in analyzing and interpreting their learning experiences in terms of the workplace.

— Plan and provide instruction that prepares individuals to enter, progress, and transfer among jobs in an occupational field or career cluster.

— Assist individuals in identifying a wide range of occupations to which their vocational instruction is applicable.

— Encourage employers to provide information that will expand awareness of career opportunities.

Instructors may also plan career exploration activities and discuss the importance of capitalizing upon certain personal characteristics in making career decisions. Career exploration often includes examining past experiences to evaluate both vocational and nonvocational successes and failures. This type of exercise can help in identifying skill strengths and weaknesses that may be important in future job decisions. Career exploration may also involve the process of values clarification, which assists individuals in identifying priorities related to life-style choices, including choices concerning careers and occupations. Career exploration activities may be included as part of a unit on life skills. Depending on the type of course, it may also be appropriate for teachers to provide instruction in specific job hunting skills. Such instruction would include locating information about job openings, completing job applications, and preparing for the interview process.

Assistance for individuals in obtaining information related to career planning is a highly important service for adults. Adult students need a variety of information about themselves and their values, skills, and interests; occupations, training and credentialing requirements; standard educational requirements; and career education services and resources. Large numbers of adults only want or need information in order to proceed with their career planning activities. However, since some adults have limited information inquiry, processing, and interpretation skills, they may need assistance in using the information. Because teachers have ongoing contact with their students, they can play a key role in helping adults access and use career planning information.

To support career planning teachers might want to provide the following information:

— A list of local resources offering career and educational guidance services,

— A list of local community colleges, colleges, universities, and trade and technical schools,

— An overview of job seeking skills including those involving resumes and cover letters, interviewing techniques, and ways to seek employment,

— A description of how to register with the Employment Securities Commission,

— A list of local unions and personnel offices for local government, public schools, and large businesses,

— A list of commercially available publications related to job hunting and career development.

Teachers may also serve as "networkers," providing links between adult career development and counseling services in both the institution and the community. Through classroom interactions, teachers are frequently able to identify individuals who need further career services. They should be knowledgeable about the variety of career services and resources available to their adult students and be able to refer them to the appropriate sources.

EVALUATING SCHOOL GUIDANCE PROGRAMS

Demonstrating accountability through the measured effectiveness of the delivery of the guidance program and the performance of the guidance staff helps ensure that students, parents, teachers, administrators, and the general public will continue to benefit from quality comprehensive guidance programs". To achieve accountability, evaluation is needed concerning the nature, structure, organization and implementation of school district/building guidance programs; the school counselors and other personnel who are implementing the programs; and the impact the programs are having on students, the schools where they learn, and the communities in which they live. Thus, the overall evaluation of school district/building guidance programs needs to be approached from three perspectives: program evaluation, personnel evaluation, and results evaluation.

Guidance program evaluation asks two questions. First, is there a written guidance program in the school district? And second, is the written guidance program the actual implemented program in the buildings of the district? Discrepancies between the written program and the implemented program, if present, will come into sharp focus as the program evaluation process unfolds. To conduct program evaluation, program standards are required. Program standards are acknowledged measures of comparison or the criteria used to make judgments about the adequacy of the nature and structure of the program as well as the degree to which the program is in place.

All students are provided the opportunity to gain knowledge, skills, values, and attitudes that lead to a self-sufficient, socially responsible life. To make judgments about guidance programs using standards, evidence is needed concerning whether or not the standards are being met. In program evaluation such evidence is called documentation. Evidence that the standard is in place might include the following:

1. A developmentally appropriate guidance curriculum that teaches all students the knowledge and skills they need to be self-sufficient and lead socially responsible lives.
2. Yearly schedule that incorporates the classroom guidance plan.

Documentation of such evidence could include:

1. guidance curriculum guides
2. teachers' and counselors' unit and lesson plans
3. yearly master calendar for the guidance program
4. curriculum materials

Sometimes the program evaluation process is called a program audit. The American School Counselor Association, for example, uses the "term" audit in its program evaluation materials. The Association has developed guidelines for a program audit for secondary schools, for middle/junior high schools, and for elementary schools.

Personnel Evaluation

Personnel evaluation begins with the organizational structure and activities of the guidance program in a school district. A major first step is the development of job descriptions that are based directly on the structure and activities of a school district's guidance program. Using the Missouri Comprehensive Guidance Program framework for example, the job description of a school counselor would include the following key duties: implementing the guidance curriculum; counseling individuals and small groups concerning their educational and occupational plans; counseling individuals and small groups with immediate needs and specific problems; consulting with parents and teachers; referring students to appropriate community agencies; coordinating, conducting, and being involved with activities that improve the operation of the school; evaluating and updating the guidance program; and continuing professional development.

Guidance program personnel evaluation is based directly on their job task descriptions and usually has two parts: a formative part (supervision) and a summative part (evaluation). The job task description identifies the performance areas to be supervised and evaluated. Gysbers and Henderson have developed an extensive listing of job task descriptors for school counselors grouped under the basic guidance program components of guidance curriculum, individual planning, responsive services, and system support plus the areas of professional relationships and professional responsibilities.

Having established that a guidance program is operating in a school district through program evaluation, and having established through personnel evaluation that school counselors and other guidance program personnel are carrying out the duties listed on their job descriptions 100% of the time, it now is possible to evaluate the results of the program. Johnson suggested that there are long-range, intermediate, immediate, and unplanned-for results that need consideration. According to Johnson, long-range results focus on how programs affect students after they have left school. Usually long-range results are gathered using follow-up studies. Intermediate results focus on the knowledge and skills all students may gain by graduation from participating in the guidance program. Immediate results are the knowledge and skills students may gain from participating in specific guidance activities. Finally, the possibility of unplanned-for results that may occur as a consequence of guidance activities conducted as a part of the guidance program also need to be taken into account.

Guidance Competency Mastery

Do students master guidance competencies? Johnson outlined the following procedures to answer this question for immediate results. First the competencies to be mastered need to be identified. Second what results (what students should be able to write, what they may be able to talk about, or what they may be able to do) are specified. Then who will conduct the evaluation is decided. This is followed by when the evaluation is done. Then criteria are established so that judgments can be made about students' mastery of guidance competencies. Finally, how all of this is done is specified.

Do students master guidance competencies? Another way to conduct immediate evaluation, to measure mastery of guidance competencies, is the use of a confidence survey. In this fonnat, guidance competencies are listed and students are asked to rate how confident they are that they have mastered these competencies. The confidence survey can then be used as a pre-post measure. Gain scores can be obtained and related to such measures as academic achievement and vocational identity.

Career Plans

Do students develop and use career plans? In making judgments concerning the career plans of students, criteria need to be identified as to what makes good plans. Four criteria are recommended; plans need to be comprehensive, developmental, student-centered and student-directed, and competency based. Based on these criteria, one way to evaluate students' career plans is to judge the extent to which the activities included in the Individual Planning Component of the guidance program lead to the development of plans that meet these criteria. A second way is to make judgments about the adequacy of the plan contents. Finally, a third way is to judge their use.

COUNSELORS AND TEACHERS AS STUDENT ADVISORS

Amid all the recent flurry of state and national reports calling for educational reform initiatives to raise academic standards, add course requirements, require competency testing, and otherwise upgrade the quality of our schools, very little attention has been given to the need for improved guidance and counseling services. Yet effective learning can take place only within a supportive environment, of which developmental guidance is a crucial component. When students have problems, they turn to those whom they know the best, and who they think can help the most. Surveys have shown that the adults to whom students of all ages are most likely to turn, after their parents, are teachers. A teacher advisor program (TAP) is therefore one very effective way of directly involving teachers in developmental guidance.

In most schools, there are far from enough school counselors or others specialists to provide a comprehensive program for developmental guidance. As it is, counselors' hands are normally full as a result of dealing with high-risk students who have special needs or emotional problems, and most other students are lucky if they can gain access to a counselor more than a few times during a school year. Yet all students, especially at the middle school level, need the support of a friendly adult who cares about them personally; someone they can confide in, who can help them deal with the problems of growing up, keeping up with their studies, and planning their careers.

Although the teachers may lack the professional training of counselors, school teachers have a long tradition of helping students with personal problems. They also interact with the students daily, and thus are in an excellent position to provide personal direction. In fact, effective teachers share many of the same traits as effective counselors: ability to empathize with students, patience and flexibility, excellent interpersonal skills, openness to new ideas, and awareness of individual differences. Good teachers also habitually promote and sustain positive group interaction in their classes, and develop a helping relationship with both students and parents. In all these ways, the teacher's role is closely allied to that of the counselor.

Elementary school teachers, who work closely with young children in a single classroom, generally accept the idea that developmental guidance is an integral part of their responsibility to students. But middle and secondary school teachers work with a larger number of students and usually spend no more than an hour a day with each class. Because their teaching is limited to specialized fields, they tend to emphasize academic skills, and have little time to spend getting to know their students or talking about students' needs, interests, or problems. Yet adolescents at the middle and high school level need personal attention and guidance as much as, if not more than, young children. A trusted high school teacher is often the student's first choice as someone to turn to in discussing personal problems.

Teachers, especially in middle schools and high schools, often feel so overwhelmed with their schedules and responsibilities that they do not have the time to build close personal relationships with their students. To be successful, a teacher advisor program must therefore be incorporated as a part of the regular curriculum. One popular approach has been to assign each teacher 15-20 advisees, and to arrange regular "homebase" or "homeroom" periods of 25-30 minutes at the beginning of each school day. The teacher then devotes at least two sessions per week to developmental guidance activities, during which students can explore their personal interests, goals, and concerns with a supportive group of peers. Teacher-advisors also hold regular student and parent conferences and keep track of their advisees' academic progress, consulting with other teachers, school counselors, and support personnel.

Structure of a Guidance Curriculum

A developmental guidance curriculum can be structured to include units that focus on the following themes:

— getting acquainted/orientation

— study skills and habits

— self-assessment

— communication skills

— decision-making and problem-solving

— peer relationships

— motivation

— conflict resolution

— personal hygiene and wellness

— career awareness and development

— educational planning

— community involvement

These units may be organized sequentially according to a school guidance calendar and the major events of the school year.

For example, orientation and study skills units would be scheduled early in the year to allow students to get to know the school and one another, and to get off on the right track academically. A self-assessment unit would follow, enabling the students to map out their personal strengths and identify the areas where they need to grow. While some of these topics can be covered in a single class period (such as "getting acquainted"), others can become recurrent focal points for group discussion, such as motivation, conflict resolution, communication skills, and study skills.

Some sessions should be carefully structured to build group cohesiveness or to introduce important developmental concepts. Other sessions should be left open-ended, allowing discussion to focus on students' particular interests and needs.

Counselor's role in TAP

Although some teachers and counselors alike fear that TAP is simply a strategy for getting teachers to take over counselors' work, it is important to emphasize that teacher-advisors can never be a substitute for professional school counselors. Rather, in a well-designed program, the respective roles of teachers and counselors must be clearly identified. An understanding needs to be reached, for example, that teachers will refer students with special needs to counselors, instead of attempting to handle students' complex emotional or behavioral problems on their own.

Teachers can also collaborate with counselors by inviting them to address their classes on special topics; such visits will create a visible bond between teachers and counselors, and thus dissuade students from attempting to play one off against the other. Furthermore, counselors can assist teachers who are having trouble managing their groups by modeling group guidance skills and serving as consultants to the teachers. In fact, counselors often assume leadership roles in TAP, coordinating the teachers and providing resources for them.

In spite of the advantages of a Teacher Advisor Program, many teachers are reluctant to support such a program, because they are either skeptical about its utility or wary of the extra preparation that such a program would involve. Robert D. Myrick estimates, for example, that in most schools 20% of the teachers would immediately support such a program while 20% would be strongly opposed. It is therefore important to move the middle 60% toward supporting TAP and developmental guidance. If most teachers are to support a Teacher Advisor Program, they must clearly understand and embrace the essential concepts of developmental guidance underlying the program and the curricular goals. They also need preparation in guidance and interpersonal skills, so that they can effectively facilitate class discussions that help students think about personal problems and explore alternative courses of action.

Second, if a TAP is to be anything more than a formality, the time commitment needs to be adequate. Group meetings of once a week or less are not likely to allow valuable helping relationships between teachers and their advisees to develop, nor do they give teachers the opportunity to establish continuity or consistency. TAP works best when it is scheduled every school day, or at least two or three times a week; otherwise, teachers tend to view TAP as an added encumbrance, peripheral to their major duties.

Besides an adequate allotment of time, TAP also must have a developmental guidance curriculum with clearly articulated objectives, and with supporting materials and activities that can stimulate student participation. If teachers have an organized guidance handbook, which they are at liberty to follow, adapt, or modify as they see fit, they are more likely to "buy into" the guidance program as a whole. Finally, teachers need to be assured of full support and cooperation from both the administration and the counseling staff, so that they won't feel as if the burden of student guidance has been unfairly shifted to their shoulders. For this reason, TAP should be monitored and evaluated by students, teachers, counselors, and administrators every year to ensure that the program is meeting its goals.

Teacher Advisor Programs compensate for the high counselor-student ratios that make it impossible for school counselors to know all students personally. But beyond this compensatory role, TAP strengthens teacher-student relationships and creates a supportive learning environment in which teachers and counselors can work together to respond to students' academic and personal needs. The major disadvantage of Teacher Advisor Programs is that not all teachers are able or willing to work effectively with students in an advisory role. Such programs are therefore often viewed as a passing fad or an infringement on academic time.

To be successful, a Teacher Advisor Program must therefore have a clearly defined purpose, reflected in a well-conceived curriculum, and it must enlist the full support of administrators, teachers, and counselors alike.

Traditional organizational patterns for school guidance have emphasized the position and duties of the counselor or the therapeutic process of counseling, at the expense of a coherent programmatic focus. As a consequence, guidance has been widely regarded as an ancillary support service, rather than as an integral part of education. This pattern has placed counselors in a remedial and reactive role, a role in which their duties were ill-defined, large blocks of time were spent working with a small number of students, and they were likely to be saddled with extra administrative and clerical duties, such as scheduling and record keeping.

In response to this widespread lack of an appropriate organizational structure, Norman C. Gysbers and associates at the University of Missouri (Columbia) developed a Comprehensive Guidance Program Model that has been adopted by schools and statewide educational agencies throughout the country, from Alaska to New Hampshire. The purpose of the model is to help districts develop comprehensive and systematic developmental guidance programs, kindergarten through grade twelve. It is also to provide guidance with specific educational content, with accountability for attaining certain student competencies. When fully implemented, the program allows counselors to devote all their time to the program, thus eliminating many of the non-guidance related tasks that they now carry out.

The Missouri Comprehensive Guidance Program Model has two major parts: structural and programmatic. The structural part has five components: Definition and Philosophy, Facilities, Advisory Council, Resources, and Staffing Patterns and Budget. This part addresses administrative aspects of the program that do not involve contact with students, but are essential in maintaining the administrative and structural integrity of the overall program. The programmatic part has four components: Guidance Curriculum, Individual Planning, Responsive Services, and System Support. The Guidance Curriculum consists of structured developmental experiences presented systematically through classroom activities, to provide students with knowledge of normal growth and development and to promote good mental health and assist them in acquiring life skills. The curriculum is organized around

(1) career planning and exploration;

(2) knowledge of self and others; and

(3) educational development.

The Individual Planning component consists of activities that help all students set goals, plan, and manage their own learning, as well as their personal and career development. Conversely, the Responsive Services component consists of activities to meet students' immediate needs and concerns, whether these require counseling, consultation, referral, or information. The System Support component consists of management activities that establish, maintain, and enhance the guidance program as a whole through professional development, staff and community relations, consultation with teachers, advisory councils, community outreach, program management, and research and development.

Comprehensive Guidance Program Model

The Comprehensive Guidance Program Model is predicated on the concept of life career development, defined as self-development through the integration of roles, settings, and events in a person's life. (The concept of "career" refers to one's whole life, and not just occupation.) The program emphasizes three domains of human growth in life career development: self-knowledge and interpersonal skills; life roles, settings, and events; and life career planning. In the self-knowledge and interpersonal skills domain, the focus is on helping students to understand and accept themselves and others, and to become aware of their personal characteristics—interests, aspirations, and abilities. Through learning about the interactive relationship of self and environment, they learn how to create and maintain relationships, and they develop personal standards and a sense of purpose in life.

The second domain emphasizes various life roles (learner, citizen, consumer), settings (home, school, work, and community), and events (job entry, marriage, retirement) in which students participate over their life span. This domain focuses on the sociological, psychological, and economic structure of their world, and encourages students to overcome stereotypes and plan for the future. The Life Career Planning domain is designed to help students understand that decision making and planning are important tasks in everyday life. Students learn of the many occupations and industries in the work world. Students also develop skills in gathering information from relevant sources and using that information to make reasoned decisions. Students are also encouraged to assess their personal values as these relate to prospective plans and decisions.

Counselors, teachers, administrators, parents, students, community members, and business and labor personnel all have roles to play as human resources in the guidance program. While counselors provide the services and coordinate the program, they must enlist the involvement, cooperation, and support of teachers and administrators for the program to be successful, for the program is predicated on an assumption that guidance is central to the educational process. To involve parents, community members, and business and labor personnel, a school-community advisory committee can be formed to provide recommendations and support services to counselors and others involved in the program.

The involvement of the teaching staff is critical, so teachers should have the opportunity to volunteer for active participation in program planning and implementation. Counselors and teachers should work together to plan the delivery of the guidance curriculum, so that guidance learning activities are presented in the appropriate content areas, and so that teachers do not feel displaced by counselors in the classroom. Furthermore, to make the guidance curriculum, individual planning, responsive services, and system support components function effectively, the program requires a new way to organize guidance program facilities.

Besides the usual individual offices for one-to-one counseling sessions, the program requires reorganization of space into a guidance center, which brings together guidance information and resources and makes them accessible to students. Such a center could also be used for such activities as group sessions and self-exploration. The guidance center could also include a library and/or computerized database, providing advice and materials for career planning, educational opportunities, community involvement, and recreational opportunities.

Following are some steps for schhols to implement a coprehensive guidance program;

1. Sell the model to the counselors in the department, since those participating in it must feel some ownership. According to Gloria Morgan, who has implemented the Missouri model in two high schools, approximately three years is needed to implement a comprehensive guidance program. Because many counselors and administrators resist change, it is essential to lay the groundwork for implementation by thoroughly discussing the program in advance with all affected staff members.

2. Develop an inservice workshop for teachers, so that faculty will understand and support the purposes of the Comprehensive Guidance Program.

3. Launch a public relations program to inform students, parents, and the community about proposed changes in the guidance program. This can be done through workshops, talks at local civic groups, newspaper articles, and even local television spots.

4. Conduct a thorough assessment of the current guidance program, including available resources, both human and financial. This means evaluating the time and task allocation of the counseling staff, and taking inventory of materials.

5. Conduct a needs assessment, including a survey of students, parents, and teachers, in order to help counselors identify important program categories and competencies in the three major areas around which the guidance curriculum is organized: career planning and exploration, knowledge of self and others, and educational and vocational development. The self-assessment and needs evaluation both provide baseline information to use in designing the new program along the lines of the model, but in a way that addresses the needs of each school.

6. Develop the guidance curriculum, introducing specific competencies sequentially. In the initial planning stages of the curriculum, it is best to concentrate on cooperative departments and teachers, and to plan the entire year's curriculum in advance, if possible. The guidance curriculum

is usually the most difficult part of the program to implement, because it must fit in with existing curricular constraints, and must overcome the reluctance of teachers to give up class time or to alter and supplement their existing instructional plans. It is thus essential to seek administrative support, be well organized, and give teachers as much advance notice as possible.

7. Establish a coherent annual evaluation procedure that assesses attainment of student competencies, personnel performance, and the achievement of program goals.

Rapid technological changes, dramatic shifts in labor force distribution, and the increasing pressures of foreign competition have made the dangers of skill obsolescence and eventual job loss a reality for many American workers. Moreover, there is every likelihood that the need for retraining will continue to increase. Economic security is coming to depend less on expertise and more on flexibility. This ERIC Digest examines why past responses to skill obsolescence are no longer sufficient, describes the elements that should be included in a comprehensive program to prevent skill obsolescence, and proposes appropriate roles of business, labor, and government in retraining.

In the past, employer-provided, job-specific training for new employees and continuing education for those who wished to advance in their jobs were often sufficient to keep abreast of technological changes. When automation resulted in massive labor market shifts, the solution to worker dislocation was often relocation. However, large-scale layoffs and plant closings in the last two decades have focused attention on reeducation and retraining. The rapid pace of technological advancement, the shrinking supply of entry-level workers, and the increasing complexity and abstractness of many jobs coupled with lower levels of general education among labor market entrants made it imperative that more attention be paid to the issue of preventing skill obsolescence among American workers.

After analyzing many successful and unsuccessful retraining and worker relocation programs, Gordus, Gohrband, and Meiland drew a distinction between "reactive" responses to changing job skill requirements (i.e., retraining programs that are begun only after massive permanent layoffs and plant closings have occurred) and "active" retraining programs that anticipate future skill deficits and provide training to upgrade workers' skills before jobs are lost and plants are forced to close.

Gordus et al. demonstrated that even exemplary programs begun only after workers' skills have become obsolete and their jobs have been lost are expensive ($800 to $3,500 per participant for vocational skills training) and their outcomes vary widely (the placement rates from six demonstration sites of a model economic readjustment assistance program ranged from 9 to 81 percent). Time is another crucial factor. Effective retraining programs—whether remedial or intended to teach workers new skills—take time to plan and implement. Program providers who must initiate retraining programs after workers have been dislocated do not have time to engage in long-term planning, and unemployed persons are often unwilling to participate in lengthy retraining programs. Because they do not have such time constraints, ongoing retraining programs geared toward persons who are currently employed can be more carefully planned and presented.

By anticipating what skills their workers will need in the future, employers can prepare their present employees to respond to changing demands imposed by technological advances and thereby avoid the disruption in operations and added expenses related to recruiting, hiring, and training new employees. Workplace retraining programs also benefit employees by increasing their basic skills, enhancing their employability, improving their job performance, and providing them with the skills needed to perform new jobs and adapt to new technologies.

Business, labor unions, and government can all play a role in funding and/or providing retraining. Funders can make their influence felt by selecting the training provider and shaping the content of training. Of course, funders retain the most control over a program when they provide the training themselves rather than paying an independent institution to provide educational services. Employers who provide their own training can increase the incentive for employees to participate in retraining by making the instruction relevant to employees' work experiences. According to Gordus et al., the most successful programs, in terms of postprogram wage raises, are those operated by employers and unions.

Federal, state, and local government funding can be combined with union or business funds to varying extents. The National Alliance of Business described the following examples of ways in which public funds can be used in privately run retraining programs to prevent skill obsolescence among persons who are currently employed: Funds provided by the state of Michigan's Upgrade Program are used to train Frost, Inc. employees in the use of flexible manufacturing systems. As an added incentive, employees are given the opportunity to purchase home computers at half price. The National Technological University's degree program offers management seminars accredited by the North Central Association of Universities and several Master of Science degrees via satellite-transmitted training through a network of 24 universities.

In Delaware, funds provided through the Blue Collar Jobs Act of 1984 are used to pay part of the costs for customized training that is tailored to companies' written specifications. Trainers are paid half before training is provided and half after it has been satisfactorily completed. At the Alabama Center for Quality and Productivity, a governor-appointed seven-person board guides curriculum development to ensure that it is responsive to business needs and helps market the program. The center operates on land donated by General Motors and has trained 3,000 GM staff in quality control.

The content of a workplace retraining program depends largely on the specific skill needs of the individual industry or company in which the program participants are employed. Gordus et al. identified the following program elements, which may be used in different combinations to meet the needs of individual employers and employees:

- A counseling/educational guidance component that provides adults with the information and skills required to develop an action plan for their own career and educational development
- An assessment system (as nonthreatening as possible) that enables educational institutions and employers to determine where training and upgrading are needed
- A support system that provides such elements as tuition assistance, time off from work for learning, a study site within the workplace, child care, and recognition of the program participants' achievements
- A basic skills program (which may require another name so as to avoid any stigma that may be attached to employees' need for remediation)
- A vocational skills program (which should integrate learning with practical application in the workplace to the greatest extent possible)
- A general skills program that includes communication and organizational skills
- Management development programs

Other elements were identified in a study of ways to persuade those in fields of declining opportunities to take advantage of retraining. The study found that workers have a limited perspective of the workplace, do not judge a job on the basis of its potential as a career path, and are adverse to taking risks. Recommendations to overcome these barriers include the following:

- Take the program down to the personal level
- Confront specific problems and concerns

— Ensure a short time frame

— Talk in terms of options and opportunities

— Create a central source of help and information

Educational aspects aside, the success or failure of collaborative programs to prevent skill obsolescence can depend on the way in which a partnership is established and the way in which a program is organized. Gordus et al. listed the following actions as being crucial to the success of retraining partnerships:

— Identification of differences between educational and corporate institutions in terms of their missions, goals, and climate so that respect for differences can be developed and supported

— Identification of mutual goals and objectives

— Clear demarcation of roles and responsibilities

— Multiple contacts among many levels of the organization so that knowledge of each other's plans and problems can be acquired

— Careful communication on both sides, including the development and maintenance of information-sharing procedures

— Flexibility based on trust and knowledge of what can and cannot be accomplished in each organization

— Rapid responses to concerns and complaints from all partners

— Development of a reward and recognition system for learners and for persons working on the programs

Diverse as the many types of retraining program partnerships may be, it is important that they include a mix of general employability and job-specific skills to prepare program participants to adapt to future workplace changes that cannot as yet be predicted with certainty.

6

Classification and Dissemination of Occupational Guidance

Infusion is an interesting concept. According to Webster, infusion refers to the act or process of steeping or soaking in water or a substance in order to extract its virtues. The Gage Canadian Dictionary uses the words "permeate," "fill with," and "inspire" to define infusion. Lately, the word infusion has been adapted by career educators to refer to the introduction of career concepts and strategies into the regular curriculum in order to instill relevance and quality to subject matter at school.

The infusion of career development and planning skills into the regular school curriculum is advocated by career leaders. Hiebert, in a theme editorial in "Guidance and Counselling," calls for an infusion or integration of career concepts across all grade levels and in all subjects. He contends that in addition to providing information about the specific subject matter, teachers may properly discuss the roles of various jobs. Whether the subject is science, health, or mathematics, students must learn that it is natural and important to ask questions about the nature of jobs in which people engage.

School counselors can facilitate infusion of career skills by consulting with teachers and by teaching units for/with them.

This approach of infusing career information into subject matter will add relevance and interest for young people and, ultimately, will contribute to the establishment of a "Career Development Culture." Over the years, the author has been involved in a number of studies dealing with the infusion of sets of skills (research, thinking, questioning) into the regular school curriculum, as opposed to teaching these skills separately. These studies have indicated that the infusion approach for education is best, as long as it is accompanied by professional development or staff training either at the preservice level (university) and/or inservice level (schools). In Alberta, to accomplish this staff training goal, a course entitled "Everyday Career Development" was created to help teachers infuse career skills into their daily teaching activities.

"Everyday Career Development" is a 3-day professional development course for secondary school teachers. "Homework" is assigned to enable educators to implement and receive feedback on various strategies. The strategies included in the course largely require an awareness of career development, rather than an entirely new set of duties for teachers. After a field-test of the course, teachers overwhelmingly reported satisfaction and confidence in their ability to implement the ideas in their math, science or English classes. A Facilitator Guide to Everyday Career Development has been prepared to help local facilitators maintain quality control when delivering the course.

METHOD OF INFUSING CAREER SKILLS

Whether they realize it or not, teachers have a strong influence on students' career development. The course "Everyday Career Development," enables them to make a conscious impact on students by using the infusion approach. Teachers learn how to connect activities in the classroom to the events unfolding in the labor market. The ultimate goal of the course is for students to have a smooth transition from school-to-school or school-to-work, assisted by a network of teachers who are infusing career development concepts and strategies into their everyday teaching activities.

The course typically is delivered in two, one and one-half day workshops with "homework" in between. The following "homework" activities are included for the teachers:

(a) review the curriculum they teach and describe how it helps students meet the workforce requirements of the new economy;

(b) identify their values, beliefs and interests and identify how these are fulfilled in their work and non-work lives; and

(c) have a class generate a list of activities and skill sets for a job sector related to a subject area.

Teachers can use a variety of methods or strategies to help students gain a better understanding of themselves in relation to the career building process. Some of these are as follows:

— Encourage students to examine and describe their school performance.

— Help students identify competencies used in school performance.

— Encourage students to talk with and observe individuals in a variety of roles.

— Help students connect their enduring visions with "the world."

In addition to infusing career development ideas in career content, teachers are encouraged to implement the ideas incidentally, i.e., make casual comments when they see students in the hall or in class. Parents can also assist by acting as volunteers. For example, in one school a parent, acting as a career technician, used a telephone hotline and interactive video disc to assist students in exploring various career paths.

In order for teachers and counselors to infuse career development into the curriculum, professional development needs to be provided. Ministries of Education have a responsibility to make professional development happen. The province of Alberta chose to use a partnership model rather than do it alone. Alberta developed a partnership with the provincial teachers' union and a private foundation (the Canadian Guidance and Counselling Foundation) to deliver the inservice. One of the guiding principles of this professional development initiative is that inservice opportunities should be available to teachers and counselors in their home locales. Local facilitators who are trained, provide this inservice around their home jurisdictions. A detailed facilitator guide is prepared for each course to promote consistency across different offerings of the same course.

Each teacher and counselor who completes a specific number of courses will receive a certificate designating them as a "career education specialist." In addition to "Everyday Career Development," other professional development courses offered to teachers explore methods in group career education and career education for special populations. These courses, in combination with "Everyday Career Development," will help ensure that teachers and counselors have the background and skills needed to implement successful infusion approach.

CONFLICT IN CAREER DECISIONS

A value conflict arises when one value can only be realized at the expense of another value. For example, an artist might believe that commercial art provides security, but little creativity. By contrast, independent artists lack security, yet enjoy opportunities for creativity. Across the artist's range of options, realizing one value seems to require foregoing another value. In stronger cases of conflict, a person's whole set of values can be divided into groups that clash with one another. In weaker cases, conflict might be limited to a few values. This digest describes the scope of career value conflict, its developmental significance, and some strategies of conflict resolution.

In three studies of conflict in career values, Cochran found that approximately one of every three significant relations among values was conflicting. In one study, 84 senior high students rated 10 personally selected options on 10 common values. For every pair of values, at least one student demonstrated a conflict. Values that were particularly prone to conflict included salary, freedom in job, security, leisure time, and challenge. For example, the promise of higher salary might tempt persons to sacrifice their free time or fear of insecurity might frighten persons away from challenges. The diversity of conflict was striking. Even without evidence from the above studies, it seems that conflict within decision making is common. Conflict prompts a decision. If an option existed that met all of one's values, a decision would be unnecessary. Whatever option is examined, there are apt to be gains and losses, and it is this struggle between what to realize and what to neglect that calls for a decision.

Developmental Significance

Individuals typically embrace career values as means or vehicles of value, not values in themselves. For example, salary may forward other values (intangible constituents of the good life), but it has no value in itself. The immediate implication is that conflicts between career values cannot be adequately resolved or understood in themselves. Rather, career values are concrete ways to pose fundamental value issues of a person's vision of a good life. For example, can one best attain a good life by increasing one's capability of acquiring goods and services (salary), by avoiding calamities (security), or by becoming a better person (cultivation of talent)? Now, when one career value conflicts with another, fundamental questions arise with some urgency. Is it better, for example, to have the goods most worth having or to become the kind of person most worth being?

Conflict provides a natural entrance to fundamental questions and meanings concerning a person's implicit vision of life, providing an exploratory depth that might help persons establish stronger priorities and make wiser adjustments. While there are many reasons for encouraging greater depth in career counseling (e.g., preparation for coping with conflict and compromise), two reasons furnish immediate significance. First, studies of midlife career change indicate the presence of intense and unresolved conflicts from earlier decisions, conflicts so significant that one can speak of a lost self. One value or set of values is realized at the expense of a core value or set of values, a loss that can eventually lead to crisis. Second, as Taylor has argued, a person's identity is defined by fundamental evaluations of what ideals should prevail in life. Becoming a person requires a capacity to articulate one's position with the depth necessary to determine compatible courses of action. In this sense, resolving conflict helps one become a stronger agent in shaping a desired life.

Conflict directs attention and motivates individuals toward a solution. According to Janis and Mann, if the conflict is significant, solvable, and if there is time, a person is apt to be motivated (e.g., vigilant) to explore options, gather information, weigh values, and strive for a solution. Below are seven strategies that counselors might consider as they counsel clients. The first four strategies emphasize dissolving conflict (making it disperse) while the last three strategies emphasize resolving conflict (settling it by resolution). Conflict is based upon judgments of options.

Often, these judgments are faulty or too extreme. In these cases, conflict might be dissolved if misjudgments are corrected. For example, the artist who is noted in the introduction might find that commercial art allows more creativity than originally thought. Corrections of judgments typically arise through further exploration of options, gathering information, and gaining experience. Corrections might also occur through the consideration of temporal changes in occupations. Beginning commercial artists might work largely under the direction of others, but over time, they may become responsible for creative projects. By suspending static judgments of occupations and by considering how occupations is change over time, conflict can sometimes be realistically dissolved and converted into anticipated challenges (e.g., to perform well enough to earn more responsibility).

Ordinarily, a conflict is limited to a range of options. For example, creativity and security might conflict with one another, but only within a particular set of options. By searching more broadly, a person might discover options accompanied by little or no value conflict. One should also consider how a value might be satisfied in other outlets, such as recreational pursuits, volunteer work, or civic participation. A variety of transient and extraneous influences can make a particular value unjustifiably prominent. A peer group, family, television, or a romantic relationship, can render a salient value, upon closer examination, as not pronounced at all. In these cases, it is important to trace the basis for a value and try to determine whether it will be an enduring desire or a momentary urgency.

Values might clash because they have been conceived narrowly, vaguely, or in a distorted manner. In these cases, values can be conceived more broadly, more sharply, or with more balance. By helping clients to refine, extend, and elaborate meanings, conflict due to faulty conception can often be reframed and minimized. Also, a more adequate set of indicators (i.e., how one could determine if an option had the quality desired) can be identified.

Personal Changes and Development

Consider a conflict between confidence and challenge. The person feeling confident in jobs that lacking challenge, might lack confidence in challenging jobs. In a case such as this, conflict could be dissolved if the person became more capable of undertaking challenges without excessive discomfort. Numerous difficulties (lack of esteem, shyness, etc.) call for personal development in order to realize other values.

As ends in themselves, two values might beat odds. However, if considered as means to fulfill one's vision of a good life, incompatible values can sometimes be made complementary. For example, salary and time-off might conflict with one another, but each might also be important in forwarding a common end such as the quality of family life. By seeing how each value complements the other as means toward a common end, a conflict is placed in perspective. A client can consider each value in preparation for evaluating options and making wise compromises. Common ends can be explored by asking clients why they prefer, for instance, higher salary.

Perhaps the most natural way to resolve conflict is to determine which value is most important. Suppose a client was faced with a choice between a job that was interesting but low in salary, and a job that was uninteresting but high in salary. Such a conflict might be resolved by whether or not salary was more important than interest. Sometimes, a priority is obvious. At other times, a person must decide which value should prevail in an envisioned course of life. The peculiarity of this decision is that a client does not decide between options, but between values, weighing their relative advantages and disadvantages for the future. Occasionally, clients can transcend a conflict by considering their priorities. For example, a client might find that the conflicting values are relatively unimportant when compared to other core values.

Families and School Counselors

Recent national surveys indicate that career guidance is a major issue for American families. In Gallup polls, for example, parents report that helping their children choose a career is their second most pressing concern. For the general public, understanding the world of work and making realistic plans for after high school are the third and sixth most important goals of education. Students themselves, according to more than 33,000 sampled in 1973 and 1983 by the American College Testing Program, have increased their involvement in career planning activities. Among the eighth and eleventh graders in the 1983 study, over 70 percent said they want even more help with making career plans. Yet despite the primary role that parents play in children's career development, school counseling programs show little evidence of tapping into this resource.

In short, career guidance has a top priority with parents, the general public and high school students. Continuing and further assistance appears to be needed, and a collaborative effort between schools and families could help meet the need. This digest briefly considers the following issues relevant to this effort: family determinants of children's career development, stages of children's career development, counselor guidelines for starting parent programs, and counselor interventions to utilize family influence.

Family Determinants of Children's Career Development

The major family determinants of children's career development can be categorized as follows: geographic location, genetic inheritance, family background, socio-economic status, family composition, parenting style, and parental attitudes toward work. Authorities in psychology and career development believe that parents are the most crucial factor in the formation of children's personalities and self-concept, and that career choices can be regarded as the "implementation" of these qualities. As children make self-assessments and receive feedback from significant others, they form educational aspirations. These in turn are a primary influence on educational achievement, the level of which is the single most important determinant of eventual occupational achievement.

Children's Career Development

In the early years of career development three basic stages occur:

(1) awareness, up to age 11, when children believe they can do whatever they like and transform needs and desires into occupational preferences;

(2) exploration, ages 11-17, when tentative choices are made on the basis of interests, abilities and values; and

(3) preparation, age 17 to young adulthood, when actual choices are made that strike a balance between personal capabilities and such factors as educational and employment opportunities and job requirements.

Stereotypes and prejudices about the appropriateness of certain careers may need to be challenged throughout this process. School counselors can start involving parents in career guidance by creating a parent resource library, distributing lists of practical suggestions, and calling a parent group meeting to get the program off the ground. Laramore offers some practical guidelines for insuring the success of the involvement program:

1. Find someone to run the program who knows about the subject and is a clear, enthusiastic speaker.
2. Advertise the program as the parents' role in their children's educational and career future. If only "career" is mentioned, parents who expect their children to go to college are unlikely to attend.
3. Don't be discouraged if only two parents come the first time. Pretend it's a roomful and give it your all. The second year, there will be 50 parents; the third, 150, and so on.
4. Elementary and middle school/junior high parents often don't realize that this is the time to begin. Therefore, in the publicity, use phrases like, "Now is the time to start your child on her/his successful future."

Counselors can provide direct services to parents and children, both separately and together, as well as indirect services through classroom teachers, school and community committees, and a variety of activities. Useful examples include the following:

1. *Conduct parent study groups*: Counselors can help parents understand their role in children's career development, the general growth and development of their children, and the relationship between the career guidance program and the total school program. Specifically, parents need up-to-date, accurate information about the following: changing career choices and broadened options for males and females, educational opportunities, wage and salary statistics, the importance and stages of career planning, barriers to the career development process, career resources in the school and community, myths in sex-role stereotyping, sex equity laws, and ways to improve communication skills.

2. *Coordinate parent resources*: Programs can be developed in which parents serve as mini-course instructors or resource persons in the classroom, teacher aides on field trips, members of advisory committees, technical advisors to counselors and teachers on developing simulated work settings, and members of curriculum development committees. Counselors can also assist parents in assuming liaison roles between the school and the working community, especially in the parents' own places of employment.

3. *Organize career activities for families*: Career nights appear to be one of the most popular activities at the high school level, although some authorities in career development question the value of a single event in a process that occurs over a number of years. Additional suggestions include parent/student workshops to facilitate career discussions, self-directed career centers for use by both parents and children, and student/parent handbooks for personal educational and vocational planning.

4. *Conduct student sessions on family influence*: For many students, as they begin to deal with issues of autonomy and independence, it is important to sort out family influences on their career development. Counselors can help in this process through a variety of techniques that are suitable for individual and group counseling or for

coursework. These include: family systems review, paradigms of family interaction, family sculpting/ choreography, family constellation diagrams, occupational family trees, and "advice, advice, and more advice"—an exploration of parental work values.

COMMUNITY INVOLVEMENT IN K-12 CAREER EDUCATION

Just as "it takes a village to raise a child," the support of the whole community helps prepare children for the complex choices they must make in a changing world. This Digest looks at how career educators and counselors involve business, community agencies, churches, and others in assisting students with the process of shaping their life careers.

Forms of Career Education

Official federal support for career education began in 1974; although funding intensity has varied over the subsequent 20 plus years, career education continues to receive emphasis in the nation's schools. The most recent programs included under the umbrella of "career education" are titled "school-to-work" and "tech prep," programs that are receiving generous federal appropriations for 1996-97. School-to-work programs, which include tech prep programs, are characterized by their focus on bridging the gap between school and work. They draw upon education and business collaboration, and partnerships between education and other parts of society. They are designed to provide "school-based learning, work-based learning, and activities to connect the two"; in this way, they engage the community in the career education and development of youth.

The coordinated support network promoted in school-to-work programs is "linked to school and relies on parents, mentors, employers, youth advocates, and social service agencies to assist youth". Whether through school-to-work or tech prep programs, businesses are increasingly approached for active involvement in the educational community. As they recognize the growing need for technically, academically, and socially prepared workers, businesses are becoming more and more enthusiastic in their desire to collaborate with schools to provide up-to-date education and training for the students who will be their future workers. Tech prep programs capitalize on the employers' need for qualified workers by drawing employers into the identification of skills necessary for employment in their industries—thus establishing benchmarks for education and skill achievement. Most partnerships between schools and businesses focus on the delivery and development of academic and vocational skills (which include skills for employability). Such collaborative efforts can help students develop relevant skills for the workplace through revised up-to-date curriculum, youth apprenticeships, and mentoring experiences.

Youth apprenticeships afford another avenue by which community businesses become involved in the career education and development of youth. Apprenticeships require a partnership between "educators—secondary and postsecondary—and business people who are willing to provide jobs and worksite learning experiences for young people". They have the advantage of taking students out of the classroom and exposing them to the rapidly changing work environment, complete with new technologies and new management processes.

Community agencies, such as the Chamber of Commerce, are also valuable resources for student career development as they afford linkage to community leaders and community-based experiences. In Austin, Texas, the Greater Austin Chamber of Commerce and the Austin Independent School District jointly administer the Austin Adopt-A-School program. The program, which began in 1983, includes every elementary, middle/junior high, and high school in Austin and over 1,500 adopters. The employer volunteers provide attendance incentives, dropout prevention, mentoring, periodic classroom instruction, parent training sessions, and teacher assistance in the form of professional development. The Motorola Teachers in Industry program, for example, offers teachers who are selected through a competitive application process 2-month summer internships with the company.

Service learning projects that link students and community organizations afford another type of exposure to career development. Such projects offer students opportunities to learn the habits and conditions of the workplace as well as the personal benefit of doing service work. "By combining community service with learning activities and reflecting on their experiences, students realize increased personal, social, and intellectual growth and preparation for work". Through a Learn and Serve America grant administered by the Corporation for National Service, inner-city parents (trained in Harcum College's Early Childhood Education Program to be volunteer tutors in their children's classrooms) receive 12 college credits in exchange for their volunteering. These nontraditional student tutors have provided more than 6,000 hours of individual tutoring to over 480 at-risk children.

Ken Hoyt's definition of career education, written in 1971, reflects the broad scope of career education: "Career Education is the total effort of the education system and the broader community to help all individuals become familiar with the values of a work-oriented society, to integrate those values into their personal value systems, and to implement them in their lives in such a way that work becomes possible, meaningful, and satisfying for each individual". Bedrock components of true career education programs growing out of this definition include helping pupils acquire both positive work values and productive work habits—the basic goals of career education.

Frequently, the career awareness focus of elementary school programs is on values clarification and the adoption of positive work habits and behaviors. One of the most recent programs designed to develop student values, behaviors, and self-concept while exposing them to community is the Feinstein Foundation's "I CAN MAKE A DIFFERENCE" GOOD DEEDS PROGRAM. In this program, students are asked to make a commitment to accomplish at least 33 good deeds, which they must record, discuss with others, and attempt to incorporate into their everyday behavior. This program is heralded by educators as one that has "made a positive contribution to the guidance, community-service, school-to-work, and other objectives for schools". The program materials, developed for elementary school children, are designed to foster community service, character development, citizenship education, and communication skills. The program is action oriented and involves home, school, and community.

Parental involvement in the career choice process of youth has traditionally focused on mentoring and work shadowing. Recent career guidance efforts have attempted to involve parents in students' career planning activities and in the documentation of experiences in the career passport. The *Career Orientation and Planning Profile* provides a folder for parents, as well as students, in which parents are instructed to keep such information as lists of teachers, school activities calendar, special projects, awards received, class schedule, PTA/PTO information, school handbook, grade reports, school correspondence, immunization record, list of organizations/clubs, test results, career awareness activities and materials, and other relevant data.

The goal of having parents keep such records about their elementary school children is to provide them with a vehicle for becoming involved in their children's career planning. "As they move through the educational system from elementary into middle/junior high school, to high school and into post high school training or work, parents have the responsibility to assure that their children develop a positive self-image, now and understand their individual skills, and help them relate these to effective educational and career planning".

Because the issue of community involvement in career education spans K-12, the collaborative efforts among schools, business, and other agencies vary. However, the elements common to effective collaborative partnerships can help the stakeholders change the way they deliver services. These common elements are as follows:

— *Involving the Right Players*: Partnerships achieve their maximum potential when the right mix of people from many organizations is involved. Involving employers of all sizes and types permits the partnership to provide a range of work experience options for students.

— *Ensuring Commitment*: The partnership must have the endorsement and support of high-level leaders from the collaborating organizations who are willing to assign time, money, and human resources to the partnership effort. Commitment can be fostered by developing a sense of ownership among the various organizations.

— *Developing a Shared Vision*: Developing a shared vision of intended outcomes that is realistic and sensitive to all partners' individual objectives is necessary to produce a genuine understanding among partners.

— *Producing a Formal Plan*: A formal plan that establishes joint long- and short-term goals and objectives as well as steps for achieving them is at the heart of a successful collaborative effort.

— *Emphasizing Performance*: Schools involved in partnerships need to adopt a private industry perspective that emphasizes performance and accountability.

— *Focusing on Common Ground*: A climate that ensures a focus on students' needs and expected outcomes should be fostered.

— *Maintaining the Partnership*: Partnerships need to be cultivated and maintained. Time and effort should be devoted to preparing for the inevitable changes that will result over the life of a partnership.

It has been estimated that 40-50 percent of what a child learns occurs in school and the remaining 50-60 percent comes from the family and community. "Without close articulation of and involvement with the family and larger community, schools will ultimately fail". Although there are many ways to involve business, community agencies, parents, and others in assisting students with the process of shaping their life careers, the efforts that are more organized and reflect the elements described here have a better chance of realizing effective collaboration among all stakeholders.

ADULTS IN CAREER TRANSITION

Job and career changes are increasingly common due to the uncertainties of the economic environment, technological changes, and new attitudes toward work. The more drastic of these transitions—changing careers—is often linked to the developmental stage of midlife. However, such changes are not limited to that age group. In fact, recent research and theory are moving away from age-related developmental models toward more individually determined stages. Other researchers are questioning the validity of linear career development models versus cyclical patterns. Still others criticize prevailing models for their lack of relevance to women and different cultural groups.

Although "midlife crisis" is a dominant image, adults experience cyclical periods of stability and transition throughout life. Sargent and Schlossberg suggest that adult behavior is determined by transitions, not age. Adults are motivated to make transitions by a continual need to belong, control, master, renew, and take stock. One explanation for transition may be found in Hughes and Graham's work in developing the Adult Life Roles Instrument. These researchers identified six life roles (relationships with self, work, friends, community, partner, and family) that go through cycles of initiation, adaptation, reassessment, and reconciliation. An individual may be at a different stage in each role simultaneously. The conflict or lack of congruence between two or more of these role cycles may spur the process of career change.

Interviews with over 500 adults uncovered differences between voluntary changers ("Questers") and nonchangers ("Traditionalists"). Questers viewed jobs or careers as vehicles for self-expression and growth; they experienced cycles of entry, mastery, and disengagement. In the disengagement stage, when self-appraisal tells them the intrinsic rewards of a job no longer satisfy, Questers seek change. In contrast, Traditionalists value extrinsic rewards (position, power, money, security) that control their career choices. They are generally less introspective and open to risk than Questers. Career change has become more socially acceptable as personal fulfillment is more highly valued.

Career decision making is seen as a series of continuous choices across the life span, not a once-and-for-all event. Thus, careers may be viewed as a spiral sequence of all life roles, with changes triggered by factors ranging from the anticipated (marriage, empty nest) to unanticipated (illness, divorce, layoff) to "nonevents" (a marriage or promotion that did not occur). Other reasons that people seek change are that their initial career was not their own choice, their original aspirations were not met, there is insufficient time for other life roles, or the present career is incongruent with changed values or interests. Longer life expectancy, changing views of retirement, and economic necessity are other factors.

Personal reactions to transition vary: Whether the career change is voluntary or involuntary, people may experience a variety of emotions such as fear, anxiety, or a sense of loss. Phases of transition may include immobilization, denial, self-doubt, letting go, testing options, searching for meaning, and integration and renewal. The close relationship between career and identify may necessitate reformulating one's self-concept when making a career change.

New Models of Career Development

The traditional linear career development model—education-employment-retirement—very likely accounts "for less than one-third of all careers". New ways of looking at life/career cycles that better explain adults' developmental diversity are needed. Leach and Chakiris elaborate on three types of careers: linear, free form, and mixed form. Linear careers follow the traditional pattern of education-work-retirement. Free-form careers include work for pay (such as permanent or temporary part-time jobs, consulting, entrepreneurial activity) or unpaid work. Mixed-form careerists are involved in transitions between linear and free-form patterns. The temporarily or permanently unemployed, underemployed, and those undergoing training or retraining in preparation for a career fall into this category. In her work with adults as learners, Cross identified three types of "life plans":

— Linear life plan—education when young, work through the middle years, leisure when elderly

— Redistribution of work, education, and leisure into recurring cycles

— Blended life plan—combining leisure, work, and study activities concurrently throughout life

She sees the trend toward longer, healthier life spans resulting in greater emphasis on the blended life plan.

Given these diverse career and life forms, the developmental tasks for each adult differ with age, social role, and culture. Age-related life-cycle theories have been criticized by Eastmond, Hughes and Smith, and others because they are often inappropriate for women and minorities. Women may accomplish the same developmental tasks as men, but often in different periods of the life-cycle. Forrest and Mikolaitis argue for the inclusion of a different component in women's career development—self in relation to others—that accounts for women's experience of the world. Ethnic minorities' career development is influenced by their differential experience of home, school, and the workplace; the kinds of transitions they undergo may not correspond to linear or age-related patterns.

These new ways of looking at life/career cycles and the transition process suggest approaches for assisting adults contemplating career change. The multifaceted approach proposed by Hughes and Graham requires recognizing the developmental stages of adults' multiple life roles and their interaction. The search for a new career involves not only matching the person to the work, but also fitting the "occupational career" into the "life career".

According to Sargent and Schlossberg, adult readiness for change depends on four factors: self, situation, support, and strategies. Counselors can help adults in transition assess

(1) self—personal responses to change;

(2) situation—changes in roles, relationships, routines, assumptions;

(3) support—does a range of sources exist? were they disrupted by transition?; and

(4) strategies—taking action to change the situation, change its meaning, or change oneself.

A variety of coping skills for managing transition are necessary. These skills include:

— perceiving and responding to transitions

— developing and using internal and external support systems

— reducing emotional and physiological distress

— planning and implementing change

A holistic approach to transition management includes the following components:

— receiving psychological, marital, and family counseling

— assessing interests, values, and skills (using gender- and culturally appropriate instruments

— obtaining information about careers

— learning about educational and training opportunities

— identifying and overcoming resource barriers such as financial need and child care

A computerized career guidance system such as SIGI PLUS (System of Interactive Guidance and Information) can also be of value. Norris, Shatkin, and Katz describe how SIGI was modified in recognition of the fact that career decision making is lifelong and, for adults, more complex. Components of SIGI PLUS encompass both occupational and nonoccupational factors, because such factors as family mobility and investment in education, training, and social/community activities may inhibit adults' flexibility in career choice. The Coping component recognizes the practical problems and barriers to training and career entry facing adults.

If, as Leach and Chakiris suggest, periodic unemployment will be experienced by most of the working population at some time in their lives, career and life role transitions will be everyone's concern. They suggest helping people make distinctions between jobs, work, and careers; place greater value on noneconomic work roles; and recognize transitions as an inevitable part of life and a continual challenge for redefining oneself.

TRENDS AND DIRECTIONS IN CAREER EDUCATION

Career education began to develop dramatically in the 1950s when the traditional occupational choice emphasis of career education began to be replaced by a broader focus on individuals and their career development over the course of their lives. The focal point of career education expanded in the 1960s when career development came to be viewed as an aggregate of psychological, sociological, educational, physical, economic, and other factors. The scope of career education became broader still in the 1970s when the concept of a career began to be understood in terms of possible personal choices related to the total life-style of an individual.

At the time of the passage of the Career Education Incentive Act in 1977, career education was seen as a means of "relating the occupational aspects of human development to all levels of learning" and of relating leisure, sex, family, and community roles to one's commitment to work. The repeal of the act in 1981 and a number of societal changes in the last decade have altered the context of career education. This ERIC Digest examines trends in the field of career education since the beginning of the 1980s and raises some key issues that may determine its future.

Hansen discusses some societal changes that affect the context in which career education operates. Rapid changes in information and technology are not only revolutionizing the workplace and occupations, but are also altering the way in which career information is acquired and career guidance is practiced. Changing family patterns, such as dual-career and single-parent families, signal the evolution of new relationships between family and work that will affect individual career choices and patterns. The "humanizing" of the workplace implies that career education must continue to emphasize the individual needs of workers. At the same time, structural changes in the economy resulting in layoffs and firings reinforce the importance of educating people about changing careers and about looking at work as one among many possible sources of life satisfaction.

The lifelong learning movement and the trend toward lifelong career development point to the need for instilling lifelong attitudes about learning early in the educational process. Other trends in career education were identified in Hoyt's surveys of the National Career Education Leaders' Communication Network. The following components of career education give an indication of its past, present, and future.

From the outset, career education has been defined in terms of a partnership between public education and the community. Public sector-private sector partnerships are a popular concept with many promising models. However, better definitions and measures of effectiveness could be developed. More also needs to be done in terms of better connections between the concepts of partnerships and educational reform and of improved awareness of the potential of the partnership concept as a tool for educational reform.

Although opinions vary as to exactly what constitutes employability, general employability skills have been deemed an important part of career education since the U.S. Office of Education's (USOE) first official policy paper on career education. Employability skills have gained popularity with the growing recognition of the fact that people will increasingly be forced to change occupations during their adult lives. What is needed now is consensus on defining employability skills and on deciding how and where they will be taught.

As occupations change and the relationship between education and work is transformed, the importance of career education as a vehicle for helping persons achieve greater career awareness and master decision-making skills is being recognized. Support for career awareness and career guidance has been particularly evident in the recent educational reform proposals. First used in the 1970s, the concept of infusing career education in classrooms has been enthusiastically received in the 1980s. Many outstanding materials for use in infusing career instruction in vocational and academic classrooms have been produced. Hoyt feels that process-oriented approaches are necessary for lasting educational reform; career education is a thoroughly tested and validated process-oriented approach.

The following steps are especially important if career educators are to succeed in making work a meaningful part of the total life-style:

— Shifting the focus of instruction in work values away from factors enhancing worker satisfaction to "employment productivity indicators"

— Recognizing the human need to work and helping students discover ways of meeting this need in other life roles

— Recognizing the need to retain the concept of the work ethic and applying it in conjunction with an emphasis on work values

— Taking advantage of the expertise being accumulated regarding the quality of working life movement.

The need for students to see a more meaningful relationship between school and work was listed by USOE as 1 of the 11 conditions dictating a need for educational reform. This need was also highly ranked by the National Career Education Leaders' Communication Network. Materials designed to enhance this relationship (such as computerized career guidance systems) are increasing in quality and quantity. However, the goal of education as preparation for work should be kept in perspective as one of several basic goals of education. The need to protect the interests and freedom of career choice of women, minorities, disabled, and disadvantaged persons has been addressed in federal legislation since the 1970s. However, Hansen describes changing attitudes toward social justice issues as evidence that bias and stereotyping still exist. She stresses that career educators should continue to fulfill an advocacy role. On the other hand, some state legislation and other laws such as the Carl D. Perkins Vocational Education Act contain efforts to improve equity for these groups.

Based on an analysis of the main trends in career education, Hoyt identifies some key issues that may shape the future of career education.

— To what extent will the focus of career education be on employment as opposed to employability? Since the early 1980s, the view has existed that keeping the focus of career education on employability will result in the greatest long-term benefits. This appears to be what is in fact happening; for example, training programs sponsored by the U.S. Department of Labor (including Job Training Partnership Act programs) are focusing more on helping clients develop employability skills rather than on creating jobs.

— To what extent can career education be used to increase partnerships between the educational system and the broader community? The wide acceptance of the concept of public-private partnerships to improve education enables a shift in focus from creating more partnerships to creating more meaningful partnerships. The first step is to make the business community and the community at large understand that the problems facing schools are not the exclusive concern of the educational system but that they are in fact everyone's problems.

— To what extent will career education be effective as an educational reform movement? One of the greatest challenges facing career educators today is persuading other educators of the value of career education as a proven process-oriented approach to educational improvement.

— To what extent will state and local leadership for career education continue to exist? State departments of education and local school systems employ fewer career education coordinators than they did in 1982. However, a relatively large number of persons charged with coordinating career education still remain, even though their job title may have changed. Other encouraging trends include the fact that there continue to be over 400 persons in the National Career Education Leaders' Communication Network each year, their opinions regarding the "health" of career education have remained fairly stable over the past 5 years, and state and local career associations are increasing in both number and strength.

Hansen presents some other ideas for shaping the future of career education:

— Systematic career/life planning programs in schools and colleges

— Increased emphasis on the linkage between work, family, education, and leisure

— Reaffirmation of the democratic goals of maximizing human potential

— More emphasis on entrepreneurship and creation of one's own career

— Better training in planning and management of change.

Career Development for Meaningful Life Work

Several years ago, a Wall Street Journal/ABC News poll reported that nearly 50% of all those working in the United States would choose a new type of work if they had the chance. Why do so many people feel dissatisfied with their work? The answer is complex and multifaceted. We live in an age where work has become "more personal than ever—when who you are is what you do—a deeper source of personal satisfaction than ever". Many are reexamining their careers in light of the growing realization that work should be more than a job. Instead of listening to internal signals, many individuals make choices about work and careers on the basis of external criteria such as income potential, status, and the opinions of others.

Although they may achieve success in these careers, they may be unhappy and dissatisfied because their work is not aligned with who they are—their "core self". Others may select careers based on their aptitudes-things they are good at doing—but just like external criteria these aptitudes may not reflect their "deep interests," that is, the things that really make them happy. According to Timothy Butler and James Waldroop, examining the terminology used to describe work can help unravel some of the questions about choosing work that is meaningful. Although the term "career" is used most frequently, the term "vocation" is more profound because it has to do with doing work that makes a difference and that has meaning.

The Latin word vocare, which means "to call," is the root of the word vocation. A vocation is a calling that one has to listen for. It is not immediately recognizable and one has to be attuned to the message for it to be heard. Finding meaningful work, therefore, involves listening for those internal signals that signify "deep interests" and then allowing the interests to lead to work that is aligned with a "core self." Traditional vocational or career guidance grew out of the needs of the modern industrial era and focused on measuring individual differences or traits and then using this information to match people to occupations. Part of this tradition was measuring job satisfaction through a positive evaluation of individuals' attitudes toward their jobs. Career satisfaction measures concentrated on correlating external job factors with global measures of satisfaction.

Job satisfaction also depended on an individual's ability to recognize and follow his or her interests. According to Henderson, when "the popular literature began suggesting deeper meaning in work...these traditional studies and assessment techniques began to have an empty ring" for both individuals and career development professionals. In response to the need to address the evolving concept of meaningful work, a new construct known as career happiness has emerged.As defined by Henderson and a number of colleagues, career happiness results when individuals find or develop careers that allow them to express their core identities and values, that tap into their true essence. According to Henderson, "Career happiness appears to have emerged more from philosophy, mythology, and psychology, than from the existing job satisfaction literature". Theories underlying the construct include the following:

- Concept of true self and its potential
- Concepts of innate self and potentiality related to processes for psychological healing
- Mythological processes for self-discovery and self-expression in career and life stage development that honor life journeys of profound purpose and meaning
- Concept of serendipity that enable individuals to take advantage of unexpected or chance events
- Optimal experience as critical determinants of personal happiness

Career happiness is connected to human development and is influenced by developmental processes. Career happiness may result "when career activities, challenges, and environments support, gently challenge, and resonate with fundamental developmental tasks," but as an individual grows and changes, activities that once resulted in career happiness may not continue to be meaningful. A study of eight people who experienced career happiness revealed that the participants had the following personality traits: a positive sense of self, self-determination, energy, strength of character, positive and productive relationships with others, and a positive relationship to the world. Work environments contributed to their career happiness by providing freedom and autonomy, challenges, a positive social atmosphere, and the opportunity to make personally meaningful contributions.

A number of recent developments in career development theory support the concept of meaningful work:

— *Constructivism*: The search for meaningful work is connected to constructivism with its emphasis on deriving meaning from experience. As a part of their career development, individuals can construct careers that are personally meaningful and self-managed. To have meaningful careers, individuals will need to reflect on their experiences and make the changes necessary to keep their careers aligned with their values and interests.

— *Career adaptability*: Career adaptability emphasizes making career changes without great difficulty to fit new or changing circumstances. It involves both an ability to cope with the predictable tasks of career development such as preparing for and finding a job as well as a future orientation that allows individuals to improve the match between their internal job description and the external world on a continuing basis. It "involves planful attitudes, self- and environmental exploration, and informed decision making,".

— *Planned happenstance*: Planned happenstance is a theory that helps individuals develop skills to recognize, create, and use chance in career development. Closely related to both constructivist notions of career development and career adaptability, it requires individuals to exercise curiosity to explore new learning opportunities, to persist despite setbacks, to meet changing attitudes and circumstances with flexibility, to optimistically view new opportunities as possible and attainable, and to take risks by being proactive in the face of uncertain outcomes.

— *Connecting spirit and work*: The idea that work has a dimension that is spiritual or carries with it a sense of harmony is connected to meaningful work. When individuals connect what they really like to do with what they do for pay and when they are absorbed in that work, they have achieved a connection between their spirit and their work. Career development plays a role in this process by helping individuals discover their needs, interests, and values and understand the nature of work and occupations, and then by assisting in bringing the two areas together. Meaning lies in how the two areas are merged. Bloch suggests the practice of intentionality—a process of using the mind to influence events outside one's self—as a way of creating career changes that will lead to more meaningful work.

CAREER DEVELOPMENT-BASED, LEARNING-TO-LEARN PROGRAMME

Today's youth face unique challenges. To cope with changing economic and social structures, young people need to be creative and adaptable, and must be able to self-manage their life-career and learning. To do this, they should acquire relevant skills, attitudes, knowledge, and motivation. They need to be able "to learn to learn." For a variety of reasons, however, many youth leave school without the competencies they need to make successful transitions into the work place. Since 80% of school leavers drop out with a "C" or higher grade average, poor performance is seldom the issue. Youth drop out of school because their studies lack meaning and/or because they have problems outside of school that they are not equipped to handle.

For example in Canada, the ENGAGE program, designed as a Stay-in-School initiative, uses a comprehensive life-career focus to address youths' continuing learning needs. ENGAGE features the following key elements:

(a) print materials designed for youth, parents, and teachers; and

(b) workshops for youth, parents, and teachers.

ENGAGE was developed to provide high-school-aged youth with the skills, knowledge, and motivation necessary to take responsibility for their life planning/learning both inside and outside school. ENGAGE assumes that:

1. Young people can effectively direct their own learning.
2. Young people are more likely to direct their own learning when they have both the motivation and the skills to do so.
3. Young people will be more motivated to learn if they see learning as meaningful and goal-directed.
4. Career building helps young people see their learning as goal directed.

ENGAGE is based on Magnusson's, Day's, and Redekopp's "Hierarchy of Self-Directed Adaptation" which posits that external interventions (e.g., counseling, coaching, teaching) should decrease in intensity as youth become more adaptable and responsible. ENGAGE focuses on four of these levels: formal instruction, consulting (entrenchment), self-help (enhancement), and personal innovation (elaboration).

— Formal instruction is the predominant learning mode that youth experience in school. Learning strategies, including study skills, are important for success in formal instruction.

— Entrenchment occurs when youth apply what they learn to "real world," non-school settings, including jobs, hobbies, or sports. At this level, youth are encouraged to be pro-active in seeking others who can help them reinforce their learning. To succeed at this level, youth need techniques for selecting and developing relationships with others that allow them to express their needs and obtain useful feedback.

— In enhancement, individuals combine external assistance with self-help activities and self-analysis. Youth learn to use self-directed learning resources, such as print products, videos, workshops, and individuals within the youth's network; use self-analysis procedures; and develop protege/mentor relationships.

— In elaborating, youth become proficient at personal innovation. Strategies here include "self-created learning" opportunities (e.g., writing and presenting), and "learning by facilitating" which includes teaching, supervising, and mentoring.

ENGAGE introduces youth to current decision-making and career development concepts and has them conduct personal, career-building activities. This is an essential component of ENGAGE because all subsequent activities are based on the results of career building. Instead of being asked to focus on "the big decision" (what they want to do with the rest of their lives), students are encouraged to look at "the big picture" of their lives. Youth learn that career building is an ongoing process requiring awareness of current values, beliefs, interests, skills, and knowledge; visioning, fluid decision-making skills, and tentative setting of shorter- and longer-term goals and intentions within their changing life contexts; and continual assessment and re-assessment of their life-career plans as both their personal life circumstances and the world in which they live continues to change.

Products and Services

ENGAGE consists of print products and workshops for youth, teachers, and parents. Youth products include the following:

— *Your Life*: A 44-page, highly visual magazine designed to appeal to young people. It uses career building principles to provide information and motivation.

— *Pocket Powerbook*: A 68-page companion to Your Life that provides "how-to," step-by-step strategies for career building, communicating, studying, self-management, and accessing support systems and networks. These booklets can be distributed to youth as "stand alone" products or used in conjunction with a workshop.

The adult products include a teacher's guide, a parent's guide, and a workshop leader's guide. The teacher's and parent's guides provide an overview of ENGAGE principles, as well as tips on how to both respond to and support youth as they take control of their learning. The workshop leader's guide is designed to help facilitators (teachers, counselors, club leaders) effectively deliver a motivational two-day workshop. Workshops have been designed for all participants in ENGAGE. The two day youth workshop is described below. Workshops for parents and teachers are independent of the youth workshops and are designed for evening sessions lasting two to three hours.

ENGAGE emphasizes direct contact with youth through a two-day workshop and subsequent follow-up sessions, where students focus on the need to develop learning objectives and maintain a "stay-learning attitude." The workshops use an active, process-oriented approach. The favorite activities are:

— *For Love and Money*: Youth are asked to list 10 of their favorite activities. The group then brainstorms ways that individuals can make money doing what they love to do.

— *Risk-Taking*: Youth are asked to invest money (candies) at a variety of stations that differ in their degree of risk. In the discussion that follows, students share the types of risks they face in their lives (which often include standing up to their peers or making important life-learning decisions), talk about what makes it okay to take risks, and what stops them from taking risks. Strategies for calculated risk-taking are then presented.

— *Negotiating Skills*: A simple four-step model of collaborative negotiating provides a tool that can be used in a variety of situations. Youth, parents, and teachers have remarked that this skill helps individuals express their needs and listen to and consider others' needs.

As part of the Stay-in-School initiative, ENGAGE workshops were started in six Alberta schools with youth who had been identified by their teachers as being at risk of dropping out of school. Upon completion of the two-day workshop, students showed statistically significant changes in perceived motivation to learn, and expressed more interest in staying in school, spending more time learning out of school, and in developing goals and plans related to learning and their life-career. About 95% of participating students indicated they would like further follow-up sessions.

7

CAREER DEVELOPMENT

Some experts who were asked to spend a day together, summarized what they knew about career development in five pithy messages. These messages would be used to promote career development in Canadian youth. What resulted is the "High Five" of career development:

1. Change is constant.
2. Follow your heart.
3. Focus on the journey.
4. Stay learning.
5. Be an ally.

CHANGE IS CONSTANT

The famous American philosopher, Yogi Berra, once said, "The future ain't what it used to be." Canadians took that statement to mean that predictions about the future are difficult because the processes of change, not just the content of change, are changing. In the world of work, for example, the role of the automotive technician is changing not only due to technological changes in cars but also due to segmentation of the industry. Therefore, the process of defining an "automotive technician" is changing while the content of the technician's work is also changing. Thus, predictions about the technician's role (or any other work role) are tenuous.

Rapid and continuous technological, economic, demographic, and social changes directly influence the world of work. As a result, the "labor market" of the past is quickly becoming a "work dynamic" that is difficult to encapsulate with occupational dictionaries, codes, or titles. For example, dozens of environmental roles exist today that did not exist at the turn of the decade. New jobs are emerging and old jobs are changing to require new skills, knowledge, and attitudes. Personal change occurs continuously as well. People grow and develop new skills, attitudes, knowledge, beliefs, networks, and other assets at varying rates. Assessment tools, the backbone of traditional career development, give the clients the impression that change is unlikely; that who they are is who they will be.

People who recognize, value, and nurture their own fluidity, will better adapt to their changing environments. Likewise, goal-setting needs to be reconsidered in light of constant change. Goal-setting can be useful, but the dogged pursuit of goals can prevent people from optimizing chance opportunities. Goals have to be seen in context with serendipitous discoveries. Gelatt's concept of "positive uncertainty" applies here.

Follow Your Heart

When change is constant, relatively stable guideposts become all the more important. The "heart" (the set of characteristics that includes values, entrenched beliefs, and interests) is reasonably stable and is well worth heeding. One's "heart" drives one's career path. Skills, knowledge, and attitudes are simply tools that allow the path to be followed. A corollary to this message is that dreaming is normal, natural, and appropriate. Career development practitioners often concern themselves with helping clients become "realistic" at the expense of their client's dreams. Many people have "unrealistic" dreams, but there is nothing wrong with pursuing them and cherishing them. Ultimately, reality will impose itself on people and trying to accelerate this process may be of little benefit. On the other hand, people can move towards their dreams when provided with the tools and strategies to do so.

FOCUS ON THE JOURNEY

One of the reasons the field has been preoccupied with helping individuals select appropriate occupational destinations is that we wish to help people find work that is meaningful and fulfilling. In doing so, however, we have tended to underemphasize the meaningfulness of the journey towards one's vision. Now, since continual change undermines the predicting of occupational destinations, we must take great efforts to help people enjoy the process: to better fulfill their values, beliefs, and interests with every decision they make. In fact, focusing on the journey means people move away from feeling a need to make "the correct decision" ("What should I be?") and move toward examining the immediate and enduring effects of virtually all decisions ("What do I want to be doing now and in the future?").

STAY LEARNING

"Lifelong learning" has become a catch phrase. However, the public's beliefs imply that nothing more needs to be done once an occupational destination is reached. We will be better able to communicate the prescription to "stay learning" when the first three messages of the "High Five" have been adopted. Learning is constant when change is constant, and learning can be enjoyable and meaningful when it is seen as part of a journey that fulfills one's heart.

Unfortunately, many people cringe in terror when they hear about "lifelong learning." People who have had limited success with formal learning are anxious about "lifelong learning" and need to know that most learning does not occur in formal settings. Individuals are continually accumulating assets (e.g., skills, contacts) through experience, but few people have a mechanism by which they can identify, record, and organize these assets. Consequently, they often do not recognize that they have undergone a tremendous amount of learning. People need ways to keep track of their learning experiences.

BE AN ALLY

This last theme brings us back to the old idea of the importance of community. Many people do not feel part of a community and do not have the wherewithal to create one for themselves. Many youth, in particular, see the labor market (or work dynamic) as something external, "out there," and distant. They do not realize that the labor market surrounds them, and is represented by their parents, neighbors, friends' parents, and parents' friends. These allies surround youth, yet the two appear unable to connect with each other. Our field and our society have stressed independence and autonomy; perhaps a reexamination of interdependence and community would be appropriate. Asking for help is not a sign of weakness. Rather, it is a sign of strength when one can identify a need, clearly express the need, and articulate how others can help one meet the need. This is particularly true when one wants to learn continually, keep up with change, and adapt to change.

The "High Five" can be described in a variety of ways. Different client groups respond to different descriptions and examples. We have incorporated these messages in a variety of products, workshops, and speeches, and we have used a variety of ways to explain them. Some examples of their application follow:

ENGAGE is a learning-to-learn system for youth that includes products and workshops for youth, parents and teachers. The "High Five" messages form the core of the system.

"Opportunities with Change" is a career development workshop for professionals, in which the concepts and activities directly follow the "High Five."

"Everyday Career Development" is a course and text for secondary school teachers designed to help them infuse career development into their day-to-day teaching activities. The course is based heavily on the "High Five."

We have found that people respond favorably to these messages. Each message has a universal quality which reaches virtually all audiences, as the following testimonials indicate. From a grandmother who read the ENGAGE materials: "Don't know how I reached this age without knowing and achieving some of the suggestions. Good for any age—real treasures. We sure do a lot of muddling along in life without knowing how to improve." Parents respond particularly favorably to the "High Five"; the messages remove some of the intense pressure they feel to help their children decide "what they are going to be."

CAREER DEVELOPMENT AND GENDER, RACE, AND CLASS

Many theories of career development are derived from theories of personality. They attempt to illuminate the interrelationship of individual personality and behavior with work and careers. However, some prevailing career development theories were based solely on research on white males from middle- and upper-middle-class backgrounds, so their applicability to women, people of color, and other socioeconomic groups has been called into question. In addition, the focus on individual psychological or personality characteristics does not take into account the wider environmental context in which people make career decisions, thus failing to recognize the constraints faced by some groups.

Some types of career development theories include trait and factor, life-span, and social cognitive. Following are some of the issues surrounding the applicability of these theories in regard to gender, race, and class.

Trait and factor theories: The basis of trait and factor theories is the assumption that there are unique traits that can be reliably measured and that it is possible to match individual traits to occupational requirements. Holland identified six types of occupations theorized that people seek work environments and occupations that match their preferred traits. However, some people question the accuracy of the instruments used to measure these traits for groups other than white males. Do they reflect understanding of diverse life experiences? Are the requirements for success in an occupation the same for people of color as for whites? For women as for men?

Research has demonstrated real differences in the abilities of different gender, racial, and socioeconomic groups, but what factors brought about these differences? According to Helms and Piper, there is "no valid reason for explaining or anticipating consistent between-group differences on the basis of race per se"; such differences may result from shared cultural socialization experiences. Likewise, "differences in abilities, achievements, personality, interests, and values between men and women do exist, [but] they are often rather small".

Life-Span Theories: Trait and factor theories tend to deal with career issues at one point in time, whereas life-span theories take a long-term, developmental perspective. The most widely known life-span theory is Super's Theory of Vocational Choice, which suggests that individuals pass through stages of vocational development involving developmental tasks at each stage; it also considers the performance of multiple roles and their interaction across the life-span. However, some studies have shown that the life stages Super outlined are not exactly applicable to women, especially as their roles have changed in the last few decades. Super considered self-concept and vocational maturity to be important determinants in occupational choices. However, the self-concept of people of color is linked to some degree to the formation of ethnic identity, the impact of which needs to be acknowledged in life-span theory. Low scores on career maturity measures may be a reflection of perceived societal barriers, restricted access to and limited opportunities in the job market, or a realistic appraisal of one's prospects.

Social Cognitive Career Theory: This theory identifies the interaction of personal attributes, external environmental factors, and behavior in career decision making. It focuses on the influence of self-efficacy beliefs and outcome expectations on goals and behavior. That is, if individuals believe in their ability to undertake an endeavor and have an expectation of the outcome of that behavior, they will behave in a way that will help them achieve their goal. However, for women and people of color, barriers such as discrimination or bias may determine outcomes independent of behavior. Self-efficacy beliefs may have been undermined by racial or sex-role stereotypes. Therefore, individuals may foreclose career options that they perceive are not truly open to them. The fact that some individuals have been able to persist and achieve in a nonsupportive environment is in some cases attributable to their high self-efficacy expectations.

Critics of the major career development theories charge that they are based on white, middle-class values; make certain assumptions (relative affluence, access to education and occupational information, free and open labor market, work as a central value); fail to include crucial structural and cultural variables; and include concepts not applicable to certain groups. For example, "the very notion of career development may be inappropriate for some ethnic minorities". "We do not even know to what extent the term career is culturally sensible to Native people". Fitzgerald and Betz question the relevance of career development to people who are permanently unemployed or underemployed. Naidoo critiques research that measures minority groups against white, middle-class norms (any differences being attributed to race) and studies that confound race with social class. However, many authors agree that these theories have some utility and need to be expanded and elaborated to include relevant variables.

Career maturity

Career maturity is the readiness to make appropriate career decisions. It has often been measured using majority populations as the norm, but research on diverse populations demonstrates that some of the variables used to measure it may not apply to all groups. Career maturity is influenced by age, ace, ethnicity, locus of control, socioeconomic status, work salience, and gender. The complex interaction of these factors affects individuals readiness to succeed in mastering the tasks appropriate to various stages of career development. Perron et al. found that minority students in Quebec had higher ethnic identity and vocational maturity earlier than the majority population but their maturity scores fell behind by 11th grade. They suggested that increased ethnic identity may lead to greater awareness of potential barriers and thus lower career maturity.

In Lundberg et al.'s study, Anglo ninth-graders had higher career maturity scores than Mexican-American students, which they attributed to the latter's limited access to information about the world of work. They also found significant differences between the two groups on the Myers Briggs Type Indicator, highlighting the key influence of personality on career maturity. Some studies fail to show that socioeconomic status (SES) has a significant influence on career maturity, but others suggest that such concepts as career exploration and planning may not apply to poor individuals who may leave school to take jobs for economic survival. Rojewski found that adolescents from low-income backgrounds score lower on career maturity measures, which he attributed to lack of access to occupational information, role models, and the perceived lack of employment opportunities, all of which influence career choice.

Although low-income youth often have high aspirations, the influence of inadequate guidance and lack of information, high school preparation, or role models affects their "fit" with the career maturity model. Career maturity research shows conflicting results for gender, some studies finding higher levels in males, others in females. Again, the complex interaction of other influences may make career maturity development different for women and men. Although women in Luzzo's study had higher career maturity scores than men, they were more inclined to perceive role conflicts and barriers as obstacles in their career development process. Women may balance their career preferences with what seems possible, regardless of whether their career behavior is appropriate for their career development stage.

Salience

Salience refers to the value individuals place on life roles (study, work service, home/family, leisure), which can change over time. In addition to these roles, the salience of racial/ethnic identity is emerging as an important dimension in explaining career development. A "Special Issue" of the Journal of Vocational Behavior explored the role of racial identity in career behavior. In this issue, Cross presented the Nigrescence model, a continuum of African American identity in which individuals range from placing low to high salience on being black. Traditional career development theory may apply to blacks with low salience (whose world view is similar to whites) but not to blacks whose world view is more Africentric. Evans and Herr found that high salient racial identity did not predict career aspirations of African Americans, suggesting the importance of considering personal identity factors.

Leong and Chou found that a continuum of acculturation/ ethnic identity influences the vocational behavior and career choices of Asian Americans. Similarly, the salience of Native Americans' world view compared to that of the dominant culture affects their view of work. The degree of acculturation, or the extent to which individuals adopt dominant cultural values, may determine the fit of traditional career development theories. For others, bicultural competence, or the reconciliation of the values of one's culture with the dominant culture, explains career development patterns. For some the salience of the family influences career behavior. Different cultures have different conceptions of the family, gender roles, and family-work relationships.

In some cultures, "career" may have a collective, not an individual meaning. "African Americans expressed greater salience in home and family than the work role". Several authors point out the great diversity in world view, ethnicity, and socioeconomic status within groups such as Hispanic, Asian, African, and Native Americans. Therefore, race/ethnicity should not be used as a primary signifier of career behavior, and it is important to look at the conditions under which membership in a particular group is salient.

ASSESSING CAREER DEVELOPMENT WITH PORTFOLIOS

The assessment of career development is a relatively new concept. In general, ideas of appropriate methods for assessing student achievement and mastery of any set of competencies are shifting. Criterion-referenced tests, which measure performance relative to a specified set of standards or tasks, are gaining favor, for example, over norm-referenced tests, which measure how an examinee performed in relation to others. At the same time, support for internal accountability, that is, determining what is worth knowing and assuring that students know it, is increasing. One response to this has been an increased use of portfolios that provide a medium for assessing student work and invite them to become responsible partners in documenting their learning.

Through portfolios, students compose a portrait of themselves as able learners, selecting and presenting evidence that they have met the learning standards for individual classes and for broader learning tasks. A student portfolio may be described as "a purposeful collection of student work that tells the story of the student's efforts, progress, or achievement in a given area. This collection must include student participation in selection of portfolio content; the guidelines for selections; the criteria for judging merit; and evidence of student self-reflection". As career development becomes an increasingly important component of educational systems, the issues of measurement and accountability are raised.

In today's workplace, employment security is becoming "employability security" — the knowledge that one has the competencies demanded in a global economy and the ability to expand and adjust those competencies as requirements change. The challenge of preparing our young people for this new workplace has generated legislative efforts to stimulate educational reform directed at creating "world class" education and a comprehensive system for helping American youth make a smooth transition from high school to productive, skilled employment and further learning. The "Goals 2000: Educate America Act" establishes eight national education goals and two national councils—one to stimulate the development of voluntary academic standards and the other to identify essential occupational skills.

The "School to Work Opportunities Act of 1994" is a strategy to implement the purpose of the "Goals 2000: Educate America Act," that is, helping all Americans to reach internationally competitive standards through educational reform. Career development is a major component of the "School to Work Opportunities Act (STWOA)." Career guidance and counseling, which are interventions in the career development process, are recognized as essential in helping students to choose their career (educational) pathway. Section 102 of the STWOA states that "The school-based component of a School-to-Work Opportunities program shall include... career awareness and career exploration and counseling (beginning at the earliest possible age, but not later than the 7th grade) in order to help students who may be interested to identify, and select or reconsider, their interests, goals, and career majors, including those options that may not be traditional for their gender, race or ethnicity."

The Act also provides grants to states to plan for and implement school-to-work opportunities systems. Renewed interest in career development has led to an equal demand for accountability. This prompts several questions. What do we want our students to know and be able to do as a result of a career development process and how will we know that they have achieved it? This legislation has placed the onus on school systems to provide the programs to help students make informed career decisions, and to provide opportunities for students to take responsibility for their career development. How will they know they have achieved these outcomes?

Two major endeavors can help schools to meet the double need of accountability and assessment. First, state and professional associations, as well as national leaders; practitioners, and career development experts, collaborated to develop the National Career Development Guidelines. The National Career Development Guidelines offer a comprehensive, competency-based approach to career development that states, educational institutions and other organizations can use in developing effective career guidance programs. The Guidelines offer the processes, content and structure for such programs. More importantly, they provide the standards or competencies for career development at four different levels—elementary, middle/junior high, high school, and postsecondary/adult. The competencies fall within three areas of career development—self-knowledge, educational and occupational exploration, and career planning. The Guidelines, already being used in over 40 states as standards or as the basis for establishing career development standards, provide nationally validated competencies that can be used in assessment.

The second significant effort has been the work of the Secretary's Commission on Achieving Necessary Skills (SCANS). In the Commission report, "What Work Requires of Schools", five areas of competencies based on a three-part foundation are delineated. Of the 36 specific skills or qualities noted, over half are commonly included in a career guidance program. This report validates the integration of career guidance and counseling into educational programs and supplies a complementary set of standards by which a career development process can be measured.

The essential criteria for measuring the accountability of a career guidance program are available. Since self-assessment and reflection are important to developing personal responsibility in career decision-making, a portfolio that sets standards and also allows for reflection emerges as the instrument of choice. Until now, most efforts to document career development have been through career planners. Career planners are usually the end product of a career development process and, as such, are appropriate for secondary education or higher but not for the student at the awareness or exploratory stages. They also do not typically provide for the self-reflection essential to an individual's ownership of the process.

"*Get A Life*: Your Personal Planning Portfolio", designed through collaboration between the American School Counselor Association and the National Occupational Information Coordinating Committee, is one instrument that sets standards and allows for self-reflection. The portfolio is divided into four sections—self-knowledge, life roles, educational development, and career exploration and planning. Each section contains competency files and personal files. The National Career Development Guidelines for the middle and high school levels are used as competencies for both program and individual assessment. Program planners can analyze the comprehensiveness of their programs by evaluating their activities in relation to the expected student outcomes contained in the Guidelines.

Individuals can determine if they have met the career development competencies through the programs offered. Within the competency file, a sign-off ascertains the strategies and the date on which each competency was addressed. In some schools, students make the decision whether, in fact, the activity or strategy presented did help them to master the competency. The personal files are a set of guiding questions that help students to reflect on their learning. The portfolio is an organizational tool that allows the owners to collect information about themselves to use in making personal, educational and career decisions. At the same time, the students are introduced to the idea that the process is lifelong, and that they must become "career negotiators", taking responsibility for their own development.

Recent efforts to improve education have led to a new look at assessment. As pedagogy has changed to focus on learner-centered education, the need to make assessment an integral, on-going part of instruction has become obvious. Concurrently, Federal initiatives to promote educational reform have required the provision of career development opportunities and have demanded accountability in this area. The portfolio concept is one way to meet this challenge by giving students ownership of their work and standards by which they can be measured. States and local districts must define the career development standards they wish to implement, allow students the opportunity to take responsibility for their career development, offer the necessary career guidance and counseling to support student learning, and assess both the program and the individual to assure that the expected outcomes are being achieved. The portfolio provides the format for the process and documentation of career development while giving individuals and programs standards for assessment.

FAMILY ROLE IN CAREER DEVELOPMENT

Family influence is an important force in preparing youth for their roles as workers. Young people form many of their attitudes about work and careers as a result of interactions with the family. Family background provides the basis from which their career planning and decision making evolve. However, within each family, the level of involvement can vary, offering both positive and negative influences.

Family background factors found to be associated with career development include parents' socioeconomic status (SES), their educational level, and biogenetic factors such as physical size, gender, ability, and temperament. In a study of the influences on adolescents' vocational development reported by Mortimer et al., the variable that had the most effect on educational plans and occupational aspirations was parental education. Mortimer et al. also report that parents with postsecondary education tend to pass along its importance to their children—a finding supported by other studies. Montgomery notes that females talented in math viewed their career choices as reflective of interests that stemmed from early family influence and educational opportunities. Marso and Pigge found that the presence of teachers in the family was a significant factor influencing teacher candidates' decisions to teach.

DeRidder, however, points out that lower levels of parent education can retard adolescents' career development. "Being born to parents with limited education and income reduces the likelihood of going to college or achieving a professional occupational goal and essentially predetermines the child's likely vocational choice". Family income is another aspect of family background that influences the career development of youth, especially for girls. One reason for this may be that families with limited economic resources tend to direct them first to the males of the family, giving less hope and encouragement for further education to the daughters in the family. Also, some parents—especially working class or lower-income parents—may hold values that place girls in the homemaker role and reflect less emphasis on occupational preparation. Given this disposition, it is understandable that the self-efficacy of girls with respect to career opportunities is linked to the economic support they can expect to receive from their parents.

Although much of the research on the role of family in vocational and career development has focused on family background, the investigation of family processes viewed in relation to life roles offers additional insight into the influences of the family. Family processes of interaction, communication, and behavior influence what the child learns about work and work experiences. Attitudes about school and work, educational and career goals and aspirations, and values have a long-term impact on a youth's career choices, decisions, and plans.

"Parents as daily models provide cultural standards, attitudes, and expectations and, in many ways, determine the eventual adequacy of self-acceptance and confidence, of social skills and of sex roles. The attitudes and behaviors of parents while working or discussing their work is what the children respond to and learn". Through the process of educating their children about life roles, parents can influence the employability skills and values that children subsequently adopt. The interaction of many individual variables in family process is a significant factor to consider in studying family influence on career development. Middleton and Loughead suggest that adolescents' career aspirations be examined from an interactionist perspective rather than a unilateral process of influence, "focusing on the context and situations in which adolescents' career development occurs".

Parents from certain minority groups have a great influence on the educational and occupational decisions of both boys and girls in the family. Two very different examples are Mexican American and Korean parents. Clayton et al. found that "Mexican American parents want more education for their children than their children want for themselves". This is especially significant from a population that typically is undereducated and has high unemployment and dropout rates and low occupational status. Although the aspirations Mexican American parents hold for their children may be high, continuing education is often unavailable due to lack of funds. In fact, "50 percent of the 8th and 12th graders and 55 percent of the community college students" in Clayton et al.'s study cited lack of funds as a primary factor in their plans for continuing education.

Mexican American parents should be made aware of the availability of financial aid that could support their children's continuing education. Whereas Mexican American parents are focused on the role of continuing education in the career development process, Korean parents focus on career selection. "The strong desire of Korean immigrants for their children to be professionals and earn money and prestige is conveyed either in a rather demanding form or in a more subtle form that is just as clear". The pressure to choose certain careers is often initiated when the child is quite young. Stories by college students of Korean descent, reported by Kim, confirm that their career choices both "explicitly and implicitly reflect the cultural model of success their parents share".

One student described how, when he was still young, his father announced at a potluck dinner that "Tim will be a lawyer and Don will be a doctor." Another student described how her father introduced each member of their family to his guests by stating what career each would pursue before any of them had made a career choice: "Ron, the future doctor; Ben, who will be an engineer before you know it, and Carrie, who is going into business". "As he announces the children's career plans proudly in public and as the guests at the party recognize and envy his success, the Korean immigrants' cultural model of success is also recognized, reinforced, and transmitted". As happens in other cultures, Korean parents distinguish between boys and girls in the careers they assign to their children. "Girls can choose careers that are considered less stressful and less demanding and that have more flexible schedules so that they can combine families with careers".

Negative Effects

Middleton and Loughead present three categories to describe types of parental involvement in adolescents' career development:

(1) positive involvement,

(2) noninvolvement, and

(3) negative involvement.

The greatest anxiety adolescents feel about their career decisions or exploration, quite understandably, is in response to parents' negative involvement. Parents in the "negative involvement" category are often controlling and domineering in their interactions with their children. The children of such parents often pursue the careers selected by their parents rather than those they desire so as not to disappoint their parents or go against their wishes. Likewise, they feel a strong sense of frustration and guilt when they do not meet their parents' expectations.

The burden of following a parent's narrowly defined expectations of success has resulted in "mental health problems, estranged parent-child relationships, or in socially delinquent behaviors". Penick and Jepsen note that "adolescents from enmeshed families may have difficulty mastering career development tasks because they are unable to distinguish their own from parental goals and expectations". Disengagement of family and adolescents has similarly negative effects. "Adolescents from disengaged families may lack familial support and interaction, resulting in limits on self-knowledge and task orientation that interferes with mastery of career development tasks".

Structuring or guiding parental involvement in adolescent career development is increasingly seen as an important element of a school's career counseling. "Previous research has suggested that educational institutions are not the only source of learning related to occupational choice and enactments in this society. It has been found that the family plays an important role in the transmission of values such as independence, ambition, career orientation and actual career choice". DeRidder suggests that counselors work directly with parents, collaborating with them and helping them to improve their effectiveness in guiding their children. He encourages parents not only to communicate about work and careers with their children, but to show faith in their children's abilities to be successful, providing them with encouragement and information. "They should help their children learn that basic work attitudes of promptness, respect, responsibility, and interest in schoolwork are expected both at home and at school".

Career development professionals can help parents by providing them with information and support. Middleton and Loughead recommend that counselors meet with parents "individually or collectively to disseminate information on how to facilitate their adolescents' career development and familiarize them with career resource materials". Within the school setting, Grinstad and Way suggest that "vocational education at all levels should be placed within a contextual framework where the work of the world and the work of the family are integrated and explored simultaneously". By increasing communication between home and school regarding career development, it is possible that the positive aspects of family influence can be enhanced and the negative aspects can be offset, improving the career development outcomes of the workers of the future.

VOCATIONAL CAREER DEVELOPMENT OF FREE AGENT WORKERS

A number of factors have converged to create a new type of worker known as free agent. Downsizing by corporations during the 1980s and early 1990s signaled the end of an era where loyalty to an organization or corporation paid off in a lifetime guarantee of employment. Technology has created opportunities for work to be done differently, including virtually. The transition to the knowledge-based economy has generated a demand for workers with certain types of skills; workers possessing such skills are in short supply now and in the foreseeable future. These factors have served as a catalyst for the emergence of workers who consider themselves free agents.

Like professional athletes or actors, free agent workers do not usually attach themselves permanently to a specific company or organization, but tend to go where their skills and talents are in demand. Because free agent workers do not usually have long-term attachments to one organization, their needs for career development must be met in nontraditional ways.

Who are free agent workers? According to Arnold Packer, "Free agents, usually young people, don't expect (or want) a lifetime career with a single employer. They have taken responsibility for charting and preparing their own professional futures. In that group, changing jobs is commonplace". Being a free agent worker is as much a matter of mindset as of mobility. Free agent workers think of themselves as having talent to sell and they shop it around for the best offer, but money alone does not ensure their loyalty or interest. How many free agent workers are there? Estimates of the number of free agent workers range from a high of 25 million to a low of 12.9 million, but these estimates include different categories of workers.

The 12.9 million figure is based on 1999 Bureau of Labor Statistics data on the number of self-employed individuals outside of agriculture; this number actually declined by 1 million between 1994 and 1999. Pink's estimate of 25 million was calculated by adding self-employed (14 million), independent contractors (8.3 million), and individuals working through temporary agencies (2.3 million). Pink refers to this combined group as the "free agent nation." Not all of the individuals included in Pink's estimate would fit the definition of free agent workers, however, because many have not voluntarily chosen to work in these categories. For the most part, free agent workers are well educated and possess high levels of skills that are in demand; they have chosen a free agent lifestyle because it frees them from organizational politics, provides them opportunities to learn, gives them more control of their time, and provides 30% to 200% more income than their counterparts in traditional jobs earn.

Changing Concepts

The model of the free agent worker has emerged during a

period when conceptions about careers and career patterns have been changing. The career development literature, for example, contains discussions of the boundary-less career, one that is characterized by independence from rather than dependence on traditional organizational career arrangements. "The typical boundaryless career is characterized by a career identity that is independent of the employer (e.g., 'I'm a software engineer'); the accumulation of employment-flexible know-how (e.g., how to work in an innovative, efficient, and/or quality-enhancing way); and the development of networks that are independent of the firm (e.g., occupation or industry based), non-hierarchic (e.g., communities of practice), and worker enacted".

A relational approach to careers is another recent concept in the career development literature. In describing the relational career, Hall speaks of the external and the internal career. Previously, the external career—the actual jobs or positions an individual held—was more important. Today, the internal career, which is the individual's perceptions and self-constructions of career events, is of greater consequence. In the relational view, career development is seen as a mutual process, a process of co-learning. The objective of career development is not mastery and independence but rather interdependence.

The relational aspects of work environments can have a powerful influence on career development because they provide opportunities for interaction, the development of competence, and a more confident self-identity. The emergence of free agent workers can be seen as a natural outgrowth of changing concepts about careers and career development. Stroh and Reilly used the term free agents to describe mangers who began systematically to manage their own careers by changing companies. Their research found that managers who followed a free agent career model fared better than those who did not. Free agent workers have boundaryless careers; their career identity is independent of an employer and it is their know-how that allows them to function as free agents. Networks are also important to free agent workers. These networks allow free agent workers to take a relational approach to career development.

Since free agents workers have nontraditional careers, they do not have access to traditional career development opportunities that are available to workers who follow more traditional career paths. That does not mean, however, that free agent workers do not continue to develop their careers. Two career development strategies in which free agent workers engage are learning and networking.

Learning

The skills and knowledge that free agent workers possess are what makes them valuable and they engage in learning on a regular basis to keep up to date. Knowing how to learn and adapt are skills that most of them possess. Free agent workers find that, in many situations, the ability to acquire the required skill rapidly may be just as essential as having a specific expertise: mastering "hot new technology in a snap is a hot skill—not knowing last year's hot new software". The term free agent learning has been coined to describe the type of learning in which free agent workers engage. Free agent learning is voluntary, self-directed and, for free agent learners, its focus is primarily on new jobs. Free agent workers engage in self-directed learning that is career specific so that they can develop competencies that promote their employability and career success. "With their focus on employability through growth and learning, free agents are essentially free agent learners-independent, highly motivated adults who take responsibility for their own learning and development, use their spare time to learn, use new approaches in learning, and self-teach using a variety of resources".

Networking

The development of networks is another career development strategy used by free agent workers. In fact, lack of contact with professional colleagues is one of the major downsides to free agent work, and some have left self-employment to escape the isolation that accompanies it. To fulfill the need for contact with others, free agent workers are developing networks. The networks, many of which are small groups, are used by free agents to succeed professionally and survive professionally.

The networks may be virtual or take more traditional forms. Some free agent workers use regular conference telephone calls or meetings to solicit and receive advice, set goals, give advice, and provide emotional support. Several women in Skokie, Illinois, for example, have formed the Strategy Group that meets monthly in a living room. At their meetings, each participant is allowed a maximum of 20 minutes to speak, with the time divided into four periods: accomplishments, struggles and dilemmas, interactive session, and making commitments for the next month. These networks help free agent workers take a relational approach to their career development and continue to develop their careers through repeated exchanges with others in significant ways.

THE TAXONOMY OF CAREER DEVELOPMENT INTERVENTIONS

Every year millions of public and private dollars are spent on career development interventions for America's teenagers. However, no comprehensive listing of these interventions exists in the professional literature. The lack of such a listing hampers both practitioners and researchers in the area of career guidance. To remedy this situation, the Career Development Research Team of the National Research Center for Career and Technical Education conducted research with the aim to

(1) identify a comprehensive list of career development interventions that occur in America's secondary schools, and

(2) create a taxonomy of the identified interventions.

Through consultation with career guidance practitioners and researchers from across the country, as well as through examination of research articles, grant reports, and program manuals, the Career Development Research Team established a comprehensive list containing 44 interventions. These 44 interventions were then rated on 5 variables (i.e., Time, Mode, Control, Place, & Size) by a random sample of the membership of the Guidance Division of the Association for Career and Technical Education. These ratings were then cluster analyzed. This analysis produced a four taxon solution. The taxa were

(1) Work Based Interventions,

(2) Advising Interventions,

(3) Introductory Interventions, and

(4) Curriculum Based Interventions.

Every year millions of dollars are spent on career development interventions in America's public schools. Such expenditures are seen as a sound investment, as it is believed that they increase the relevance of education for the nation's youth. However, despite these benefits, no one has attempted to construct a taxonomy of career development interventions that occur in secondary schools. The production of such a taxonomy would benefit school counselors, administrators and other school personnel in three ways. First, this taxonomy would standardize career guidance language in terms of both content and structure. For instance, does the term career major mean the same as career pathway? Without a standardized language, it is difficult to engage in meaningful professional dialogues and conduct research.

Second, this taxonomy would provide school counselors with a parsimonious framework to judge where their school's career guidance efforts are underdeveloped. Moreover, school counselors can use this taxonomy to map their school's progress in the underdeveloped taxa. Third, this taxonomy would make it possible to compare the efficacy of specific types of interventions against other types (e.g., school-based curricula vs. work-based learning). The current lack of knowledge about the comparative efficacy of career development interventions leaves school counselors with no alternative other than employing an inefficient and expensive "shotgun" approach to career development for America's youth.

Given the benefits mentioned above, some counsellors set out to discover the underlying taxonomic structure of career development interventions that occur in secondary schools. The first step was to develop a comprehensive list of career development interventions that commonly occur in these schools. They examined research articles, grant reports, and program manuals in order to develop this list. Drafts of this list were circulated to career development experts around the country for feedback. Then they incorporated their feedback and a final list of 44 interventions was set. Amazingly, the list represents the first comprehensive articulation and demarcation of the universe of career development interventions.

The next step in creating this taxonomy was to decide what dimensions to use in assessing the 44 interventions. A total of 13 dimensions that can be used to describe school-directed programming were considered. However, to keep the survey a doable length, they decided to limit the rating dimensions to the five they felt would be the most "robust". By robust they mean the dimensions that lead to the most homogeneous taxa possible. Their selection of the five was done conceptually and was guided by Saylor and Alexander's influential text on curriculum planning. In particular, they were influenced by their six level model of factors that influence "the actual experiences provided pupils by the school". They rated as most robust those variables that occurred on the factor level that Saylor and Alexander held was most closely linked to actual student experiences. These five dimensions were

(a) duration of the intervention [Time],

(b) pedagogical style [Mode],

(c) location of intervention [Place],

(d) size of the intervention group [Size], and

(e) control of the intervention's application [Control].

Our next step was to create a survey that asks career guidance professionals to assess the 44 interventions across the 5 dimensions. They sent this survey to a random sample of the membership of the Guidance Division of the Association for Career and Technical Education. The survey required participants to select the binomial descriptor that "best" represented an intervention. Brief definitions were provided for each descriptor. Specifically, for the Time dimension, the participant could circle S for Short (1 hour to 2 weeks) or L for Long (greater then two weeks). For the Mode dimension, the participant could circle P for Passive (listening, reading, viewing) or A for Active (hands on).

For the Place dimension, the participant could circle S for School Based (on campus) or C for Community Based (off campus). For the Size dimension, the participant could circle G for Group (small group and above) or I for Individual (a student). Finally, for the Control dimension, the participant could circle Y for Youth Directed (control over time/scope/location) or A for Adult Directed (control over time/scope/location). In total, each participant made 220 ratings. The final step was to submit these ratings to a statistical procedure called cluster analysis. Cluster analysis is a multivariate statistical technique used to determine naturally occurring groupings or categories.

At its most basic level, cluster analysis is the application of a set of rules (i.e., algorithm) for the dividing up a proximity matrix in order to form groups of similar objects. In this definition, the term "proximity matrix" refers to a matrix of similarities or dissimilarities between objects. Cluster analysis is commonly used to create taxonomies in a wide variety of fields. Application of cluster analysis to career development interventions in secondary schools produced a four-taxon solution.

Taxon 1: *Work Based Interventions*: "The class of interventions designed to promote student self-efficacy and motivation through sustained and meaningful interactions with work sites in the community." Historically, this class of interventions has been limited to Career and Technical Education students. However, one of the benefits of the School-to-Career movement in American education is that this class of interventions is beginning to be opened up to all students.

Taxon 2: *Advising Interventions*: "The class of interventions designed to provide direction, resolve impediments, and sustain planfulness in students about their goals for the future." Eminent career development theorist Donald Super felt that planfulness was a core element to successful career development in adolescence. This taxon was the only one of the school-based taxa described as delivered on an individual basis.

Taxon 3: *Introductory Interventions*: "The class of interventions designed to awaken a student's interest in their own personal and professional growth." This taxon was similar to the fourth taxon with one exception. The modal Time variable descriptor for this taxon was "Strong Short" and the modal Time descriptor for the fourth taxon was "Strong Long." This difference emphasizes the introductory and preparatory nature of this class of interventions.

Taxon 4: *Curriculum Based Interventions*: "The class of interventions designed to promote core student knowledge and skills through means and content relevant to the world of work." As noted in the previous section, the distinguishing characteristic of this taxon of interventions versus the other school-based taxa is its long-term nature. The interventions contained in this taxon represent the school-based complements to the interventions that are part of the Work Based Interventions taxon.

IMPORTANT FUTURE DIRECTIONS FOR CAREER DEVELOPMENT

Career development in Canada is undergoing exciting changes.

Many good initiatives have been sponsored by provincial and federal government departments. With CAMCRY Stay In School, Youth Services Canada, and Youth Internships, substantial financial resources have been invested. Excellent programs have been developed. Many well-trained professionals are now working in the area of career development. Equally important, many others now see the need for career development and are actively supporting it. Career development is moving into the mainstream and gaining a greater profile within professional circles.

The need for career development is enormous. High unemployment is a global problem and Canada's figures fall within the mid-range. There is agreement that the "old way" of "one job for life" is no longer a reality for most people. It is possible that, in the future, there will not be enough paid employment for all. Therefore, there is a need to build on, and extend what we have accomplished, in order to meet the challenges of the future. It is dangerous and inappropriate to "crystal ball gaze," but it is possible to suggest some issues that will need to be addressed, and outline some of what is—or will need to be, on the horizon, in order for career development to remain a vital force.

1 *The meaning of "career success" needs to be reconceptualized.*

Baby boomers, the largest demographic group in Canada, have been taught to believe that a stable career is good—if people work hard, and earn a good education, they will be assured of work, will be able to choose any job, and may remain in that job as long as they want. Success is defined in terms of "upward" mobility—mobility through, or upward into another organization.

Now the rules have changed. Companies are downsizing. There is massive unemployment and a surplus of qualified workers in many areas. Quota systems in most universities prevent many youth from getting into the program of their choice. Those who do get the program they want may find there are no jobs available in that area when they graduate. There is a dramatic increase in part-time jobs, contract work, and "portfolio people."

The meaning of "career success" needs to be revised so that people are able to view themselves as successful, despite changing circumstances. People are not necessarily failures if they "only find part time work" or if they change jobs every 2-3 years. While it is true that some people lack the skills to maintain permanent work, it is also true that others are forced to change jobs by system factors beyond their control. Therefore, it is important to develop a mind set that does not automatically assume that there is something wrong with people who change jobs frequently. Moreover, it will be important to legitimize the satisfaction and feeling of success which people derive from unpaid work. The current bias towards occupations requiring a university education automatically excludes 80% of the population from entering "high status" jobs. More value must be placed on technical occupations, apprenticeships, trades, and other skilled work. Such alternatives may then be seen as legitimate "first choice" options for workers.

2. *People need expanded skills sets to succeed in the work place.*

Expanded skills sets are described in several sources. The Conference Board of Canada underscores higher order thinking, personal management, and team working skills. Borgen and Amundson outline a youth empowerment model that facilitates successful transitions. In addition, it is important that people learn how to be self-motivated, how to recognize opportunity in changing circumstances, how to find ways to promote satisfaction in their current jobs (focusing on the positive), and how to manage their self-talk so that it coaches facilitative behavior, productive thinking, and motivating affect. It is also be necessary to develop skills in marketing oneself, to enhance skills and attitudes that promote being flexible, and to foster skills for determining one's generic transferable skills.

3. *The needs of workers in transition must be recognized.*

Many people are in life roles in which they feel trapped. Such people as these who are between jobs, women returning to work, workers changing to more satisfying jobs, and workers wanting to renew their enthusiasm for their current jobs. Programs and methods need to be developed to assist these people in making transitions to more meaningful situations.

4. *The needs of older workers in retirement must be recognized.*

With increasing numbers of people nearing retirement age, and with firms offering early retirement incentives, it will be important to change the concept of retirement from a transition to "doing nothing" to a planned change in focus." This may involve a gradual reduction of job hours while a worker explores other sources of satisfaction. It may also require formal career planning for the post-retirement career/life options. Most people who enjoy retirement find that they are busy pursuing non-paid work as sources of satisfaction (the term "volunteer work" is not a coincidence!).

5. *The scope and practice of career development needs to expand.*

The term "career/life" development acknowledges that career issues cannot be separated from other life issues. The domains of career counseling, career guidance, and career education need to be updated. Following are some point:

— Career education will take place mostly in school classrooms, with a focus on developing knowledge, skills, and attitudes generic to most career/life transition situations. Increasingly, the focus is on an infusion model where career education becomes a component of several school subjects, English (e.g., resume' writing), and science (e.g., being aware of career possibilities in chemistry), and so forth.

— Career guidance (people often need a guide) will take

place largely in small workshops and have a skill-training focus. Most European countries call this "careers guidance." In Canada, it's sometimes called "counseling," "workshops,' or simply "group work." In some cases, guidance may be individualized, but the focus will be either on skill training, or marketing, or placement.

— Career counseling may involve individuals or groups, but the agenda will include complicated skill sets or long-standing problems, such as contextual situations or client barriers.

6. *Alternative delivery systems need to be developed.*

A revised delivery system will make career guidance/counseling accessible to all, across the life span. This may involve the promotion of a "Career Development Culture." Just as "Participaction" increased the awareness of the importance of physical fitness for health, promoting a "Career Development Culture" will help people take charge of their career/life paths. There may be a need for periodic "career check-ups," where workers at all levels and in all jobs take stock of their career direction and map out their future career/life plans. Part of a new delivery system may include the three-component model of self-help, group work (guidance), and individual work (guidance or counseling), which is summarized by Kellett and Conger.

7. *The scope of practice of those working in career development will need to be expanded.*

Counselors need to break out of the traditional mold which emphasizes individual client interactions. Many client problems are more amenable to group intervention. Working with third parties (families, employers, other agencies) is increasingly important in helping clients achieve their goals. Practitioners need to become adept at marketing their programs, and the results of their interventions, to the public, and to their clients, supervisors, managers, and co-workers. Social action also has a legitimate role for career development practitioners, such as wheel chair access in public buildings for handicapped clients.

8. *There is a need for standards of training and service delivery.*

Currently there is no accepted training standard for those working in career development and no guidelines for quality assurance in service delivery. A multilevel set of standards should be developed to assure clients that service providers (classroom teachers, school counselors, agency counselors, contract trainers, and so forth) have appropriate training to deliver services. Commensurate with this, guidelines are needed to guarantee that adequate services are offered in career development. This will ensure that quality control procedures are in place to monitor and evaluate the outcomes from each respective group.

9. *Evaluation approaches need to be modified and more readily accepted.*

The scope and context of evaluation needs to be expanded to include ways of tabulating the things that counselors do to keep clients motivated, gauge client progress, and teach clients how to be more aware of their successes. Increasing accountability concerns will make it important to develop non-intrusive ways to use naturally occurring events as evidence of client success. Currently, the profession is not good at this because people have applied little collective creativity towards developing valuation procedures. As devote more energy to evaluation new methods will begin to emerge.

8

Guiding Students with Special Needs

For a number of years, studies have reported that people with disabilities have lower work force participation rates than the general public. Since work is highly valued in our society, scholars have been interested in determining why this is so. They have suggested that one factor is a lack of transitional, vocational programs for young people with disabilities and experts have recommended creating programs based on the unique characteristics and needs of the target population. "Thresholds" is one such program, developed to meet the transitional and vocational needs of young people with physical disabilities.

Before leaving high school and entering the world of work or other post-secondary settings, young people with physical disabilities must master a number of career developmental tasks in relation to their disabilities. Practitioners and researchers have suggested that many aspects of Super's "life-career rainbow" are applicable to young people with disabilities. Super has combined situational and personal determinants with life-roles and life-stages to explain career development across the life-span. During the school-to-work transition, most young people have entered Super's exploration stage, which fosters the exploration of personal characteristics and career opportunities.

As career opportunities and realities are clarified, young people make tentative career selections, test them through fantasy, discussions, and/or work experiences, and consider them as possible life-roles.

Many potential barriers exist for young people with disabilities. For example, these young people may not obtain the same amount or variety of pre-vocational work experiences; they may lack training in basic skills such as job search, job maintenance, mobility/transportation, and self-advocacy skills; schools and other career counseling agencies may lack specialized personnel; society may have lower performance expectations for them. Unless vocational programs incorporate activities that examine the concept of disability, and the accompanying barriers, they will not prepare people with disabilities to enter and succeed in the work world.

THRESHOLDS

"Thresholds" is designed to enhance career development for young people with physical disabilities. Physical disability is defined as a restriction to perform communication, personal care, locomotor and/or bodily activities in a manner or within the range considered normal for a person. The severity of the restriction produces observable performance difficulties, which may be augmented by aids, appliances, and/or another person. "Thresholds" is intended for qualified facilitators working with 15-18-year-old adolescents with physical disabilities, who have just begun exploring who they are and how they fit into the world of work. This program provides an initial step to career exploration—is not a job search.

"Thresholds" has three parts: In Part A, participants reflect on their interests, capabilities, and values, and then practice communicating these personal characteristics to others. In addition, they examine ways in which people with disabilities have successfully bridged the gap between school and career. In Part B, young people explore the world of work. They formulate questions to investigate specific careers, determine if these careers meet their personal needs and directions, test their questions in a mock interview, refine them, and try them out in a formal interview. In Part C, participants examine barriers to career success. They identify their own barriers and contemplate strategies to overcome them. They also consider ways in which other people with disabilities have confronted career barriers. Finally, they revise their personal plans for addressing barriers and formalize action plans to achieve their career goals.

"Thresholds" includes 12 sessions of 80 minutes each and consists of group and individual activities. The facilitator, who may be a teacher, career counselor, occupational therapist, or social worker, leads the participants through the activities. The program is detailed in a facilitator's guide and a participant's handbook (grade 7 reading level).

Facilitator Characteristics

In order to implement "Thresholds" successfully, facilitators require a number of attributes. Consider the following points:

— People with disabilities often face barriers that negatively affect their self-concept, self-esteem, and self-efficacy. Recognizing the true potential of persons with disabilities and appreciating the possible effects of frequent, negative experiences can help to minimize the impact.

— Counselor attitudes can influence their clients. Examining personal and professional attitudes towards disability and persons with disabilities could benefit facilitators.

— Over the last 2-3 decades, persons with disabilities have challenged society's perceptions of them. The challenges have encouraged members of society to change their attitudes and expectations. Facilitators should be aware of this history and be sensitive to the need for further social action.

— Participation of people with disabilities in the labor force is low. Therefore, knowledge both of the realities of the world of work and the factors that influence young people with physical disabilities is important.

"Thresholds" was based on a needs assessment and was field tested in two urban settings. In the first field test, a social worker and a vocational counselor guided three males and five females (ages 14-18) through the program. In the second test, two career counselors worked with 10 males (ages 15-18). Pretest-posttest differences in the first setting showed a significant improvement in vocational decision-making abilities. In the second setting, significant improvements in vocational decision-making abilities and self-appraisal skills were also observed. Participants in the first test had a poor understanding of career decision-making strategies, but a good understanding of who they were, prior to entering the program. In the second setting, participants had limited understandings in both areas. Therefore, the initial characteristics of the participants seemed critical in determining whether or not notable improvement would occur.

SEX EQUITY IN GUIDANCE AND COUNSELING

Societal changes over the past 15 years have brought a new awareness of the need to expand opportunities for women and minorities. Sex equity received a big boost with the passage of the Education Amendments of 1972 and the Women's Educational Equity Act. Several legislative and private initiatives gave impetus to the creation of hundreds of programs in schools, colleges, and communities to reduce bias and expand options for girls and women. These have been complemented in recent years by a few programs which address new options for boys and men.

There seems to be agreement that counselors should play a major role in helping to remove barriers and create options for both sexes and that nonsexist counseling is essential for optimal growth of students. Yet, it is clearly not the role of counselors alone. Indeed, all types of personnel have collaborated or worked independently to achieve sex equity. Project BORN FREE (Build Options, Reassess Norm, Free Roles through Educational Equity), a multimedia training program for counselors and educators working with children, youth, and adults, was one of the first to link career development, sex-role stereotyping, and social change and to emphasize changes in roles of both women and men. While interest grew in sex-equity throughout the 70's, by the 80's, a call for new school reform totally ignored sex equity issues, and from 1980 on, emphasis on sex equity in education began to diminish. While much progress had been made, the problem was far from resolved.

There is no doubt that new options have opened up for women and that the equity gap has begun to close in secondary school subjects, in higher education access, and in the workforce. Nonetheless, problems remain, especially for girls and women who are minorities, poor, disabled, and outside the opportunity structure. Counselors and educators are in a position to provide clients and students with realistic information concerning future life role options and to help them with adequate preparation for these future roles. In doing so, it is essential that counselors and educators possess accurate information on important societal trends. Recent data indicate that:

— Women today comprise 44% of the labor force;

— The average woman can be expected to work about 30 years of her life;

— In 1986, of the married couples with families, over half were dual earner couples;

— Most single parent families are maintained by women.

— In the year 2000, 80% of new entrants into the workforce will be women, minorities, and immigrants.

While the interventions of the past 15 years doubtless have had an impact on sex equity (and program evaluations and statistics attest to this), there is abundant evidence that the impact of socialization on sex-role attitude is deepseated, and a huge gap still remains between attitudes and reality. For example, according to recent studies, the expectations of adolescents and young adults concerning their future life roles are in sharp contrast with the statistics on current societal realities. When Herzog and Bachman investigated the sex-role attitudes of 3,000 high school seniors, they found relatively traditional attitudes toward family roles. Both males and females were opposed to women with small children working outside the home. They also expected a traditional division of labor, with women primarily responsible for the children and men bearing financial responsibility for the family.

Similar findings are reported in an extensive study of 14-18 year old Minnesota high school students regarding their plans for future educational, work, and family roles. These studies, and numerous others, have shown that young people's career choices still reflect stereotypical views of what is appropriate for their gender, although they may know a wide range of choices is open to them. Discrepancies between adolescent expectations and realities would suggest that, as educators and counselors, we need to continue to prepare students and clients for a rapidly changing society and to aid them in developing their values, skills, interests, and life choices apart from sex role stereotypes.

Sex-Equity and Counselor Attitudes

In working with clients and students to prepare for and to make choices about life roles, it is essential for counselors and educators to be aware of their own biases and stereotypes and how these attitudes may influence their work. Broverman, Broverman, Clarkson, Rosenkrantz, & Vogel investigated the extent to which counselors and other mental health workers held stereotypic sex-role attitudes. The results of this, now classic, study reflect stereotypic views of men and women and equate the characteristics of a mentally healthy adult with those of a healthy male, implying very different standards of mental health for women and men.

The attention given to counselors' sex-role attitudes in the past two decades raises questions about what impact this has had on present counselor attitudes. Using methodology similar to Broverman et al., O'Malley and Richardson found, in contrast, that the subjects perceived healthy adults as possessing characteristics stereotypically associated with both men and women. However, similar to Broverman et al., counselors continued to respond in a stereotypic manner when asked to predict characteristics of an adult man or woman. In spite of mixed results, it appears that some counselors and educators continue to have stereotypic expectations of female and male clients and students.

The combination of societal changes and continuing, though more limited, interventions has made it necessary for counselors and educators to begin to rethink the current status of sex equity and their role in it. The new face of sex equity issues includes the following:

- Recognition that sex role and stereotyping issues affect men as well as women.
- Emergence of diverse family types, including two-earner families, single parents, and blended families.
- Growing recognition of the linkage between work and family and implications for life career planning and division of labor.
- Movement toward holistic life planning which emphasizes balance in life roles and a more integrated approach to life planning.
- Recognition of the need to challenge continuing examples of attitudes and behaviors which devalue girls and women.

Counselors as change Agents

Counselors and educators committed to the development of human beings and the utilization of human potential, as well as to democratic values, can, if they are willing, assume a much more proactive role in effecting positive change. The following recommendations suggest ways in which counselors and educators can be change agents for sex equity:

— Examine their own attitudes and practices to assure that they have eliminated the subtle as well as blatant attitudes and stereotypes regarding both sexes.

— Assure that new knowledge about the changing roles of women and men, work/family intersection, stereotyping and socialization, and gender equity are a visible part of curriculum and programs.

— Advocate for public policy changes that bring policies more into consonance with the changing realities of women and men in work and family.

— Influence career guidance programs to include more about life roles, purpose and meaning in life choices, and integrative life planning—not just occupational choice and the paid work role.

— Teach students, teachers, and prospective teachers that they can be positive agents for change in developing more egalitarian relationships between women and men.

ADULT CAREER COUNSELING

Adult career counselors have traditionally dealt with the concerns of re-entry women or employed men and women who are questioning the direction of their current occupation and looking for possible career alternatives. However, other groups of people now appear frequently in the adult career counselor's office: older adults who are looking for post-retirement careers; displaced workers, both white and blue collar, whose jobs have been eliminated through such events as plant closings, farm foreclosures, and business mergers or failures; and dual-career couples whose needs are more complex than those of an individual doing career exploration. However, other groups of people now appear frequently in the adult career counselor's office: older adults who are looking for post-retirement careers; displaced workers both white and blue collar, whose jobs have been eliminated through such events as plant closings, farm foreclosures, and business mergers or failures; and dual-career couples whose needs are more complex than those of an individual doing career exploration.

Another trend is the movement of career planning into the corporate setting as businesses and other organizations begin to offer counseling and career planning at the work site. Since keeping abreast of changes in occupational trends and labor market projections is an important component of a career counseling program another important development is the use of computers, which provide both interactive guidance programs and up-to-date occupational information. All of these trends necessitate expansion of the adult career counselor's skills, knowledge base, and roles.

Adults who require retirement counseling are often seeking full- or part-time careers. Those who wish to find part-time work are usually trying to make ends meet or hoping to fulfill personal needs such as the desire to contribute to society or the need for affiliation. Goals of retirement education may include:

1. a positive attitude toward retirement and potential for continued success and growth,
2. a personal plan for retirement,
3. planning, decision-making, and interpersonal communication skills,
4. a deeper awareness of having control over one's own future.

Retirement planning has traditionally focused on financial planning. Many newer programs also include the interpersonal or lifestyle aspects of adjusting to retirement. Retirement specialists must add to their counseling repertoire an understanding of career development for the increasing numbers of older clients who wish another career; and they must add an understanding of the aging process as well as of key retirement issues.

Large numbers of displaced workers are facing decisions about new careers and confronting a job search for the first time in their lives. Many of these people moved into their previous work without much conscious thought, and find themselves ill equipped to plan and develop new work lives. In addition, family resistance to change may further disrupt a worker's ability to take action on his/her own behalf. Counselors need to target their strategies to the different psychological stages experienced by most displaced workers. According to Greenwood, "Stage three, when the dislocated worker is actively seeking a job, is the true 'in-transition' time and emotional support is critical. If jobs are not found quickly, apathy, frustration, disillusionment and deep depression are likely to set in."

Amundson & Borgen focus on the intervention strategies appropriate for the three stages of the unemployment cycle. Loss and search interventions can include:

(a) understanding clients' feelings and challenging them to view their job loss from different perspectives,

(b) assisting in the resolution of conflicts related to the loss,

(c) developing a realistic view of skills and strengths,

(d) evaluating with clients their options and job search approaches,

(e) continuing to support clients,

(f) developing specific action plans, and

(g) practicing necessary skills for implementing the plans.

Burnout strategies should include validating client feelings, building self concept, and identifying new approaches to the job search.

Dual-career Couples

Increasingly career counselors are being sought by dual-career couples who have complex career planning issues because of their interdependence. In the past career planning has been viewed as an individual activity, but for both men and women in dual-career relationships career decisions cannot be made without taking into consideration the connection between work and family roles. Consequently, both spouses must be involved in the career counseling process to deal with the issues of balancing roles and demands, juggling responsibilities, and the careful planning of career transitions.

The adult career counselor must be aware of the career, gender role, and marriage-family dilemmas of couples in career transitions who are experiencing the stress and conflict which accompany disequilibrium. The career counselor who works with dual-career couples must understand the developmental stage of:

(a) each career in the family,

(b) the "couple" relationship, and

(c) the family.

In the past, career counseling programs for adults have been delivered in academic institutions, community agencies, and private offices. The workplace is now emerging as an additional setting for these services. Profit and non-profit sectors realize the benefit of conserving both human and financial assets and of saving recruitment, training, and outplacement costs. Career assistance is being provided not only for people these organizations plan to terminate, but also for those they want to keep, e.g., valuable employees who are dissatisfied or people whose productivity has slipped for a variety of reasons but whom the organization wants to keep.

Providing career counseling in the workplace also allows individual employees to improve their job classification and become aware of career path opportunities within the organization. Additionally, it aids an employer in improving employee relations and productivity. The better placed an employee is, the greater his or her satisfaction. Career development assistance is being provided by outside career counselor consultants hired by an organization, career development specialists who are members of an organization's human resources team, or managers within the organization who have been trained in career pathing and monitoring. Zunker proposes that these programs should include:

1. experience, skills and interest identification,
2. values and needs clarification,
3. education/training, occupational and life planning.

As in other trend areas, providing career development programs at the work site demands additional skills of the counselor—particularly expertise borrowed from human resource management and training and development. The career development specialist in the workplace must also possess knowledge and skills in the following areas:

1. adult learning and development,
2. training program design,
3. group facilitation,
4. consulting skills.

The major concern of counselors providing services in academic or community settings is with the needs and goals of the individual. The counselor providing these same services in the work site must often take into consideration the needs of the organization as well. This may require redefinition of the counselor's role and increased emphasis on counselor ethics.

CAREER EDUCATION COUNSELING FOR MIGRANT STUDENTS.

The high mobility and concurrently high dropout rate among migrant students have attracted a great deal of attention, and a number of programs have been developed to make the educational process more compatible with lifestyles of migrant students. However, unless students participate in such programs, they have little meaning. Although special consideration must be given to the factors of high mobility and dropout rate that characterize the migrant student population, career education itself is essentially the same for all students. The guiding principle for all should be to prepare students for life in the working world. To this end, career education counseling incorporates three major elements: career exposure, work preparation, and basic skill development.

Career exposure seeks to promote self-awareness, to provide job and role information, and to teach decision-making and goal attaining skills. Self-awareness activities consider the values, talents, and desires of the student and include close self-examination of the student's own physical, emotional, and mental being. The most effective career decisions will be based on knowledge of special talents and limitations. All youth should understand that each person is an individual with unique abilities and unique opportunities to share them. Self-awareness can be encouraged not only in specific self-awareness sessions in a formal career education program but also in learning experiences in all areas of school life.

Information on jobs and roles is an important part of career development. It may include the skills and tasks, tools and equipment, training and formal education, and placement and advancement opportunities for various occupations. Job and role awareness ensures that students will make occupational choices based on true and complete rather than false or inadequate information. Decision-making and goal-attaining activities provide a structure for reaching goals by making decisions and following through with sequential activities which ultimately lead to goal attainment. Thus, students are guided through processes in which they formulate their goals in tangible terms; investigate available resources; consider all options and probable outcomes; make a decision; plan, act or review their progress; and ultimately reach their goals.

For the most part, migrant youth know one type of work—migrant agricultural labor. They must be made aware that there are other options. Therefore, all students should be provided not only with written information but also with direct experience in a variety of occupations through interview, shadowing, and work experience programs. The student prepares for the interview by first reading about an occupation and then talking to professionals in that occupation. Shadowing provides the student with the opportunity to follow a professional in his or her work activities for several days. The work experience component allows the student to spend a number of weeks or months working alongside a professional. The student is paid for the time involved and the work performed. Thus, the student can participate in a new work experience while building basic skills and discussing career issues with a counselor or teacher. Such a setting also provides practice in employment interviewing, resume writing, and other work preparation activities.

For youth who have left school prior to graduation, as do many migrant students, career education counseling must be accompanied by programs which provide training in basic literacy, English as a second language (when needed), and content area studies. Following is a brief description of some existing programs.

1. Adult Basic Education (ABE) is for those who have left school and need basic literacy, second-language training, and/or basic mathematical skills.

2. General Equivalency Diploma (GED) programs are for those who have the basic skills but lack a high school diploma.

3. Giving Rural Adults a Study Program (GRASP) is a method by which adults who cannot participate in a traditional daytime schedule of studies may still be able to participate in an ABE or GED program. GRASP programs may use the rural library or the post office system to deliver units of study which the student completes at home. Friends or neighbors may be used as tutors.

4. Portable Assisted Study Sequence (PASS) programs began in California as an option for the migrant student who did not wish to leave school but who encountered severe difficulties in completing the course credits due to frequent moves. PASS provides units which may be completed independently or with the help of a tutor. Upon completion of a given course of study, high school credit is issued by the PASS sponsoring school.

Programs which promote self-awareness, provide job and role information, and encourage the development of decision-making skills beginning as early as kindergarten prove beneficial. As the students progress through high school, interviewing, shadowing, and work experience programs can be added. Often these activities serve to demonstrate the usefulness of remaining in high school to prepare for productive roles in the world of work.

Because of continuing mobility, migrant youth often do not participate in such community activities as scouting, church, and city-sponsored youth groups. Therefore, the advantages provided by such groups should be included in a migrant career education counseling program. Also, both ABE and GED programs must be made available in a non-traditional and creative manner to accommodate the transient lifestyle of migrant youth. Career education must be approached through short units which can be completed in limited periods of time. The alternative programs described above and others have been developed to mediate the effect of the high dropout rate among migrant, as well as other, students.

Those tutors or teachers who are most often in contact with the migrant in-school youth must be prepared to support such students with career information and guidance, preferably incorporated into language arts and content area studies. The teacher, tutor, and/or student can benefit form the support of a trained career education counselor, who should be responsible for reviewing currently available programs and training the tutor and teacher to work with the student. Counseling of secondary school students and those no longer in school is also an important part of the counselor's role. Community professionals and workers can help by speaking to groups of students. They can also bring reality to career education by participating directly in interviewing, shadowing, and work experience projects. This community support has the side effect of promoting greater community understanding of the unique qualities and attributes of migrant youth and families.

CAREER COUNSELING OF GIRLS AND WOMEN

The need for quality standards for the delivery of career counseling services, and for the articulation of competencies required for practitioners delivering these services, is gaining increasing attention in Canada and elsewhere. Work has focused on generic standards and competencies and guidelines pertaining to specific populations. One important contribution to these efforts in Canada is the guidelines for career counseling of girls and women developed by the Collaborative Action Working Group on Counselling. The guidelines which follow were based on the guidelines, policies, and standards in the professional literature and those provided by governments and counseling associations. The guidelines were a key component in a strategy to promote labour market equality that was endorsed by Ministers Responsible for the Status of Women and Ministers with Labour Market Responsibilities in all provinces.

Career counseling is understood to include services and programs designed to facilitate individuals' development and their ability to make optimal choices regarding their roles in occupational, familial and social structures. Responsible professional practice requires counselors to be knowledgeable about the effects of gender in human development and to apply such knowledge in career counseling with girls and women. In order to ensure responsible professional practice, jurisdictions must require all individuals involved in career counseling with girls and women to adhere to the following guidelines:

1. Counselors are aware of the assumptions underlying various theoretical approaches to the practice of career counseling and recognize that such theories may apply differently to women and men. Counselors continue to examine theoretical bases and assumptions underlying their practice to ensure that they utilize theories and models which are free of sex bias and sex role stereotypes and promote the realization of full potential by girls and women.

2. Counselors ascribe no preconceived limitations on the direction or nature of potential changes or goals in counseling with women. In particular, counselors ensure that career choice is an open process and that no individual is limited by gender-or by race, age, disability, ethnicity, sexual orientation, or religion-from the exploration of any career option.

3. Recognizing that the use of male terms as gender-neutral reflects bias against women, counselors use inclusive and gender-fair language in all oral and written communication and ensure that resources used to assist clients with decision-making are gender-fair. As an extension of this principle, counselors also avoid the use of generic adjectives to describe women with handicaps (e.g., blind, deaf, and so forth) in order to avoid excessive focus on the disability; descriptive phrases (e.g., women with visual handicaps) are used as a much-preferred alternative to the more generic adjectives.

4. Counselors are knowledgeable about support services available to women (e.g., child care, legal aid, health care,

transportation, emergency services) and assist clients in accessing community resources which are suited to their needs. Where significant gaps are identified in support services available to women, counselors may initiate or act as catalysts for the development of such support systems in their communities.

5. Counselors continue throughout their professional careers to gain knowledge and awareness of social, biological and psychological influences on female development in general and their career development in particular. As part of their ongoing professional development, counselors continue to inform themselves about specific issues which may have an impact on the career decision-making of girls/women (e.g., balancing vocational and family roles, issues related to training and employment of women in non-traditional occupations, family violence, sexual harassment and sexual assault), as well as acquiring knowledge which is relevant to counseling particular sub-groups, such as women with disabilities, women who are culturally different, long-term welfare recipients, and female offenders.

6. Counselors understand that the source of client difficulties often rests not only in the woman herself but also in situational or cultural factors which limit her concept of self, her aspirations and the opportunities available to her. Counselors recognize and are sensitive to the impact of stereotyping, prejudice and discrimination on the basis of gender—as well as race, age, disability, ethnicity, sexual orientation and religion—and work to counteract the negative effects of such attitudes and actions.

7. Counselors are aware of and continually review their own values and biases and the effects of these on their female clients. Counselors assess and monitor their own activities to ensure gender-fair practices, as well as participate in professional development programs, consultation and/or supervision to assist in identifying and working through personal biases and issues which have a limiting effect on their work with female clients.

8. Counselors support the elimination of sex bias within institutions and individuals, by promoting fair and equal treatment of all individuals through services, programs, theories, practices and treatment of colleagues and clients which recognize the full potential of each.
9. Recognizing that there are circumstances where clients will have a preference for a same- or opposite-sex counselor, whenever possible, clients will be given the opportunity to choose the counselor with whom they will work.

The Working Group felt a need to go beyond suggestions for counselors to include guidelines for jurisdictions employing counselors. Factors like access to training, supervision, and tools to assist delivering appropriate services for girls and women were seen as essential components in a strategy to promote labour market equality. The following specific measures to be taken by federal and provincial jurisdictions were included in the report:

1. The jurisdiction is committed to providing or accessing the training and/or professional development that supervisors and counselors require to enable them to apply these principles effectively.
2. Each jurisdiction ensures that sex-fair language and balanced depictions of women appear in all publications and resource materials.
3. Counselors will be given an opportunity for supervision/consultation to occur on a regular basis to assist them in working through conflicts and issues which arise for them in their work with clients.
4. A process will be put in place to monitor the implementation/application of the guidelines.

The following recommendation was later endorsed by provincial Ministers:

— It is recommended that each jurisdiction develop a policy and guidelines for the provision of career counseling to girls and women which reflect the principles and guidelines developed by the Collaborative Action Working Group on Counseling.

— It was hoped that the guidelines would be reviewed by professional associations of counselors and adopted, or adapted to their particular contexts. The Feminist Network of the Canadian Guidance and Counselling Association is intending to take leadership in this initiative.

CAREER COUNSELING FOR ABORIGINAL YOUTH

Education philosophies originate within specific socio-cultural contexts, which are characterized by unique problems and issues. Historically, Canadian Aboriginal peoples have been denied the opportunity to develop need-based, culturally relevant programs. Instead, government has used education systems to undermine Canadian Aboriginals' tribal organization, their forms of leadership, their spiritual beliefs, their health system, and their economic system. The result is a legacy of poverty and deprivation.

In hoping for a brighter future of self-government and self-determination, Aboriginal communities have placed great hopes and expectations on their youth: "From our children will come those braves, who will carry the torches to the places where our ancestors rest...This is how the void will be filled between the old and the new ways". This vision is becoming a reality. In search of their identity, many Aboriginal youths are reclaiming their culture - not as an attempt to return to the past, but as a resolve to participate in society as equals, and on their own terms. The complexity and uniqueness of career-related issues pose a formidable challenge in the development of career-counseling programs for Aboriginal youth. Program planners must recognize that most of the answers and solutions for a successful program rest within Aboriginal communities. In keeping with this community-based view, "Career Counselling for Aboriginal Youth: The Journey Inward; The Journey Outward" was developed.

Planning should involve all program stakeholders and should also acknowledge that many unknown cross-cultural variables need to be incorporated into the planning process. Thus, program development should be participatory and open to change as the various planning components evolve. The aim of the planning model should be to facilitate self-determination and social change by espousing mutual respect and sharing as key components of the planning process. Planning and decision-making responsibilities should be shared and control should be negotiated on an on-going basis by program development team members.

To meet the needs of Aboriginal youth, as well as the aspirations of their home communities, the following key components should be considered by program planners:

— The program development team should include representation from the agency or community requesting the program, the institution which will offer the program, and resource people with career counseling expertise. In order to focus on the program's outcome vision, invite an Aboriginal Elder to guide the program planning team.

— Negotiate the terms of reference for team member participation and/or leadership in all planning activities—possibly two or more subgroups working on various planning components simultaneously, based on their areas of expertise and/or interest. The planning team should utilize consensus decision making on an on-going basis as the various planning components are integrated and finalized.

— Establish a community advisory team to be involved in all planning activities.

— Conduct a comprehensive literature review of all topics relevant to career counseling and Aboriginal youth. Include a review of previous and existing programs which successfully integrated cultural imperatives.

— Select the agencies, communities and/or groups for data collection and identify the specific members to be surveyed, e.g., youths, parents, teachers, leaders, Elders, counselors. Note that each Aboriginal community is quite distinct in terms of size, geographical location, proximity to a large center (versus isolation), accessibility (by road versus aircraft), history, cultural practices (versus adaptation of mainstream society's practices), and so forth. Ensure that the sample is representative of the youth who will participate in the program.

— Plan, develop, and field test research instruments. In some cases, focus groups, community meetings, or one-on-one interviews may be more appropriate and useful than surveys and/or questionnaires.

— Collect field test data. Ensure that researchers are familiar with the language and protocol of each community and solicit the support of local leadership before beginning the research. Ideally, the researcher should be a member of the planning team and should spend 5-7 days in each community. A journal of relevant experiences and/or observations is a useful supplement to formal survey findings.

— Analyze the findings and consider how they relate to the literature review. Present a summary to the community advisory team and discuss the implications of the findings on the design of the career-counseling program.

— Based on the research summary and the input from the community advisory team, develop manuals for the program facilitators and participants.

— Conduct and evaluate a pilot program and make appropriate revisions.

The above process was utilized to develop "Career Counselling for Aboriginal Youth: The Journey Inward; The Journey Outward" to prepare counselors to work with Aboriginal youth. The key program content came from surveys and focus groups conducted with the youth themselves. They shared fear of failure in the mainstream educational system, unresolved hurts from family violence and/or family break-up, inability to survive the prejudice and discrimination in the "outside world," and, most of all, confusion about their culture and identity.

In order to address these issues, the program is based on the traditional concept of a vision quest, and focuses on

(a) enhancing self-esteem,

(b) healing past hurts, and

(c) modeling Aboriginal values by integrating Aboriginal imperatives and rituals into the program content and delivery process.

The training consists of two 1-week modules: In Week One, "The Journey Inward," counselors enhance their understanding of Aboriginal adolescent difficulties and barriers by exploring their own adolescent experiences and assessing how these factors affect their clients' career development. In Week Two, "The Journey Outward," the counselors integrate the knowledge gained in Week One into a holistic counseling model which

(a) incorporates appropriate cultural imperatives and practices,

(b) utilizes community-based resources, and

(c) reflects the socio-economic realities and aspirations of the First Nations' communities.

The "Facilitator's Manual" provides a step-by-step guide, detailing the background information, the philosophy of the program, and daily activities. The "Participant's Manual" provides the program outline and relevant resource materials.

STUDENTS WITH LEARNING DISABILITIES

Students with learning disabilities (LD) or attention deficit hyperactivity disorder (ADHD) approach the transition from high school to college with an array of learning strengths and needs.

They need to understand their own abilities and guide their own transition planning by looking at various postsecondary options. If college is the path chosen, investigating postsecondary programs to find the right match is a crucial step. In general, postsecondary support services are less intensive than secondary special education services. Students need to become experts on how to engineer their academic success, a process that requires experiences that build self-insight, self-advocacy, and resourcefulness.

The Individuals with Disabilities Education Act (IDEA) requires that the Individualized Education Program (IEP) team consider post-school goals when the student is about to enter high school at about age 14. Beginning at age 16 (or younger, if appropriate) a statement of transition services needed by the student must be included in the IEP. High school experiences, both academic and social, greatly influence future options for all students. For adolescents with disabilities, these experiences are pivotal. Transition plans should be grounded in the student's goals and vision for life as an adult, career interests, extracurricular and community activities, and the skills the student needs to progress toward his or her goals. Planning should include preparation for proficiency tests and other assessments needed for postsecondary academic work (e.g., SATs), as well as the development of self-determination and self-advocacy skills.

During the last 2 years of high school, diagnostic testing should be conducted to further define the LD or ADHD. Colleges require documentation of a disability (i.e., results of tests indicating the presence of a disability) in order to provide support services; having an IEP or Section 504 plan in high school is not enough documentation to obtain services from colleges. Students entering postsecondary programs will need to present current assessment data in order to receive accommodations at college. Even for students who have struggled academically in high school, postsecondary education may very well be a possibility. Students who wonder whether college is a realistic option can explore summer pre-college courses for high school students who have completed their junior or senior year. Alternatively, students can take a college course the summer before they enroll to get to know the campus, learn how to use the library, and sharpen their study strategies and time management skills.

Students must understand their strengths and learning needs not only to be successful in coursework, but also to identify the accommodations they will require. For example, will they need academic support services such as math labs, writing workshops, reading courses, computer labs, tutoring, or counseling? Will they want to take courses to improve social skills, study skills, learning strategies, communications skills, or assertiveness? Understanding and using technology can be another key to success. Computers and related technologies are expanding opportunities and increasing instructional access for numerous individuals with LD and ADHD. Students should consider both instructional technology (e.g., computers, tape recorders, or videos used as a means of instruction) and assistive technology (technology used by individuals to compensate for specific disabilities).

Assistive technology is most effective if it accentuates an individual's strengths and minimizes areas of need. Selecting appropriate technology for an individual should take into account the individual's learning profile, the tasks and functions to be performed, the specific technology, and the contexts of use. For example, word processors with text-to-speech, outlining, word prediction, and speech recognition capabilities offer assistive capabilities depending on a person's specific disabilities. Technology is like any other tool: The challenge is to find the technology applications that work best for the individual and learn how to use them. This takes an investment of time and money, but the payoff can be increased productivity and creativity.

Legal Rights

Once students with disabilities graduate from high school, they are no longer eligible for services provided by the school system and will not have an IEP. If they have been receiving rehabilitation services as part of their transition plans, they can continue to receive them. They will have an Individual Written Rehabilitation Plan (IWRP) and may be eligible for services such as postsecondary education, counseling, and vocational evaluation and assessment. The Americans with Disabilities Act (ADA) bars discrimination against students with disabilities in the college application process. Once admitted, students may request reasonable accommodations to allow them to participate in courses, exams, and other activities. Most colleges and universities have a disability support services office to assist in providing accommodations.

Desirable Charaateristics of a College

Once the student's strengths, learning needs, and level of support needed have been delineated, it is time to look at the characteristics of colleges that might be a good match for the student. Consider various types of colleges: two-year colleges, public community colleges, private junior colleges, four-year colleges and universities, as well as graduate and professional schools. Students with LD and/or ADHD can succeed in all types of schools, including the most prestigious. Students must determine the characteristics of colleges that will make them happy and support their success. For example, how big is their high school? Will they feel more comfortable in a larger or a smaller college? Will they be happier in an urban or a rural area? Can they meet the academic requirements? Should they find a college that doesn't impose rigid prerequisites? Should they consider enrolling part-time rather than taking a full course load? What are their academic and extra-curricular interests?

In looking at colleges, students may also want to consider whether progressive attitudes toward instruction prevail. Colleges that are using instructional techniques and electronic technology in a flexible way can increase students' success. For example, if courses are web-based so lecture notes or videos of presentations are available online and can be viewed multiple times, then students have natural supports built into a course.

Like all students preparing to choose a college, students with LD or ADHD must identify colleges that appear to have the desired qualities and select a few candidate colleges for further investigation. They need to visit colleges, see the right people on campus, and be prepared to ask the right questions. Students with disabilities must also look at other factors. They should investigate the support services offered by candidate colleges, discuss them with college staff (e.g., personnel in the Office of Disability Support Services), and verify that the services advertised by the college will actually be available to the student. For example, is tutoring available? Will extended time be allowed for taking tests? Is someone available to help with taking notes or preparing written work? Will college policies allow extended time to complete a course of study so that fewer classes may be taken over a longer period of time?

Furthermore, students with LD or ADHD must decide whether and to whom to disclose the presence of the disability. To obtain support services, students must self-disclose their disabilities to the Office of Disability Support Services. That office will notify professors of the necessary accommodations. Students are not required to give faculty information about a disability, but to obtain the best course work accommodations, they must be able to explain their needs to instructors. Therefore, students will want to investigate specific classes before they register for them. Some strategies for becoming informed about classes are listed below:

—*Participate in orientation programs*: These programs provide opportunities to become familiar with campus life and to ask questions of continuing students and advisors about classes, faculty, resources, and services.

— *Don't procrastinate*: Do not wait until the last minute to begin gathering information about courses and professors. Most Offices for Disability Support Services will allow students with disabilities to register a few days before other students.

— *Talk to other students*: Other students are an excellent source of information about classes and professors.

— *Audit classes*: It is possible to observe a class for a limited period of time to determine whether this is the right class. Students who audit a course are not responsible for exams or assignments.

— *Check the Internet*: Most colleges and universities offer an increasing amount of information, including the course syllabus (outline of the course), objectives, textbook, readings, and assignments.

— *Meet the professor*: Professors have scheduled office hours to answer questions about the course. Getting the textbooks and reading list ahead of time also allows students an opportunity to get a head start on the course.

For many individuals with LD and ADHD, the transition to adulthood will be a time of positive self-discovery, but it will take trial and error. Goals and successes can sometimes be elusive, and the hidden nature of LD and ADHD can pose special challenges. Careful preparation for the transition to college can help.

STUDENTS WITH DISABILITIES IN CAREER AND TECHNICAL EDUCATION.

Career and technical education (CTE) can provide significant benefits to students with disabilities. CTE teachers need to be aware of the rights of students with disabilities and of the planning process involved in meeting their needs. In addition, CTE teachers must know what role they play both in planning and in providing instruction. CTE teachers often need background information on the details of disabilities and the accommodations required.

Research shows that students with disabilities in secondary CTE programs were less likely to drop out and more likely to be employed, to have paid competitive jobs, and to work full time after high school. However, CTE that included only simulated work experience in classroom settings did not appear to lead to optimal employment outcomes. Students with disabilities who had paid or unpaid work experience in high school had better employment outcomes—higher wages, more hours, more continuous employment. Furthermore, students with disabilities mainstreamed into regular CTE or academic classrooms obtained paid competitive jobs more often and felt better prepared to keep their jobs. Qualitative studies reviewed by Eisenmann imply that integration of academic and vocational curricula promoted meaningful engagement and inclusion of students with disabilities by increasing persistence, academic achievement, and postsecondary engagement.

Rights of Disabled Students

Four key federal laws define the rights of students with disabilities. Two federal civil rights laws, the Americans with Disabilities Act of 1990 and Section 504 of the Rehabilitation Act of 1973, require access for students with disabilities to all federally funded programs and prohibit discrimination based on disability in any aspect of public education programs. The 1998 Perkins Act requires equal access for special populations, including students with disabilities, to all vocational programs, services, and activities and prohibits discrimination based on special population status. The Individuals with Disabilities Education Act (IDEA), as amended in 1997, establishes the right of students with disabilities to a free appropriate public education, including special education, related services, and transition services.

The Individualized Education Program (IEP) mandated by IDEA draws on the results of a comprehensive evaluation of the student's educational needs at least once every 3 years. The IEP must identify the student's current level of educational performance; measurable goals and objectives; special education, related services, and other accommodations to be provided; and the extent of participation with nondisabled students. The IEP must also specify how the student's progress will be measured, how parents will be informed of progress, and the extent of modification in state- and districtwide tests. Beginning at age 14, the IEP must include a statement of transition services the student will need to reach postschool goals; beginning at age 16, the IEP must include a statement of transition services to help the student prepare for leaving school.

IDEA requires that six participants be involved in the IEP meeting: the student (if appropriate); a parent (and family if desired); at least one of the student's special education teachers (or related services provider, if appropriate); at least one of the student's regular education teachers; a representative of the local educational agency; and other agency personnel with knowledge or expertise to meet the student's needs. The planning process involved in IEP development includes three steps. First, the abilities, needs, interests, and preferences of the individual student are determined. Second, individual postschool goals are developed based on abilities, needs, interests, and preferences. Third, instructional activities and accommodations, modifications, and supports appropriate to the student's postschool goals are identified.

A variety of individuals must work together in an effective IEP team, including special education, CTE, and academic teachers, program support staff, guidance counselors, and school administrators. Other personnel are included as appropriate to meet the individual student's needs—for example, speech, occupational, or physical therapists; adult service providers such as rehabilitation or independent living counselors; and employers or postsecondary education representatives. Effective planning for activities and services that benefit students with disabilities and improve postschool outcomes involves several broad practices. Planning should be proactive, focused on individual students, and driven by students and parents; it should involve student assessment, life skills development, and accommodations.

Planned educational activities should focus on school- and work-based experiences linking high academic and workplace standards, with integrated academic and vocational curricula for employment skills and specific occupational instruction. Family involvement should be facilitated by training to increase parents' knowledge and skills in advocacy, planning, support, and legal issues. Business, labor, and government and community agencies should be actively involved to provide resources, training sites, and mentoring for students and educators. Finally, program policy and structure should support needed partnerships, philosophy, planning, evaluation, and human resource development.

Role of CTE Teachers

CTE teachers are only one member of the team that plans and provides educational activities and accommodations for students with disabilities. In IEP development and transition planning, CTE teachers' role is to provide information, support, and assistance to others who lead the process. However, CTE teachers play a primary role in providing instruction through school- and work-based experiences and activities linking the two and in integrating academic and vocational instruction; in that role, CTE teachers should receive support and assistance from others.

Special educators typically play the primary role in identifying educational activities and accommodations that suit students' interests, aptitudes, abilities, and postschool preferences. Trained vocational assessors, if available, may use formal assessment tools, or special educators can conduct informal assessments using data in school records; interviews with students, families, and previous instructors; or published interest, aptitude, or skills instruments. CTE teachers may be able to provide program inventories or assessment tools to establish a student's readiness for specific occupational courses.

CTE teachers can also provide information on the instructional demands (e.g., prerequisite basic, interpersonal, reasoning, and learning-to-learn skills) and setting demands (e.g., independent work, self-monitoring, ability to stay on task). In particular, CTE teachers can provide CTE-specific information. That information would include occupationally specific courses of study, cooperative education, apprenticeship, and career guidance and counseling services. CTE teachers would also provide any formal program entry criteria (e.g., prerequisite courses or entry-level skills along with tests to assess them). Although students with disabilities must meet standard program entry requirements, entry testing must allow any accommodations listed in a student's IEP for test-taking (e.g., extended time, use of a reader).

CTE teachers have a larger responsibility in providing instruction for students with disabilities, particularly school-based experiences. CTE teachers must plan and provide school-based instructional activities that correspond with the goals and objectives of students' IEPs, including classroom and lab activities to teach occupationally specific skills and work-related behaviors. Planning activities that integrate academic and occupational instruction requires collaboration and coordination between CTE and academic teachers. CTE teachers must also evaluate and grade students' attainment of the IEP objectives on which instruction is based.

In addition, CTE teachers must either provide the instructional accommodations and modifications specified in each student's IEP or work with special education personnel who do so. CTE teachers also have an important role to play in providing effective work-based experiences for students with disabilities, which can include field trips, job shadowing, school-based enterprises, career-related camps, apprenticeships, internships, cooperative education, work-study, and part-time job placement. CTE teachers may share responsibility for contacting local employers; arranging sites and experiences that meet employer and student needs; orienting employers to work-site roles (coaches for instruction, mentors for social initiation and inclusion); visiting sites to observe student work; and monitoring student progress, work, and difficulties. Perhaps most important, CTE teachers must plan and provide the connecting activities that link school- and work-based learning—feedback sessions, discussions, journal writing, student presentations, projects, or portfolios, for example.

Disabilities and Accommodation

To meet the needs of students with disabilities, CTE teachers need background information on students' disabilities and on appropriate accommodations. In particular, CTE teachers may need to correct stereotypes—for example, that entrepreneurial training and business ownership are not appropriate options for students with disabilities. Accommodations can include modified instructional methods (e.g., repeat and summarize key points, use audiovisual aids, conduct oraltesting or alternative assessments) or equipment. CTE teachers should identify the assistance available from special educators, tutors, paraprofessionals, or volunteers (e.g., providing print materials in alternative formats, monitoring student work, answering questions, developing teaching aids).

So in a nutshell, CTE teachers are one member of the team that helps students with disabilities participate fully and meaningfully in high-quality educational programs. They play a key role in providing a strong mix of all school programs—academic, functional, occupational—carefully linked to each other and to work experience, delivered with customized accommodations to meet students' individual needs, and embodying the same high expectations they have of all students.

9

Effective School Counselling Strategies

The roles and functions of school counselors are notably complex and multifaceted. Sink and MacDonald noted that these roles have changed over time, and that both internal and external demands on school counselors have increased significantly. Further, they noted that school counselors have primarily become "crisis-oriented, reactive, focused on remediation over prevention, and overburdened with nonguidance-related clerical and administrative tasks". Recent efforts at renewal of the profession focus on the implementation of comprehensive developmental counseling and guidance programs. Although the goal of these programs is often preventive in nature, the reality of life for many children includes events and circumstances—ranging from parental divorce to person and substance abuse to the challenges of blended families—that place them at risk and require remediation as well.

DEVELOPMENTAL COUNSELING AND THERAPY

School counselors need a repertoire of interventions to address the myriad of challenges present in the schools. A review of articles in Elementary School Guidance and Counseling for a 20-year period revealed that only one in four articles had treatment issues or interventions as a primary focus. Among these articles, the most frequent interventions were group guidance and group counseling, followed by parent education, individual counseling, and teacher consultation. Strategies for counseling young people simply are "not well known in the field". If school counselors are to be effective in meeting the needs of the broadest array of students in the school setting, interventions that are structured, creative, and brief, and that allow counselors to understand and conceptualize the client's view of reality, must be promoted. One such strategy, which incorporates a model for assessment as well as intervention, is Developmental Counseling and Therapy.

Cognitive Development of Children

Piaget proposed a theory of cognitive development to explain the manner in which children construct knowledge and how this process changes over rime. He believed that children "naturally try to make sense of their world', including physical as well as social phenomena. Children consistently create and test theories to explain the world they observe. At critical points in their development, new ways of thinking or constructing knowledge emerge. These new ways of thinking are described in terms of four qualitatively different ways of making meaning or of knowing the world around them: sensorimotor, preoperational, concrete, and formal operational.

The sensorimotor stage spans the period from birth to 18 months. Thought begins in activity, and this is when the earliest form of thinking and problem solving emerges. While engaged in the sensorimotor stage, children's cognitive structures develop as a result of their interactions with the environment through organization and adaptation of information. The intellectual activity based on sensorimotor experiences during this stage provides a basis for all future intellectual development. Children experience pre-operational thought from one and one-half to about 6 years of age. During this stage, children recognize that a mental image can represent a physical object without the object being present.

Pre-school children are capable of this type of thought, but have no systems for categorizing and organizing objects in their environment. Thoughts in the pre-operational stage tend to be inflexible and irreversible, and children engaged at this intellectual level are often egocentric as they only view the world from their point of view. The transition to concrete operations occurs about the time children enter school, and this stage of thinking continues until adolescence. Concrete operational children are able to reason logically about situations and events. In the later parts of this stage, linear thought processes result in the experience of if/then thinking, or causal reasoning. At this point, earlier life events that lacked consistency and order become parts of the whole operating system for the child.

In addition, cognitive conceit, which occurs when children have too much faith in their reasoning ability, can be present. Piaget proposed that the stage of formal operations, reached during adolescence, continues throughout adulthood. This new type of thinking is abstract in nature, and allows for testing of hypotheses and examining alternates prior to taking action. As is true of earlier stages, the transition to formal operational thinking can extend over many years; thus, during the middle school years in particular, children may be expected to evidence both concrete and formal operational thought processes seemingly simultaneously. Further, with only 75% of all persons reaching fully formal operational thinking, the thought processes experienced by children, especially concrete operations, will likely be seen in adults as well. In fact, Ivey proposed that the types of thinking identified by Piaget repeat themselves in both children and adults. This cyclical process and the stages that comprise the cycles provide a foundation for understanding DCT.

Developmental Counseling and Therapy

Ivey developed Developmental Counseling and Therapy based

on a metaphorical use of Piaget's theory and cognitive stages. DCT incorporates concepts from individual developmental theories such as those proposed by Kohlberg, Gilligan, Kegan, and Erikson; family theories such as those of Duvall and Haley; and multicultural theories including racial and sexual identity development. Similar to other constructivists, Ivey proposed that developmental theory and counseling can be integrated. He carried this theory further to develop a systematic model that incorporates understanding the meaning of a client's cognitive developmental functioning, assessing the nature of that functioning, and selecting interventions in an intentional manner to address specific needs of clients in relation to identified and co-constructed issues.

Similar to Piagetian theory, DCT identifies four modalities of cognitive-emotional development that people fluctuate and flow between throughout the life process. These modalities of development are cyclical and not mutually exclusive, such that it is possible to function in more than one simultaneously. Moreover, the preferred modality is situation specific. A person can prefer one modality in one set of circumstances and another modality in other circumstances. An inability to process an issue from the perspective of one or more modalities constitutes a developmental block, and counseling becomes a process of removal of such blocks.

The four developmental orientations in DCT include sensorimotor, con crete, formal operations, and dialectic/systemic. Sensorimotor refers to the experiencing of feelings, with particular emphasis on the idea that feelings are physically embedded and represent an in-body type of experience. In the concrete modality, people can relate linear, sequential details of lire experiences, and in the later aspects of this stage, can engage in causal reasoning (i.e., if/then thinking). The formal operational modality is one in which people are able to see their patterns of behavior, thought, and feeling and to reflect on the meaning of those patterns. The dialectic modality is reflected in the ability to take multiple perspectives and see multiple aspects of people and situations.

In addition, persons who think dialectically are able to view themselves in systems and understand the impact of systems and multiple interacting systems (e.g., gender, culture, family) on their behavior and functioning. Developmental blocks, defined as the inability to experience a particular event or circumstance in one of the four modalities, may be experienced atone or several levels with regard to specific situations or issues. For example, an individual whose father died when she was 7 years old may, as a teenager or adult, experience a sensorimotor block as she has difficulty expressing emotion around the event. This may happen because of her difficulty at age 7 to process grief in a helpful manner.

However, she may be able to recount the details of his illness and the family response (concrete), explain her pattern of dealing with loss (formal operational), and explain the way that she responds in relation to how other members of the family respond (dialectic). Or, this same individual may, as an adult, be unable to "let go" of relationships, and fail to understand how earlier models of loss and grief influence how she reacts as an adult. Ivey would describe her as operating under a powerful system of "rules" for responding to situations, rules that were learned in her family. Again, since not all individuals achieve fully formal operational functioning, many adults may seem to have developmental blocks in formal and dialectic modalities. The process of DCT, as an intervention, helps these adults overcome their blocks.

On the other hand, because children are unlikely to think dialectically, a lack of dialectic thinking is not necessarily a developmental block. Children in the elementary grades may be expected to be primarily concrete, but may be helped to think in an early formal operational mode and sometimes in the dialectic modality as well. The assessed cognitive-developmental level plays an important role in designing an intervention plan for the client. Ivey and Ivey and Ivey noted that counselors can identify the primary cognitive-developmental level of clients after the client speaks 50 to 100 words in the initial interview. Or a structured assessment (which is also an intervention) may be employed to help the counselor identify preferences for modalities and developmental blocks and help the client examine his or her assumptions and develop new ways of thinking about problem situations.

Counselors may choose to match a client's preferred cognitive orientation to establish rapport or to mismatch that preference in order to promote developmental change to new orientations and new ways of constructing meaning. Following an assessment of the client's preferred modalities and possible developmental blocks, the DCT model provides a useful paradigm for planning and implementing appropriate interventions to facilitate change. Ivey linked preferred theories and interventions with each of the four modalities, noting that the selection of an appropriate intervention will most likely result in successful outcomes. For example, a client functioning in the sensorimotor modality, or a client with a block in this modality, may benefit from interventions that involve the body and senses such as relaxation, music therapy, or Gestalt interventions, which help clients experience emotions in the present.

Clients who are primarily concrete respond most quickly to problem-solving methods, including reality therapy and behavioral interventions. Formal operational clients may best be helped using interventions such as client-centered approaches, while dialectic clients may find systemic approaches, racial or feminist identity development, and networking strategies to be most effective. The selection of interventions is based on a developmental assessment which may be structured or unstructured and which works equally well with adults and with children.

Using DCT with Children

Although children, especially in elementary school, are primarily sensorimotor and concrete in their thought processes, they are capable of both formal and dialectic thinking. Thus, it is possible to design interventions using DCT with even very young children that help them develop new ways of constructing knowledge and making sense of the world around them. Some specific strategies and interventions that can be effective in assessing the preferred cognitive modalities of children, designing treatment plans, and both identifying and removing developmental blocks are discussed below.

Sensorimotor modality

While operating in this modality, primary functioning is based on sensory experiences, including seeing, hearing, and feeling. Attention span often is short (even in adults) and frequent physical movement is common. To work with student or to remove developmental blocks to functioning in this modality, here-and-now experiences and interventions such as play therapy are needed. The goal is to connect the child with the physical experiences that are motivating or causing behavior but which remain at a preconscious or blocked developmental level. Children who are sensorimotor typically express their concerns in a random or hyperactive manner, change the topic often, and sometimes exhibit irrational or magical thinking patterns that may be combined with egocentric thinking.

In addition, a child's behavior might reflect a short attention span and continual body movement. An example of a sensorimotor student is a first-grader who shows his sadness about his parents' divorce by talking about his desire to just get them to come to his baseball game together so they can see how much fun it is to be together again (egocentric thinking). He goes on to say that then they would take him and his sister to Disneyland for a week and everyone would have fun (magical thinking). Alternately, a student who is coping with parental divorce by pulling pieces of her hair out is reflecting the experiencing of strong emotions through body actions.

Concrete modality

This modality is evident when the student offers detailed descriptions of people, places, and events. Emotions are likely to be described in the past tense instead of felt in the present. At the later stages of concrete functioning, the child can engage in if/then thinking, which connotes causality, whereas he or she cannot in the early stages. Concrete clients understand their own point of view, but have a difficult rime seeing situations from another person's perspective. Thus, students functioning in tnis mode of operation can explain events in great detail, but may have trouble explaining why these events occur. They may be stuck on linear descriptions, providing an endless array of details about other things, and have difficulty with if/then thinking; consequently, controlling their own environment seems impossible to them. Usually, they are unable to understand the place of emotions in their lives.

In general, most children until about the age of 9 construct meaning in very concrete terms. Children in the early concrete stage typically respond with few words when asked questions, and children in the middle concrete stage often generously expand on the details of several components of the experience they are describing. During the later stages of concrete thinking, children are able to engage in causal (if/then) thinking. An illustration of a primarily concrete student would be a third-grader who can describe in detail an argument she had over throwing a ball at someone who made fun of her. However, she cannot identify her role in contributing to the need for a subsequent visit to the principal's office (lack of if/then thinking), nor does she understand the inevitable consequences associated with throwing an object at someone who she believes has instigated the conflict.

Formal operational modality

As children reflect on their concrete descriptions of events, circumstances, people, and their actions and reactions, they often can identify patterns and repeating patterns in the way they feel and think. Once patterns are identified, children may be presented with a choice either to continue their pattern or to change. Ivey and Ivey cautioned that children are often underestimated by adults, who consider formal thought not possible for them. What seems to be true is that, left alone, children may not think in formal ways, but they can do so when helped by school counselors who are patient and creative. While engaged in this developmental orientation, students are able to describe their own feelings and sometimes describe their patterns of feelings. As they begin to recognize patterns in repeated behaviors and/or thoughts, they are engaging in formal thinking.

Although formal operational thought can appear as early as the third grade, it typically is not evident until middle school. An example of a formal thinker would be a fifth grader who can describe how his pattern of negative behavior in the classroom affects the other students and the teacher. He is able to describe the phenomenon that when he gets bored, he starts to talk to or annoy the other students in the class. He can describe how the other children see him as annoying and how his teacher perceives him as disobedient and rude. He can also describe his feelings of boredom and inferiority.

Dialectic/systemic modality

This DCT perspective requires that individuals abandon an egocentric outlook on life and recognize themselves as a part of multiple and interactive systems. Younger children may not become fully dialectic in their thinking, but they can be encouraged to both imagine and consider the feelings, thoughts, and perspectives of others. Individuals who think dialectically are aware of how the environment affects them and others around them, and they can challenge their own way of operating in and integrating these systems. They can recognize others' views as distinct and apart from their own. In general, younger children do not examine life from this perspective.

Adolescents may begin to think dialectically; however, egocentric thought patterns (the opposite of dialectic) tend to remain at least sporadically through most of the adolescent years.

As dialectic/systemic thinkers, children taking this orientation see themselves as a part of systems and are able to learn how they are affected by and also affect these systems. Two of the most predominant systems affecting children include families and schools. An example of a dialectic/systemic thinking student would be one who understands how his father's substance abuse affects the differing behaviors he chooses at home and at school. Dialectic thought can be encouraged through application of DCT principles and in particular through use of Ivey and Ivey's structured developmental assessment interview.

Developmental Assessment Interview

The developmental assessment interview is a structured clinical assessment that helps a student discuss present issues from the perspective of each of the four developmental modalities. Counselors conducting the interview are able to determine the child's primary or most comfortable modality, assess developmental blocks, and use the interview questions as a means of intervention relative to the problems expressed. The interview usually begins by asking the child to talk about what happens when he or she focuses on a particular issue such as a recent fight at home or school or their parents' impending divorce. By listening to the response, the counselor can identify the student's preferred cognitive modality and begin to assess the presence of developmental blocks. The sequence of questions guides the student through the four developmental modalities.

According to Ivey, clients present at different modalities, depending on the particular problem or situation. Knowing this, counselors are able to match or mismatch the particular modality as part of the intervention plan in order to help the client heal and see the situation from other perspectives. The interview questions progress beginning with questions regarding the clients' sensorimotor functioning and ending with the client's dialectic/ systemic development. Open-ended questions, paraphrasing, summarizing, and other techniques are used to expand responses within each of the four modalities. Ivey presented questions specific to each modality. These questions are appropriate for children as well as adults.

To promote sensorimotor experiencing, school counselors may ask the student to "Pretend this (problem situation) is happening right now. Can you image that? Tell me what you are seeing as this is happening." The goal is to help the student describe the experience as if it were happening in the present and to tell what he or she is seeing, hearing, and feeling. Because feelings are physically embedded, it is important to ask the student if he or she can tell you where in their body they are feeling a sensation and to describe that sensation. To help a student explore a problem in the concrete modality, counselors may ask for an example of another time the child felt the same feeling that was talked about in the sensorimotor discussion.

By asking questions (such as: "Who was there? .... What happened?" "What happened just before that?" and "What happened next?'), the counselor can help the child provide a detailed, linear description of an event. In the late concrete phase of the interview, the student can be asked to explain how the sequence of events is linked by being prompted to explain whether this type of circumstance happens a lot, and if so, is it common that "If this happens, then that outcome follows." To promote formal operational thinking, it is important to ask questions such as: "Has this ever happened to you before?" "Does this happen for you a lot?" and "Is this a pattern?" Students are often able to identify their repeating patterns when asked questions such as these.

Although not all children will be able to think in a dialectic manner, a variety of questions may be asked in an effort to help them do so. For example, the school counselor could ask: "How do you make sense of all of this?" "Does this happen a lot in your family?" "What does that mean to you?" and "How might someone else describe what is happening?" The developmental assessment interview allows the school counselor to understand how the student constructs meaning in relation to life events. Once that understanding has been achieved, interventions may be structured to help the student change. Both the interview and intervention processes are co-constructed and tailored to the developmental capabilities of the child. The following rive-stage process may work best with younger children:

— Start with a focus on establishing rapport
— Define the problem (with special emphasis on recognizing strengths)
— Outline goals
— Generate alternatives
— Follow up with the child

SOCIAL INTEREST AND COPING RESOURCES IN CHILDREN

Today, children, just as adults, experience higher levels of stress than ever before. Negative life events such as community and school violence, domestic terrorism, poverty, divorce, poor parenting skills, and school problems such as academic difficulties or friendship problems are a reality for many children. These stressful life events can cause emotional and psychological problems. Furthermore, children have little control over their environments and therefore may not be able to actively prevent or seek alleviation from stress. Still, some children, regardless of stressful life experiences, show high levels of resilience. That is, they seem to show a tremendous ability to actively handle life's demands.

Kern, Gfroerer, Summers, Curlette, and Matheny found that social interest and belonging were related to adults' perceived coping resources. Studies consistently indicate that children with increased psychological stress are significantly more likely to be ill, to need hospital treatment, and to use health services than children with lower levels of stress. Several studies have shown that adverse life events and other types of stresses "significantly increase a person's susceptibility to acute and recurring upper respiratory tract infections such as asthma, and other viral infections". Stress compromises the body's immunology responses thereby increasing the risk of somatic diseases, especially those that result from the weakening of the body's natural defense mechanisms. The most severe stressful life events are often unpredictable and unavoidable and involve loss such as parental separation, death of a parent or other close person, or a close friend moving away.

Other stressful life circumstances include poverty; poor housing; family, community and national violence; parental physical infirmity; parental psychiatric illness; parental alcohol dependence; family discord; and school problems such as academic hardship or friendship problems. Infants and toddlers tend to react to stressful situations with impairment of physiological functions, such as disturbances of feeding and sleep, with relatively global expressions of anger or fear, as in temper tantrums, or with withdrawal and avoidance behavior. School-aged children demonstrate their difficulties through altered interpersonal relationships with peers and family members, through impairment of school performance, by the development of specific psychological syndromes, such as phobias or psychosomatic disorders, or by "regressing" to earlier, more "childish" modes of functioning.

Pitzer suggested possible signs of stress are "bedwetting, complaints of a pounding heart, stomach upset, queasiness, decline in school achievement, demand for constant perfection, downgrading of self, extreme worry, irritability, lying, nightmares, overeating, poor sleep or eating habits, teeth grinding, difficulty in getting along with friends, and withdrawal from social activities." Curlette, Aycock, Matheny, Pugh, and Taylor summarized the considerable physical, psychological, and behavioral problems caused by stress, explaining that stress is "best viewed as the inequality between perceived demands and perceived resources". If the demands are perceived to exceed an individual's coping resources for stress, the body reacts by gearing up for an emergency.

Stress researchers argue that it is not the environmental demands that determine the individual's stress level, but the individual's perception of his or her ability to cope. Most researchers now agree that only if an individual's coping resources are perceived as inadequate by the person would environmental demands actually become stressful. In other words, difficult life events and situations will only become stressful if the individual perceives that he or she does not have the coping resources available with which to handle the stress. In addition, researchers have also suggested that personality types or traits interact with one's coping resources. The same may be true for children. Carson and Swanson suggested children's coping styles, approach, and their families' approach to stressful events are more critical to the adjustment to stress than the stressful events themselves.

While there is a plethora of literature on the impact of stress in adults there is less written about the effects of stress on children and about the coping resources children use to handle this stress. Coping resources are believed to help lessen the negative effects of stress. Coping resources are factors that are in place prior to the occurrence of the stressor. These factors can be drawn upon to cope, thereby lessening the cost and making the individual more resistant to stress. There is a wide range of coping resources useful to individuals in combating stress. For example, problem-solving, cognitive restructuring, physical exercise, and social support are all resources that are believed to lessen the demands of stress. It is the individual's perception of his or her ability to use such resources to cope that can lead to a general resistance to stress.

Social Interest

Adler believed that it was essential for individuals to possess an active approach to confronting problems and the demands of life and that social interest was critical for such an approach. The Adlerian Psychology construct of social interest is uniquely related to the topic of children's stress, yet there is little written about the rote that social interest plays in alleviating and or moderating stress in children."'Social interest' is at the heart of Adlerian psychology and is widely considered the central concept of Adlerian theory". Manaster and Corsini stated that Alfred Adler believed that mental health, or one's "personal success in life", was a function of one's social interest. Other related definitions of social interest include understanding, empathizing with, and acting on behalf of others, sharing, helping, cooperating, and taking responsibility, and the capacity for transcending the limits of self.

Social interest is thought to be the key factor in a healthy, functional personality. Adler believed that social interest was the cornerstone of mental health. In adult populations, a lack of social interest has been found to correlate with certain pathologies. Social interest has been negatively correlated with depression; the Schizophrenia, Psychopathic Deviate, and Social Introversion scales of the Minnesota Multiphasic Personality Inventory; potential for child abuse, and an external locus of control. In a study using criminal offenders, Daugherty et al. found that offenders with low social interest, as compared with those with higher social interest, "were more likely to be unemployed, to have new felony arrests, or to be re-incarcerated" at the time of a 20-27 month follow up.

There also appears to be a relationship between coping and social interest. Crandall found that social interest was related to personal adjustment and that it reduced the effects of stress on psychological symptoms and even provided some immunity to the effects of stress. Leak and Williams found that "social interest encourages an active approach to life's problems". While the construct of social interest and its usefulness in adult populations is found often in the literature, it is not found in the literature regarding youth populations. Instead the term belonging, which is an indication of individual's social interest, is commonly cited in the literature concerning children and adolescents. In children and adolescent populations, belonging has been associated with being liked, accepted, and respected by other students and teachers; students' expectations of academic success; students' intrinsic interest in schoolwork and grades; and teacher ratings of student effort. Crandall states that students who feel a sense of belonging have an enhanced sense of worth and self-confidence.

School connectedness, or belonging, plays a critical role in the success or failure of today's middle and high school student. Beck and Malley report that "most children fail in school not because they lack the necessary cognitive skills, but because they feel detached, alienated, and isolated from others and from the educational process". They go on to say that currently, there is unprecedented alienation and apathy among our youth. Furthermore, Sonnenblick stated that students who do not feel a sense of belonging at school are at risk for gang involvement and dropping out of school.

Resnick et al. stated that a feeling of connection to school is the best predictor of adolescent well-being. Mulvey and Cauffman reported that "students who are committed to school, feel that they belong, and trust the administration are less likely to commit violent acts than those who are uninvolved, alienated, or distrustful". From this evidence, it appears that children with social interest, or a strong sense of belonging, cope better with stress than children with lower levels of social interest. Blom, Cheney, and Shoddy noted that stress-resistant children who possessed effective coping skills had a variety of behavioral characteristics. "Behaviors such as empathy, understanding the points of view of others, helping others, good verbal skills, good attentional processes, reflectiveness, problem solving, inner locus of control, frustration tolerance, and success appear possible to teach.".

Social interest is manifested in these behavioral characteristics. Social interest is not an inborn trait; it is rather a trait that must be consciously developed. Former studies and definitions of social interest and coping resources appear to demonstrate that social interest and coping resources are directly related. Kern et al. used the Coping Resources Inventory for Stress and the Basis Adlerian scales for Interpersonal Success—Adult Form to demonstrate that social interest correlated positively with coping resources in adult populations. Evidence suggests that social interest moderates an individual's coping resources.

ROLE OF COUNSELORS IN PREVENTING VIOLENCE IN SCHOOLS

Recent, highly publicized school shootings have had a tremendous impact on the public's perception of school safety. These events have prompted school officials to consider prevention strategies for targeted violence in schools. School officials are increasingly turning to school counselors for help in identifying and providing interventions for students who may pose a danger to others. School counselors are meeting this challenge by providing violence prevention activities, assessing students' risk of engaging in violent behavior, and providing appropriate interventions when the potential for violence exists.

There are two ethics documents that inform the practice of school counselors: the Ethical Standards for School Counselors (American School Counselor Association [ASCA]) and the Code of Ethics (American Counseling Association [ACA]). Ethical standards require school counselors to inform appropriate authorities when a student's behavior is indicative of clear and imminent danger to others. Yet, the best means of accurately determining whether a student is potentially violent has been the subject of much scholarly debate. Accordingly, the ethical standards recommend that school counselors consult with colleagues when working with students who may be at risk for violence. Though school counselors are ethically obligated to respond to and work to prevent imminent school violence, they are also required to consider the welfare of potentially violent students. When school counselors decide to take action to prevent potential violence, the ethical standards direct school counselors to inform students of the actions to be taken in order to clarify expectations and minimize confusion.

Furthermore, school counselors have an ethical duty to keep informed about laws related to the rights of their students and ensure that their students' rights are protected. School officials, including school counselors, have a legal obligation to take action when students pose a danger to other students. In 1999, the United States Supreme Court commented on school authorities' duty to address school violence. The Court explained that school personnel are on notice that they can be held responsible for failing to protect students from student-on-student violence. Though the legal duty of school personnel to protect students from harm is clear, courts have been reluctant to find school authorities liable in school violence cases.

This trend is evident in courts' recent decisions about the culpability of school personnel in cases related to multiple homicides perpetrated by students in school settings. For example, in August 2000, a federal court in Kentucky dismissed the claims filed against school personnel in the West Paducah, Kentucky, school shooting. The court found that the perpetrator was the only responsible party for the shootings in spite of evidence that the student assailant showed students his guns when he brought them to school and wrote of homicidal and suicidal thoughts in school papers.

In late November 2001, a federal district court in Denver dismissed the lawsuits of families of victims alleging that school officials, including school counselors, failed to recognize warning signs from the student assailants . These warning signs included a violent Web site and a videotape made for a video production class portraying Harris and Klebold enacting a scenario in which they shot students with the motive of revenge. Additionally, in both psychology classes and creative writing classes, Harris and Klebold expressed their anger, hatred, and intent to kill, and wrote that they possessed firearms. According to the pleadings in the case, these communications demonstrated a serious threat of harm to students at Columbine High School and school administrators, counselors, and teachers were negligent in their failure to respond. However, the judge ruled that the warning signs were not enough to predict the impending violence. Victims' families report that they will appeal the court's decision to dismiss their case.

Though school counselors have yet to be held legally accountable for school violence, school counselors still find themselves legally vulnerable because of their role in determining whether students pose a risk of harm to others and deciding on appropriate interventions with these students. Thus, school counselors are wise to keep up-to-date on current court decisions related to school personnel and school violence. School officials, including school counselors, have been held liable for failing to protect students from foreseeable harm. Courts have consistently found that school personnel have a duty to exercise reasonable care to protect students from foreseeable harm. Courts have explained that students' violent acts were foreseeable if students threatened to do harm, especially if students have engaged in violent activities in the past. Current case law also indicates that any indicator of potential violence needs to be taken seriously. Accordingly, courts are supporting the temporary removal from the school setting of students who exhibit indicators of potentially violent behavior.

For example In Brian A. v. Stroudsburg Area School District, a federal district court considered the case of a 15-year-old student who was expelled because he wrote a note stating, "There's a Bomb in this School bang bang!!". The incident took place only a few weeks after the Columbine school shooting. The student claimed that he wrote the note as a joke and forgot to throw it away. In making their decision to expel the student, school officials considered the fact that the student was on probation because of an incident that involved blowing up a shed on the property of another school. The court held that school officials' act of expelling the student was a reasonable response to a bomb threat, especially considering the student's previous delinquent acts.

In addition to evidence of the student's intent to do harm and the student's prior violent history, courts have taken into consideration recent school violence when determining if school officials have acted reasonably when faced with a student's threats of violence. In Lovell v. Poway Unified School District, a federal appeals court considered the appropriateness of a 15-year-old student's suspension after she allegedly threatened to shoot her school counselor because she was dissatisfied with her schedule. The student defended her actions by stating that she "merely uttered a figure of speech'" and immediately apologized for her inappropriate behavior. The student did not act in a physically threatening manner toward the counselor, and yet the counselor reported that she felt threatened by the student because the counselor had witnessed the student's volatile nature and lack of impulse control on other occasions. The court commented, "in light of the violence prevalent in schools today, school officials are justified in taking very seriously student threats against faculty or other students". The court upheld the student's suspension.

Other courts have considered students' constitutional rights and focused on whether threats of violence made in school settings were believable. Though threats that present a "clear and present danger" have never been afforded first amendment protections, some courts are still finding that for a threat to be punishable, the threat must meet the objective "true threat" test. According to these courts, a "true threat" is a threat that a reasonable person in the same circumstances would find to be a serious and unambiguous expression of intent to do harm based on the language and context of the threat.

For example the application of the "true threat" doctrine is illustrated in D. G. vs. Independent School District No. 11, Tulsa County Oklahoma. In this case, the court considered the suspension of an 11th grade student for writing a poem about killing a specific teacher. The student explained that she was upset with the teacher at the time and she wrote the poem to express her frustration. The student did not intend for the teacher to see the poem. Neither the teacher nor the school administrator considered the threat to be a "true threat" because the student had never been engaged in or threatened to engage in violent conduct at school. But, the school had a "zero tolerance" policy for student threats. The court held that the student's suspension was appropriate while the threat was being investigated; however, the court added that once a psychologist determined that the threat was not a "true threat," the school was violating the student's constitutional rights by not allowing the student to return to school.

Similarly, in Lavine v. Blaine School District, a student sued school officials, including his school counselors, after being expelled because of a poem he wrote. The poem contained suicidal and homicidal imagery including a passage depicting a school shooting, 28 people dying, the shooter feeling no remorse, and the perpetrator shooting himself. The English teacher who read the poem was concerned and notified the school counselor. The school shooting in nearby Springfield, Oregon had just occurred. In a previous school year, the student admitted to the school counselor that he had thought about committing suicide. Suicidal ideation is highly correlated with violent behavior. The school counselor was also aware of recent, serious problems the student was having at home and that the student was reportedly stalking the girl with whom he had just broken up.

The student had a discipline record which included a fight and an incident of insubordination to a teacher. Based on these facts, the principal expelled the student. After the student's removal from school, the student was evaluated by a psychiatrist who found that the student could safely return to school. Though the student returned to school, the student's father sued school officials claiming that his son's expulsion had violated his son's constitutional rights. Addressing this claim, the court stated that recent school shootings have "put our nation on edge and have focused attention on what school officials, law enforcement and others can do or could have done to prevent these kinds of tragedies". The court continued by stating that "the school had a duty to prevent any potential violence on campus".

Considering the facts of the case and the recent school shootings, the court held that school personnel acted reasonably by removing the student from the school environment until a psychiatrist evaluated the student and determined that the student was not a danger to himself or others. Case law related to student suicide also has legal implications for school counselors as they engage in violence prevention and intervention activities. As in school violence cases, in student suicide cases educators' liability emanates from their responsibility to keep students safe from harm. Thus, the reasoning of courts addressing student suicide could be applied by analogy to school violence.

In student suicide cases, courts have found that school personnel need to take seriously every threat indicating suicidal ideation. School counselors have a duty to use reasonable care to attempt to prevent a student's suicide when they are on notice of a student's suicidal intent. Courts have found that students' writing assignments, such as disturbing entries in students' journals, could make a student's suicide reasonably foreseeable. Courts addressing school violence could also find that a student's disturbing writing assignments were evidence of premeditated violence. In student suicide cases, courts have also addressed the need for educating school personnel in suicide prevention, noting that without such education, school personnel are likely to underestimate the lethality of suicidal behaviors.

Just as courts are beginning to expect school personnel to be educated in suicide prevention, courts could find that there is an expectation that school personnel be knowledgeable about violence prevention as well. According to current school violence and student suicide jurisprudence, school counselors are justified in taking every threat of violence or suicide seriously. Yet, some courts have recognized that not all threats are serious threats to do harm. School counselors play a vital role in assessing these threats and working with administrators as they determine whether to remove a student from school because of a violent threat. According to legal dictates, threat assessment includes determining whether the language and context of the threat indicate a serious intent to do harm.

A school counselor's previous interactions with the student are relevant in this determination, especially if the counselor has noted volatile behavior or the student has indicated suicidal ideation. Finally, school counselors need to consider other corroborating evidence such as the student's history of violent behavior. It is important to note that judges do not expect school counselors be perfect in their prediction of school violence. Assessment of risk is not an exact science. School officials are also not expected to anticipate random acts of violence. Consequently, school counselors are only expected to act reasonably to prevent foreseeable school violence. In determining what actions are considered reasonable, courts have found that school counselors are expected to exercise the degree of care that would be exercised by other school counselors with similar education and experience. School counselors are only exposed to legal liability if they fail to exercise reasonable care in preventing foreseeable school violence.

INDEX